FRANCHISING

FRANCHISING

SUMIT KATI

Reprint: 2011

Himalaya Publishing House

MUMBAI • NEW DELHI • NAGPUR • BENGALURU • HYDERABAD • CHENNAI • PUNE • LUCKNOW • AHMEDABAD • ERNAKULAM • BHUBANESWAR • INDORE • KOLKATA • GUWAHATI

First Edition : 2010
Reprint : 2011

blished by	:	Mrs. Meena Pandey for **Himalaya Publishing House Pvt. Ltd.,** "Ramdoot", Dr. Bhalerao Marg, Girgaon, **Mumbai - 400 004.** Phone: 022-23860170/23863863, Fax: 022-23877178 **E-mail: himpub@vsnl.com; Website: www.himpub.com**
anch Offices	:	
New Delhi	:	"Pooja Apartments", 4-B, Murari Lal Street, Ansari Road, Darya Ganj, New Delhi - 110 002. Phone: 011-23270392, 23278631; Fax: 011-23256286
Nagpur	:	Kundanlal Chandak Industrial Estate, Ghat Road, Nagpur - 440 018. Phone: 0712-2738731, 3296733; Telefax: 0712-2721215
Bengaluru	:	No. 16/1 (Old 12/1), 1st Floor, Next to Hotel Highlands, Madhava Nagar, Race Course Road, Bengaluru - 560 001. Phone: 080-32919385; Telefax: 080-22286611
Hyderabad	:	No. 3-4-184, Lingampally, Besides Raghavendra Swamy Matham, Kachiguda, Hyderabad - 500 027. Phone: 040-27560041, 27550139; Mobile: 09848130433
Chennai	:	No. 85/50, Bazullah Road, T. Nagar, Chennai - 600 017. Phone: 044-28144004/28144005
Pune	:	First Floor, "Laksha" Apartment, No. 527, Mehunpura, Shaniwarpeth (Near Prabhat Theatre), Pune - 411 030. Phone: 020-24496323/24496333
Lucknow	:	Jai Baba Bhavan, Church Road, Near Manas Complex and Dr. Awasthi Clinic, Aliganj, Lucknow - 226 024. Phone: 0522-2339329, 4068914; Mobile: 09305302158, 09415349385, 09389593752
Ahmedabad	:	114, "SHAIL", 1st Floor, Opp. Madhu Sudan House, C.G. Road, Navrang Pura, Ahmedabad - 380 009. Phone: 079-26560126; Mobile: 09327324149, 09314679413
Ernakulam	:	39/104 A, Lakshmi Apartment, Karikkamuri Cross Rd., Ernakulam, Cochin - 622011, Kerala. Phone: 0484-2378012, 2378016; Mobile: 09344199799
Bhubaneswar	:	5 Station Square, Bhubaneswar (Odisha) - 751 001. Mobile: 09861046007
ndore	:	Kesardeep Avenue Extension, 73, Narayan Bagh, Flat No. 302, IIIrd Floor, Near Humpty Dumpty School, Narayan Bagh, Indore - 452 007 (M.P.). Mobile: 09301386468
Kolkata	:	108/4, Beliaghata Main Road, Near ID Hospital, Opp. SBI Bank, Kolkata - 700 010, Phone: 033-32449649, Mobile: 09910440956
Guwahati	:	House No. 15, Behind Pragjyotish College, Near Sharma Printing Press, P.O. Bharalumukh, Guwahati - 781009. (Assam). Mobile: 09883055590, 09883055536
by	:	HPH, Editorial Office, Bhandup (Megha)
ted by	:	Super Art Home, Mumbai.

PREFACE

Today many people are well travelled and well informed about the various brands which have made their presence felt across the world. When the same people travel across or are at their home town would like to experience the same brands in the similar manner. This gives humorous opportunity to the company/organization/manufacturer/brands as they already have a ready market for their products and services. Thus, it is common business sense that they should cater to these markets. But it is easier said than done. It is not so easy for any organization to just venture into any of the markets. Thus, the better way of growing within such markets would be by identifying partners, with whom synergies could be drawn for a win-win situation. In other words franchising would be one of the best ways for an exponential growth of the company.

I have earlier spoken about the win-win situation, thus, indicating that there is a lot of value for the person who would take the franchisee. The world of franchising gives immense opportunities to a self-starter/entrepreneur, in other words it gives an opportunity to own already proven business with all the support and past records.

Just imagine whenever one enters a MacDonald's across the globe, one would find the same ambience and the service across. Though the food would be customized in accordance to the local taste, the service experience for the customer is the same across. Thus, franchising does not end by just benefiting the franchisor and the franchisee, the main beneficiary is the customer. The customer experiences the same kind of products, services and most of the time even the ambience.

In this book I have not only penned down the criteria for the franchisor and the franchisee also addressed the major concerns along with the synergies between them. The reader will get an overview of the major aspects of the world of franchising.

I would also thank Miss. Priti Parikh who has added value to this book by not only collating the various inputs but also given a different perspective to the same.

Overall the book would touch upon the different perspectives on concerns, approach is for the same along with the legal and global perspective of the 'World of Franchising'.

– Author

CONTENTS

Chapter 1
FRANCHISING - INTRODUCTION

Objectives

After going through this chapter, you will be able to understand:

- The definition and the concept of franchising
- Types of franchising
- Benefits and pitfalls of franchising

Structure:

1.1 History of Franchising

1.2 Definition of a Franchisee

1.3 Definition of a Franchisor

1.4 Franchising in India

1.5 Summary

1.6 Self Assessment Questions

Mr. Menon an NRI, was very happy to return to India, though he knew that it would be a very short stay but was very enthusiastically looking forward for his stay. In a recent business newspaper he had picked the news which very confidently stated that 'India was on the growth trajectory with 8% GDP growth'. Mr. Menon was proud to be an Indian. Mr. Menon had left India in the late eighties to pursue his dream and had dreaded experiences of the licenses and regulations that existed in India those days.

Now in 2009 with not much to peep in the global economy, he was amazed to see the change in the Indian economy and the Indians themselves. As soon as he landed he used the **Meru cab services** from the airport pick-up. He decided to stay at **Orchid hotels** (a franchised hotel chain). From an instant face massage he droped at **Shehnaz Hussain** Beauty Parlour. He was in India to set up a liaison office in India. Having no experience in India, he decided to avail the services of a franchised Business Service Provider, **Crestcom.** He was overjoyed when he came to know about the local **TGIF (Thank God It's Friday)** operating with the same American standards in India. He appreciated the food, as it tasted exactly the same as he had at the Times Square Junction, New York. He was glad that the **Manish Malhotra** designed clothes were available all across the country, and they are franchising at an international level. He knew that the clothes designed by him were a rage in the US and he couldn't afford to miss this golden opportunity.

What one would notice is that all these companies have expanded gradually and made their presence by franchising. Franchising, as a way of expansion in India was little known till the 1990s. Franchising in the US was initiated by the fast food industry, whereas in India it was IT Education industry who led to its evolution. Today, franchising has forayed into all industries from Food, Management education, automobiles and fuel to lodging and Child Care. In the United States almost half of all retail sales are made through firms operating under the franchise system like McDonald's which has a brand franchise. Franchising is becoming increasingly popular in India as well.

1.1 HISTORY OF FRANCHISING

The earliest signs of franchising in the United States dates back to the 1850's just after Isaac Singer invented the Singer Sewing Machine. During his search for an effective and affordable way to distribute his product for his company, the Singer Sewing Centre, Singer ran into problems that prevented his company from becoming successful.

The first problem was a lack of capital for manufacturing the machines. Secondly, no one was willing to buy these sewing machines without first being taught how to use them, which required efforts that most traditional retailers could not provide. Singer's solution was to charge licensing fee from business people who would own the rights to sell the machines in certain geographical areas. They would also be responsible for teaching consumers how to use the machines, thereby creating sales opportunities. Using the licensing fee to fund manufacturing, the company was then able to afford to build the machines and then ship them directly to their newly formed distribution network.

Singer's idea got noticed, and over the next several decades, many other companies began to copy and enhance his business model. At first, companies like Coca-Cola introduced franchising into their bottling and manufacturing areas in order to reduce financial risk.

Later, companies such as McDonald's and Burger King took franchising to a whole new level by creating some of the largest franchise networks in the world. Today, there are thousands of successful franchise companies with outstanding business models that provide products and services to consumers and businesses all around the world.

According to Franchising in the Economy, 1991-1993, a study done by the University of Louisville, franchising helped to lead America out of its economic downturn at the time. Franchising is a unique business model that has encouraged the growth of franchised chain formula units because the franchisors collect royalties on the gross sales of these units and not on the profits. Conversely, when good jobs are lost in the economy, franchising picks up because potential franchisees are looking to buy jobs and to earn profits from the purchase of franchise rights.

Franchising

Webster's Dictionary defines "franchise" as

(1) A privilege or right granted to a person or a group by a government, state, or sovereign.

(2) Authorization granted by a manufacturer to a distributor or dealer to sell his products.

The word "franchise" comes from Old French meaning privilege or freedom. As economies evolved, so did the concept of franchising. It is believed that our current concept of franchising comes from the mid 1800s when a major German ale brewer granted certain taverns the exclusive right to sell their ale.

The International Franchise Association (IFA), the major trade association in franchising, defines franchise as a "continuing relationship in which the franchisor provides a licensed privilege to do business, plus assistance in organizing, training, merchandising and management in return for a consideration from the franchise."

Franchising is a successful method of distributing goods or services to consumers. The franchise system owns the right to the trademark of the business. The franchisee purchases the right to use the trademark and operating system.

Most people associate the word "franchise" with fast food restaurants. But, there are many more types of franchise businesses, including everything from advertising to automobile repair, printing services to party supplies and many more.

1.2 DEFINITION OF A FRANCHISEE

An individual or a company who purchases and runs a franchise is called a "franchisee."

In other words franchisee is the party in a franchising agreement that is purchasing the right to use a business's trademarks, associated brands and other proprietary knowledge in order to open a branch. The franchisee must follow certain rules and guidelines already established by the franchisor. In addition to paying an annual franchising fee to the underlying company, the franchisee must also pay a portion of its profits to the franchisor.

1.3 DEFINITION OF A FRANCHISOR

The entity or person owning the rights or license of the business. Franchisor is the person who grants the license or permission to the various franchisees. **In other words franchisor is the entity or person owning the rights or license of the business.**

Franchisor and the Franchisee work with each other and help each other grow. The responsibilities are shared among themselves and a few are as mentioned below:

	Franchisor	Franchisee
Site Selection:	Probably oversees, may choose	Chooses with approval
Design:	Provides prototype design	Implements design; pays
Employees:	Generalized recommendations	Actually hires, supervises and fires
Menu:	Set by franchisor	Changed only by approval
Prices:	Recommendations, possible caps	Decides actual prices
Supplies	May offer bulk purchasing program Lists approved suppliers or Lists quality requirements or Requires supplies from franchisor	Complies with program
Advertising:	Designs national program Requires or suggests local amounts	Pays into advertising fund Gets franchiser approval
Quality Control:	Sets standards; trains franchisees; Inspects	Trains employees, carries out systems

1.4 FRANCHISING IN INDIA

India is a vast country with a population of more than one billion people. Following its phased opening of the many stifling government regulations starting in the early 1990s, the economy is doing extremely well with an achievement of attaining a GDP growth rate of 8 to 9 per cent annually in the last few years and a similar increase projected in the coming years. The economy is backed by strong fundamentals, with a vibrant and well regulated stock market, financial institutions, excellent local financial and banking institutions and a government that is now open and willing to accept foreign investment and other inputs. The services and manufacturing sectors with double-digit growth rates are doing exceedingly well and India's lead position in the information technology domain is well-recognized all over the world.

India, with its huge market and growing demand in all sectors of the economy, is an extremely attractive proposition for entry of foreign brands through the franchising route. The key attractions for this are:

- **Lower Capital Requirements:** Franchising provides a favorable model both for U.S. and Indian business interests to expand and establish their brands without having to risk large sums of money because there are many potential franchisees in India who have the capacity to finance the business or to expand the current business.
- **Huge Market:** The size and geography of India is ideally-suited for business through the franchising model, particularly in the services' sector of the economy. Combining with people with local market knowledge can be an enormous help in dealing with meeting the market needs of the diverse country that India is.
- **Cultural Empathy:** Franchising is an eminently-suited business model for the entrepreneurial psyche of an average Indian businessman who loves to have ownership and control of operations and, being family-oriented, finds it an attractive proposition to pass on the business to future generations.
- **Laws and Language:** With English as the commonly-spoken language, the ongoing relationship between the franchisor and the franchisee becomes much easier to manage. This helps to build the spirit of partnership through easy communication. The current Law of Contracts and the Trademarks Act provides sufficient protection for a foreign franchisor in the event of emergence of any legal issues.

Franchising is in its early stages in India, and has become increasingly popular as a means of doing business in the past few years, both in terms of international franchise and domestic ones. As a result, the Franchising Association of India was set up in Mumbai, in 2000 which has links with other such associations around the world. The Franchising Association is still considering whether it should have a Code of Conduct or whether they should press for specific legislation in relation to franchising. The difficulty with a Code of Conduct is that not all franchisors and franchisees are members of the Association therefore it is difficult to enforce.

Early Entry of Foreign Players: Regarding the background, international soft drink and hotel franchise arrived in India as early as in the 1960s, but in 1977 the Government of the day had expelled foreign brands from India. The foreign brands started returning gradually from the mid 80's. In the 1990's as the market opened, foreign franchise started coming in gradually, and faced many hiccups along the way especially KFC, Schweppes, etc. Since then there has been progressive entry of international franchise, some have been successful and others not so fortunate. The well-known franchise relating to soft drinks, ice-cream parlours or restaurants include Pepsi, Coke, Baskin Robbins, Movenpick, Subway, McDonalds, TGIF, Geoffry's, Taco Bell, Pizza Hut, Pizza Piazza, Dominos Pizza, O'Brian's Sandwich Bar, Ruby Tuesdays and Barrista. Retail franchise include Marks & Spencer, West Side, Evita Peroni, Pepe Jeans and Adams. Courier companies like Air Action and DHL are there along with computer and software related franchise. The Government has liberalised the rules and regulations in relation to the retail industry and a boom in this sector is on its way.

Indian Companies Adapting The Frnachise Model: Franchising has also become a popular method of doing business within India with the franchisor granting numerous unit franchise in a wide range of areas. This has been the case in respect of IT education and franchise such as APTECH, NIIT, and STG. Then there are local food chains like Chawla's, Nirulas, Nilgiris, Coffee Day, Café Nescafe, and Sagar Ratna. Health clubs like VLCC have come up along with hair and beauty parlours who often sell their products like Shehnaz Hussain, Biotique and Habibs. There are numerous cargo and courier companies like Blue Dart, ADL, Dartmail, Blaze Flash, First Flight, Professional Couriers and DTDC. Clothing retail outlets especially for designer clothing include Bentley, L.F Couture, Ritu Beri and Deewan Sons. Other retail chains include Shopper's Stop, Lifestyle and Ebony. There are Indian travel agencies which now want to franchise abroad like Uniglobe or expand locally like Travel Port. Now the major area for local franchise seems to be healthcare with Apollo Hospitals and various diagnostic centres. Shehnaz Hussain beauty saloons and products are already an international franchise, and slowly other Indian franchisors are likely to look to expand internationally with the easing of restrictions by the Government especially since 2000.

It took some time for international franchise to become acceptable because of certain attitudes of Indian businesses towards foreign franchise whereby they could not understand why the Indian party had to make all the investments in India and on top of that had to make hefty payments in foreign exchange to the Master franchisor. Indians feel the foreign franchisor or business should also invest, participate and have some interest in the development and success of the entire business. If the brand name is very well known worldwide and the product is marketable in India, then the attitude can significantly change, as it is obvious that the local business would profit just by riding on the back of a well known brand. If the brand is well known in another country but not in India or to Indians traveling abroad, then it is difficult to convince an Indian businessperson to pay lump sum payments or royalties as its worth is not the same in India. That again can be overcome if the product or service provided by the franchise is in short supply in the country and important to its development. Market research and pilot projects can assist in assessing the prospects of any international franchise in India.

The lower the price, a product or service can be sold at, the more customers they are likely to have. Some products may be designed to appeal to the masses and other high price items can be marketed just for a select clientele like those in big business, professions, the film industry or celebrities. Expensive cosmetics and beauty therapy from abroad is for the latter. The needs of the affluent has been already met with many expensive products in the market, however, there is still scope in the retail sector for cheaper goods in terms of clothing or cosmetics. In the soft drink and fast food sector, Coke, Pepsi, McDonald and Pizza Hut have already captured the mass market.

It is not difficult to spot malls. Organised retailing though only at 2% of the retailing, will take off in a very big way. The Indian middle class has been slowly expanding, it now buys consumer appliances, thanks to the economy growth of over 8 per cent, the stock market crossing 2,000 index, forex reserves surpassing 100 billion USD, and the increase in disposable income. Today, over 33 million Indians can afford the best services and products and over 310 million Indians buy consumer appliances.

India offers lot of potential for the franchising community. Apart from Indians being very entrepreneurial, franchising as a way of doing business has been well accepted.

Today, we can find international names like Gold Gym, Subway, Hilton, etc., in many parts of India.

In many instances the products sold by the franchise outlets may have to be significantly tailored to local taste, which may go against the franchising concept or principle that outlets should be identical, and a customer should find identical quality of goods. If one goes to a McDonalds or TGIF or Pizza Hut in India, the food tastes different and the menus are geared to local taste and culture. For instance, Indian people like spicy food, and beef and pork have to be absent in the menu to avoid offending religious sentiments. In relation to restaurants and pubs, even if families would like to go together, the licensing laws in many states prohibit entry of persons less than 21 years to go to an eating place or restaurant where liquor is sold. Regarding retail franchise involving clothing, the children's wear and men's wear is similar to any other western country except that the material has to suit the tropical climate and relatively milder winters. The women's fashion however, is significantly different with the majority wearing salwar kameez or saris. Western clothes like suits, trousers, skirt and tops for women are becoming popular among teenagers and women in cosmopolitan areas of large cities.

A foreign franchisor needs to be aware of local culture and customs, and when deciding on franchise fees or other payments they have to consider realities about the buying power and people's habits about spending and not make assessment on the basis of population numbers. Research should be done on the viability of any product or service in any given state in India.

Types of Franchise

The types of franchise have evolved over a period of time in accordance to the change in the demand of the market environment. In our scope of discussion we will understand the overview of the following mentioned types of franchise;

(1) Business Format Franchise

(2) Product or Trade name franchise

(3) Dealership and Distributorships

(4) Licensees

(5) Agencies

(6) Manufacturing Franchise

(7) Unit franchisee

(8) Master franchisee

(9) Regional franchisee

(10) Multiple franchisee

(11) Developers

There are business format franchise and product or trade name franchise. Under product and trade name franchise there are distributorships and dealerships, agencies and licensees. It should be noted that some franchise are actually multi-level marketing plans. Most, but not all franchise guarantee exclusive territorial rights. Franchise agreements can be from five to twenty years, and there may be penalties for terminating the contract prematurely.

(1) Business Format Franchise: This is the most popular form of franchising, thus, these are what most people think of when you say franchise. It is a business established under an agreement that the franchisee has the right to market a product or service using the trademark, ideas and products of the franchiser for a fee and a percentage of the gross monthly sales. It operates under the Franchiser's business philosophy. In this type of franchise the "franchiser" provides the product, trade names, management training and support, advertising, operating procedures, quality assurance standards and facility designs. The company will usually provide a significant amount of assistance to the business owner in starting and managing the company. A good example of this for home based businesses would be MacDonalds.

(2) Product Franchising or Trade Name Franchising: This type of franchising only involves a product, trademark and royalties in the contract, but the franchiser does not regulate the method in which the franchisee conducts his business. The manufacturer grants a franchisee the authority to distribute goods by the manufacturer and allows the owner to use the name and trademark owned by the manufacturer. The franchisee must pay a fee or purchase a minimum inventory of stock in return for these rights. Examples of Product Franchise include: Mobil, Goodyear, Baskin Robbins, and Ford Motor Company, etc.

(3) Dealership and Distributorship: These product or trademark franchise own the rights to sell the franchiser product under their own trademark rather than the franchiser's name, with no restrictions on how the business is run.

(4) Licensees: These product or trademark, a license to make and sell the franchiser product with few, if any, restrictions on how to run their business.

(5) Agencies: These product or trademark franchise own the rights to sell products or services on behalf of a supplier. A good example of this may be vending machine franchise.

(6) Manufacturing Franchise: These types of franchise provide an organization with the right to manufacture a product and sell it to the public, using the franchisor's name and trademark. This type of franchise is found most often in the food and beverage industry, but can be applied to other industries. Examples of Manufacturing Franchise include: Coca-Cola.

(7) Unit Franchisee: This franchisee is granted the right to operate one unit or outlet of the franchised business - a unit franchise. This is the simplest and most common form of franchising. A single franchisor may ultimately have several hundred different unit franchise.

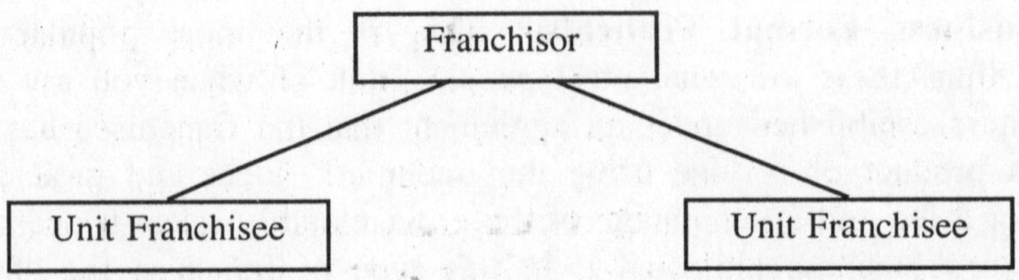

(8) Master Franchisee: A master franchisee is granted the rights to a substantial territory - usually a whole country. It will then grant unit franchise to unit franchisees throughout the territory. The master franchisee is in many ways similar to a franchisor. The term "sub-franchisor" is therefore sometimes used instead of master franchisee and unit franchisees referred to as sub-franchisees. This is the structure adopted by many franchisors to enter a new country. The master franchisee needs to have sufficient drive and resources to fully exploit the territory and control the unit franchisees territory.

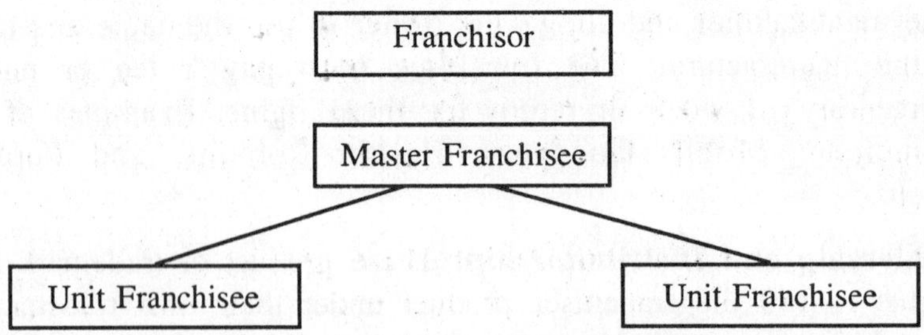

(9) Regional Franchisee: In a geographically large area a franchisor or master franchisee may decide that it is commercially appropriate to further divide the territory up with separate "regions" and grant a master franchise for each separate region.

These franchise are known as regional franchise or sometimes area franchise. The area term is commonly used in large countries such as the USA, where regional franchise for one or several of the different states are felt to be appropriate.

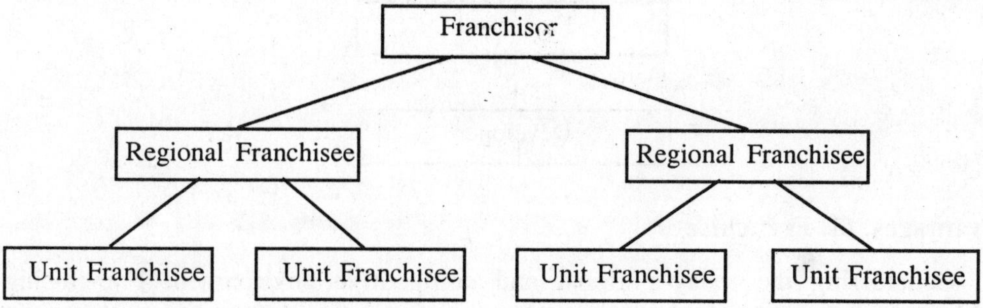

(10) Multiple Franchise: Some franchisees operate not just one unit, but several. These are referred to as multiple franchise and usually have a large number of individual unit franchise agreements - one for each unit.

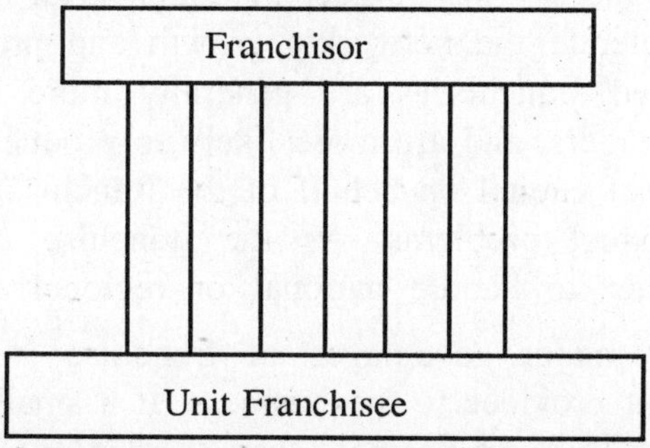

(11) Developers: Rather than be a master franchisee and sub-franchise to unit franchisees, large corporations sometimes prefer to exploit their territory by opening outlets themselves. These are known as developers. They have a single developer agreement which allows them to open many units. In practice, master franchisees also usually run some of their own outlets in the territory.

Developers therefore need to have considerable financial and other resources.

Large corporations often find it culturally difficult to easily accept that working with franchisees means working with independent business people who cannot simply be "hired and fired". They are therefore more likely than anyone else to be developers.

Even master franchisees should operate one or two "pilot" operations themselves so that they become fully familiar with the business at an operational level and can "localise" it to improve its chances of success.

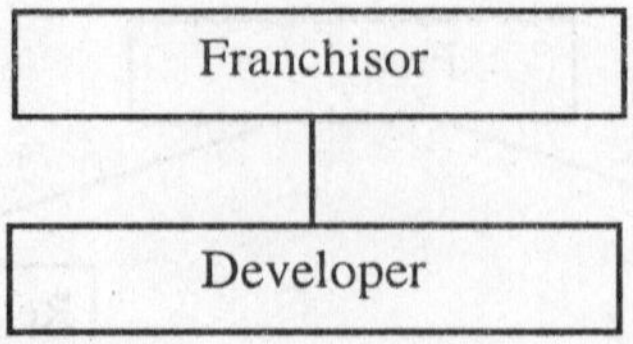

Advantages of Franchise

Considering the today's global and competitive environment Franchising could be beneficial for both the franchisor and the franchisee. In simple terms the franchisor can expand their reach as well as network and also capitalize on the strength's of the franchisee.

- The main advantage of franchising to the franchisor is that it allows the latter to increase its number of outlets with minimum capital outlay and so accelerate the network's growth and probably its profitability. Self-employed franchisees are generally more highly motivated than salaried managers, and are more likely to produce better results for less expenditure of capital on behalf of the franchisor. Less staff will mean fewer personnel problems. As the franchise network grows it will become easier to handle national or regional customer accounts.
- One of the major advantages of franchise is the established name recognition it provides to the business. If a small business is associated and linked with a big-business then there is a high probability that the small business would propel due to the firm backup and support of an established big business. Running a small business under the franchisor's name and organization is very beneficial for businesses that can't afford much finance and capital investment for their own business.
- Another major advantage of franchise is that when a business is associated with a franchisor then the big-business themselves help in corporate marketing of the small industry or business they are providing support for. Having the interest of big-budget industries in a low-budget business is a very effective marketing tactic and these franchise policy ensures the proper marketing of a small business.
- An advantage of franchise is the bulk purchasing power it gives to small business and industries. Since most of the initial financial burden is

provided to the business once it's franchised by the franchiser therefore this enables the business to buy equipments, products and other necessities to run the business with ease and without worrying about the financial investment.

- A major advantage of franchise is the training and management facilities the franchisor provides to the business. A company which provide capital and investment to any small business have vested interest in the success of the small business. Therefore the companies that provide franchise ensure that the business in which the money is being invested is run and managed properly. The big-businesses and industries provide all the necessary training to the small business staff and provide additional resources and decision-making capabilities to a small business.

Disadvantages of Franchise

- The disadvantage of franchising to the franchisor is that it has to control and co-ordinate a network of semi-independent businessmen and ensure that they build and maintain a favorable image for the whole franchised operation. This means that the franchisor's own role changes drastically.
- Disadvantage of franchise includes the indulgence of a big-business into a small business. The effective control that a small business owner have, often hinder when franchising in done. Any decision which is to be made is to be consulted and approved by the franchisors. This limits the authoritative control of the small business owner to a great extent.
- Another disadvantage of franchise is reaching a general agreement on terms and conditions. There are several occasions when the terms and conditions imposed by the investors and franchisors are biased and getting a firm deal with the companies safe-guarding the interest of both parties is a complex task.
- A disadvantage of franchise is that the much time is required while selecting a franchise. A complete and thorough research is required to select the right franchise and to determine whether it would work for the business or not.
- Another disadvantage of franchise is that this is a complex procedure and there are numerous instances during the business when heated discussion and disputes occur between the small business and franchisor.

1.5 SUMMARY

Franchise is defined as,

(1) A privilege or right granted to a person or a group by a govrnment, state or sovereign.

(2) Authorisation granted by manafacture to a distributor or dealer to sell his products.

Franchising is a successful method of distributing good or services to consumers.

India, with its huge market and growing demand in all sectors of the economy, is an extremely attractive proposition for entry of foreign brands through the franchising route, due to lower capital requirments, huge market, cultural empathy and laws and language.

The Types of Franchies have evolved over a period of time in accordance to change in demand of the market environment, such as Business Format Franchise, Product or Trade Name Franchise, Delarship and Distributorship, License, Agencies, Manufacturing Franchise, Unit Franchise, Master Franchise, Regional Franchise Multiple Franchise and Developers.

The main advantages of franchising, is that it allows increasing the number of outlets with minimum capital. If a small business is associatated and linked with the big business then there is a high probability of small business would propel, as the big business helps in corporate marketing of the small industry or the business. the advantage is a training and management facilities provided by the franchisor. However, the disavantages could be the franchisor's own role changes drastically, and indulgence of a big business into a small one. Selection of franchise is not only a cumbersome procedure, but also a time consuming factor.

1.6 SELF ASSESSEMENT QUESTIONS

(1) Define

(a) Franchise

(b) Franchisor

(c) Franchising

(2) Explain in detail, 'Franchising in India.'

(3) What are advantages and disadvantages of Franchising?

✠ ✠ ✠

Chapter 2

MERITS AND DEMERITS OF FRANCHISING

Objectives

After going through this chapter, you will be able to understand:

- The importance and merits for giving a franchise
- The importance and merits for becoming a franchisee
- Key drawbacks of owning a franchise
- Key drawbacks of giving a franchise

Structure:

2.1 Franchisee's Benefits

2.2 Franchisor's Benefits

2.3 Demerits of Franchisee

2.4 Demerits for a Franchisor

2.5 Summary

2.6 Self Assessment Questions

The very concept of franchising is expansion of a business enterprise through a network of franchised units instead of setting up its own branches and sub-units. Franchising accrues multiple benefits of low capital expenditure; personal commitment and motivation and reduced daily involvement.

Franchising brings benefit for (1) Society, (2) Franchisees, and (3) Franchisor

Society in general should benefit from franchising because of

(1) Decreased economic concentration

(2) Lower failure rates for franchised businesses

(3) Increased opportunities for minorities and women

2.1 FRANCHISEE'S BENEFITS

(1) **The trademark of the franchise and the product sold appear to be valuable, and the franchisee is willing to pay something to sell these commodities.** The franchisee's business benefits from the benefit of a name and reputation (a brand image) and goodwill which are already established in the mind and eye of the consumer. With renowned franchisee such as McDonald, Peter England, Allen Solli, Pizza Hut, etc., the customers are fully aware of the products and they are sure to get what they sought for. They flock at such outlets. Simply because of the name of the brand of such items.

(2) The franchisor often gives managerial advice to the franchisee. The franchisee's lack of basic or specialized knowledge and experience is overcome by the training program of the franchisor. A reputable franchisor will help a franchisee in almost all possible ways as per convention – such as assisting to find out a prominent and suitable area of operation, acquiring a commercial property, supplying equipment, machinery, furniture and fixtures and stock as well as imparting training to the franchisee and experience at pilot operation. The original business logo with the correct colour matching and size and even the franchisee employee's lapel badge should be made available. A comprehensive hands-on service is more convenient for a franchisor to open a franchised unit as it would be save much time and cost also. An experienced franchisor is fully aware of what to do and what not, where as a small trader who is new in the business has to see and experience a lot, even how to negotiate and reach a settlement on the part of a premise, dealing with suppliers and managers, etc., for the first time. All these are time consuming and at times may land in painful learning process and getting vulnerable to committing huge and costly errors. Such assistance may enable a franchisee to set up and carry on as a franchisee without the slightest experience or knowledge of a particular business or trade. The franchisor must always be easily accessible, and ever ready to pass on relevant information to franchisees as the need be. Any intending, change in format or strategy with regards to the existing business must be freely discussed with the franchisees before taking a firm decision. To launch a venture without

any relevant information and date would eventually be a failure. There are many a factors he requires to know about lest he may face unending problems.

(3) The franchisee will usually need less capital than he would, if he was to set-up a business independently. The franchisor often makes capital available to the franchisee in some form-either by consigning for a bank loan or by actually buying the plant and leasing it to the franchisee. Also, franchisors are less risky borrowers and hence, the franchisee can save here. Some acknowledged banks are reluctant to have business dealings such as loans, overdrafts, etc., to fresh comparatively not so well known business establishment even though their advertisement catch a lot of channel. They ascertain that the owner is financially well of making a good market share as well as profit. With a proven franchise system, raising finance is not a big problem. All leading banks offer special financial package to franchisors worth a name than they would to a small time trader.

(4) In a way the franchisee becomes an entrepreneur and opens business with substantial assistance at both preopening and post-opening by the franchisor. The franchisee has the incentive of owning his business with the additional benefit of continuing assistance from the franchisor. It is ethical on the part of a franchisor to provide all probable help for a franchisee over and above supplying the operating manual and troubleshooting experts to solve any problem that may arise. The franchisee should further have full access to the franchisor's research and development (R&D) facilities; and must be given chance to take part in training programmes; update as and when changes in the format or strategy takes place and undertake both local and national advertising campaigns. With such far-reaching and well-coordinated back-up support the franchisee will be able to concentrate on running his day-to-day business. He will not have to worry on devising a variety of policies, systems and procedures every now and then. An independent trader has to make decisions that are innovative and far-reaching select alternative courses of action, etc., constantly. The operating costs of a franchisee will be comparatively lower than that of a lone business person who will not be getting the facilities of a group R&D as well as bulk buying and advertising options. The franchisee invariably receives the benefit, on a national scale (if appropriate), of the franchisor's advertising and promotional activities. The franchisee may receive the benefit of the bulk purchasing power and negotiating capacity which are available to the franchisor by reason of the existence and size of the franchised network. However, no franchisee should consider that because he is coming under the umbrella of the franchisor he is not going to be exposed to any risk at all. The franchisee has the benefit of continuous research and development programmes designed to improve the business. The franchisee is the proprietor of its own business and

owns the tangible assets of the franchise outlet. What it does not own is the goodwill. Like any other business proprietor the franchisee buys materials, pays rent and staff salaries and takes the profit of operation, less royalty and service fees. Subject to various restrictions, it can sell its business when it wishes (usually subject to the franchisor's pre-emption right and on condition that the purchaser is approved by the franchisor). What makes the franchise different from any other business is that it gains from the franchisor the entire business concept with full training, assistance in every aspect of setting up and running the business, and access to necessary materials and supplies. In essence, it can be said that the franchisee does not have to worry about what to do or how to do it, but merely follow the developed concept. This makes failure less likely.

Advantages of Franchise Ownership

The benefits of franchise ownership are only as strong as the franchise he selects. Generally speaking, the benefits can be classified in several broad areas:

(1) Overall Competitive Benefits: The public has become accustomed to a certain level of quality and consistency from brand name franchised locations. The consumer knows the level of quality they will receive in every location they visit. This brand identification often provides the new franchisee with an established customer base accustomed to shopping under the company's brand and that makes it easier to compete with the well-established independent operators and even against other well-established franchised competitors.

(2) Pre-Opening Benefits: Franchisors have made mistakes. Another advantage of franchising is that they have survived their mistakes and can guide their franchisees not to make the same mistakes. Upon joining an established franchise system new franchisees generally receive comprehensive initial training in the operating of the franchise system, its product, services and methodologies. While the cost of entrance into a franchise system includes a franchise fee - often cited as a disadvantage, the franchisee benefits from a host of services including operation manuals, site selection, store design, construction programs and reduced cost of equipment to name just a few. Additionally, they have not only their franchisor as a seasoned partner to ask questions to but the network of other franchisees within the system that can be of assistance. In essence, the major stumbling block for pre-destined failure is removed by the franchisor — lack of preparedness. Most independent businesses don't fail because their product or services were inadequate, But they fail because they did not anticipate problems. Chief among these is working capital. Well developed franchise programs ensure that before they accept a new franchisee that they have adequate capital, even after servicing their debt and taking into account seasonally adjusted cash flow. Without this guidance many independent operators fail soon after opening.

(3) Ongoing Benefits: In exchange for paying an ongoing royalty and other payments, franchisees generally receive continual training programs and other ongoing home office and field support and assistance. Group purchasing power is a major benefit of well-developed franchise systems. Frequently buying groups established by the franchisor allow the franchisees to benefit from a lower cost of goods, equipment and supplies than that available to independent operators. Leveraging off the contributions of the entire franchise system, franchisors are able to create professionally designed point of sale, advertising, grand opening programs and other marketing materials that independents could never afford. Franchise programs can also afford to continue to modernize the system through ongoing research and development and the test marketing of new products and operating programs. Franchising is a critical mass business both with a market and system. The spending power of the individual combined with their fellow franchisees within their market and the rest of the system enable franchisees not only to dominate local markets and established independents but also to compete effectively against the established large chains.

2.2 FRANCHISOR'S BENEFITS

The franchisor can earn a reasonable profit without becoming involved in high capital risk or in the day-to-day detail and problems which arise in the management of scattered outlets. Thus, with low capital expenditure the franchisor gets a lot of benefits. The franchisor spends the initial cost for organising and marketing a franchise system. Then on, each franchised unit is set up and run with franchisee's money. Usually a good amount goes for the commercial property where the franchisee sets up his unit. This money is paid by the franchisee and no part of it is borne by the franchisor. Likewise, the fixtures and fittings and repairing and paintings charges are also met by the franchisee. Even the expenses towards developing the individual franchisee are covered by the franchisee's front-end fee and the royalty payments. These may not add up to a considerable amount in the earlier period. But once the business picks up, the benefit turns out to be quite significant. The franchisor utilizes the franchisee's finances and expands his business without spending much. The franchisor's capital expenditure is very low. Regardless of this low capital cost the franchisor earns not only a comfortably lucrative income through royalties but also establishes his product and its trade logo in the highly competitive market. In real terms a franchisee reduces to be a mere agent in the long run where as the franchisor, without having to cough up a large capital amount towards setting up franchisee units reap the benefits. He is safe from the risk of financial loss in case a franchisee unit fails to pick up. But generally, the franchisor provides all help and appropriate advice to the franchisee as and when the need arise. Through appointing franchisees, a franchisor is free from two restraining factors of running a business establishment – limited funds and high risks. These two factors hamper the growth of a business proposition. A franchisor is able to expand the business more rapidly through franchising than opening up new units. This also enables a franchisor to enlarge his business potential to a great extent. He can take it from local level to national and even international level using a minimum of risk capital and management resources. The franchisor acquires the advantages of bulk buying facilities and improved payment terms too. He can create a win-win situation in the market due to the vast sales and service network throughout the country as well as abroad. This will no doubt, lift him up to be a market leader.

(1) The franchisee invests money, time and effort in buying the franchise. He/she will launch and maintain the business and will become a self-employed and independent entrepreneur. The franchisee often raises the required finances through loans from banks and borrowing from financial institutions incurring a hefty monthly payback installment by way of capital and interest. He has to sacrifice all sorts of luxuries to a certain extent to meet his obligations. If the venture fails he will be facing bankruptcy. On the contrary if the business franchisee turns out to be a success and more and more profits pour in and his standard of living also goes higher. Thus, the fear of getting bankrupt on one side, in case of failure, and the desire for a luxurious life obviously make a franchisee work harder and more dynamic. The main advantage of franchising to the franchisor is that it allows the latter to increase its number of outlets with minimum capital outlay and so accelerate the network's growth and probably its profitability. Self-employed franchisees are generally more highly motivated than salaried managers, and are more likely to produce better results for less expenditure of capital on behalf of the franchisor. Less staff will mean fewer personnel problems. As the franchise network grows it will become easier to handle national or regional customer accounts.

(2) When a sub-unit fares well, the franchisor too earns more. He has less to worry than a non-franchisor businessman. No jostling for him to form head offices to branches spread across the country. He has to be in constant contact with the franchisee. The rest of the worries are coolly transferred to the franchisee who is all the more obliged as otherwise he would be at the receiving end. The franchisor is free from motivating his managers, to fix targets for the staff, supervise them, decides on commissions, perks and other incentives to boost sales of his products and all other activities associated with a business

proposition. Avoiding all these headaches, the franchisor is all set to create a more stable network of outlets. The franchisee not only puts all his efforts and energy to make the venture a success, he himself becomes a shrewd, manager and businessman by seeking ways and means of cutting costs, improving efficiency, eliminating unnecessary expenditures and increasing the turnover. The franchisor will find it easier to exploit territorial areas which are not already within the scope of his organization and franchisees with local interests, community involvement and knowledge come into the picture. The success of a franchisee motivates a franchisor to seek more and more franchisee and expand his empire. Speaking in business terms, Sky is the limit for a franchisor.

(3) Reduced Daily Involvement: The franchisor provides a franchisee with his business format as also all the relevant initial services. But it is left to the franchisee to run the venture. The franchisee is responsible for the day-to-day administration, stock control, managing the staff and all relevant activities within the strict framework and guidelines given in the Operating Manual. Once the franchisee masters the system of conducting the business, the franchisor is almost free from his daily involvement. He monitors the goings on and provides the franchisee with suggestions and advice as per the latter's requirements. The drastic reduction in administrative workload permits a franchisor to run his organisation with minimum effort. Work loads apart from this he is miles away from the usual worries and headaches of a business magnate. He will also have enough spare time to select more and more appropriate franchisees and study the ever changing market trends and adopt appropriate measures to check the situation and set right things. He will be able to carve out a new strategy or think about innovative technological changes and improvement in the existing system of operation. A reputable and established franchisor who successfully created a chain of franchised outlets will be well known in the business circle and earns a great respect. Thus, through the various franchisee outlets he becomes well recognised. He earns an image and good-will. He becomes famous all over his operating area and earns a standing solely due to the market share he dominates through the franchisee network which otherwise would have been possible only after years of operation and toil. Instant possession of a memorable name and status automatically lead to increased sales and profits at a faster rate than he would have derived from a small enterprise of his own.

2.3 DEMERITS OF FRANCHISEE

Just as the two sides of a coin there are certain drawbacks and shortcomings too. A franchisor meets with certain disadvantages or drawback when compared with operating a self-owned business. They are: loss of ownership; lower profits and more and more interdependence.

(1) Loss of Ownership: A franchisor owns the business format. He controls the activities of the outlet making the franchisee follow the guidelines and strictures laid down in the operating manual and through a regular vigilance and compact franchisee agreement. Yet, the outlet business is owned by the franchisee as long as the agreement is in force. The franchisor is not a commander. His role is reduced to that of a guide or an advisor. He is forced to toe the line through a radical approach. This is because of the franchisor-franchisee relationship which is remarkably different from that of an employer-employee relationship. Within a franchise both – the franchisor and the franchisee – are equals; earning mutual benefit. So, it is evident that the mutual cooperation and coordination is most important for the success of a franchise. The franchisor explains, discusses and places suggestions instead of commanding and instructing. In due course, a franchisee gains experience and his confidence gets boosted up. He may start questioning certain policies and conventions prevalent in the business. Gradually he/she may tighten the reins and demand a larger say in matters of decision-making and even a change in the business strategy altogether. The franchisor has to be very much diplomatic and tactful in dealing with such a situation, lest the communication, cooperation and mutual trust may collapse.

(2) Lower Profits: Just as in the case of setting up an altogether new enterprise, franchising too have to face certain teething problems. The finance crunch will be one of the difficulties of a franchisor at the initial outset, as expenditure supercedes income. Organising a franchise unit, advertising and marketing, etc., becomes a costly affair for the franchisor who has to depend on the namesake front-end fee and low initial royalty incomes. The situation calls for a substantial cash reserve as working capital. Further, there is no guarantee that a certain franchisee network may follow through. As in any business, the franchisor also has to be patient throughout the gestation period. More such franchise establishments will put the franchisor in a difficult spot managing with insufficient royalty payments in the initial stages. The royalties that form a certain percentage of the turnover will be smaller than the net profit accruing in a franchise outlet. Thus, the franchisor will earn a lower income from a franchisee than from a self-owned business unit. This low income coupled with the initial negative cash flow may tempt a franchisor to search for a speedier and larger financial gains. Though such a step may seem to be lucrative, in the long run it may prove futile. An inadequate and impoverished strategy may reduce the initial expenditure but it will end in a shaky and destabilised franchise network. Demanding a high up-front fee will enable to recover the expenditure incurred more quickly, but will distance the potential franchisee from making a business alliance with the franchisor. So also, asking for a higher rate of royalty may show an upward mobility of income with immediate effect but may end in disaster later on, for few franchisees would come forward to accept an outlet with a meagre profit as a major part of the income will be going to pay the high royalty. Hence, a franchisor has to be ethical while fixing the front end fee and the royalty percentage. He has to sustain early money problems which are unavoidable and integral part of a franchise. Therefore a franchisor ought to have a strong financial background and support so that he/she can withstand the heavy initial expenditure as well as losses towards break-even. It may take a considerable time to reap the rewards, quite possibly, a few years.

(3) Interdependence: The success of a franchisee has heavy dependence on mutual trust and cooperation between both the partners of the agreement. It is not only desirable but a must that a strong bond should prevail between the two. The franchisor has to supply a perfect and complete business format, tested and a proven business system, help in setting up the franchise unit, help, suggestions and advice to the franchisee as and when required. On the part of the franchisee, it becomes mandatory for him/her to follow the laid down terms and conditions in letter and spirit. If either party lacks responsibility the effort and network would be jeopardised. A franchisor is fully aware of his role and has to be ever ready with suitable solutions for any untoward problems that may worry a franchisee. This puts the franchisor in a tight corner and at times will turn out to be stressful. The fact that the franchisee is fully dependent on the franchisor for his survival makes the latter be on his/her heels. So he must have the correct know-how and appropriate skills as well as troubleshooting capabilities. These measures would definitely lead to a successful franchise. On the contrary, sticking on to outdated policies and practices or selecting unworthy unscrupulous franchisees, etc., will ruin the franchisee leading to bankruptcy of both the parties. At the same time, the franchisor had to be vigilant not to be ruined by a deceitful franchisee. A careful selection of franchisees will solve this problem. A franchisee must be competent trustworthy as well as motivated to work really hard. Over ambitious candidates should be eliminated at first instance as such people may introduce changes in their outlets which they feel comfortable with but may not be feasible for the well-being of the business as a whole. It will be a tedious task to supervise such rebellious as well as incompetent franchisees.

(4) Hard Work and Effort: There goes a common belief among many of the would-be franchisees that franchising is an easy way out to get rich fast. But it is not that easy reaching and negotiating for a suitable property, getting permission from the government authorities, raising funds, availing godown facilities, and so on for setting up a unit. Nor does the franchisor do everything as it is believed to be. The franchisee will be fully involved from the very inception to running the business daily – getting sufficient stock, displaying them prominently, dealing with the customers, attending to their queries and doubts, handling of irresponsible and arrogant staff, maintaining proper accounts and a lot of related activities. The franchisee's involvement is most necessary for the success of a franchise. Often a franchisee will be required to spend late hours and that too all seven days a week. He will be fully engrossed himself in day-to-day affairs of the unit. It will be tedious and monotonous to keep the premises spick and span, maintaining the books of every part of trading, giving instructions to staff and sales persons, collecting the stock and so on and so forth. He cannot have many a holidays, has to forgo social functions and gatherings – all these become mandatory at least for the initial years till the business is smoothly on track. Financial commitments and sacrifices will also have to be made as per the situation demands. It will be a slow process to gain profits. To finance the project a franchisee needs to arrange through loan, overdraft or mortgage which are to be repaid every month on installments without fail from the initial meagre profits. Thus, he will see himself in a tight corner and will be forced to keep himself from luxuries and fantasies for a considerable period of time.

(5) Constant Payments: After meeting the initial expenditure the franchisee has to make regular royalty payments to the franchisor in continuing back-up support. This royalty payment in the initial period when the turnover is considerably less and mounting costs brings the franchisee-franchisor relationship to a tight spot on many an occasion. The franchisor will be after the franchisee to try and improve the performance in spite of the fact that he is putting in his best. As per the stipulation of the franchise the franchisee could be coursed-into take up commercial activities such as advertising and other promotional activities which would, no doubt, boost up sales, but this will not be adding up to profit due to the heavy costs involved in taking up such a step. Even the small payments will have an adverse effect on the franchisee till he starts to get good sales and profits go up. This becomes severe during the seasonal lull such as in the rainy season when sales plummet. These constant continual payment for a long period becomes an irritant for a franchisee especially when after he gets experience and the franchisor is nowhere to be seen.

(6) Inflexible Rules and Procedures: The franchisee is under obligation to operate strictly as per guidelines laid out in the operations manual, which call for uniform standard to be maintained so as to keep the success a routine matter. The franchisor checks up in every detail to ensure that the procedures are strictly and religiously followed throughout by the franchisee. If found otherwise, the franchisee could be ousted by terminating the agreement as a last resort. Having to operate under the vigilance of the franchisor may be extremely irritating at times. Sometimes, the franchisee will be reduced to be an elegant manager with full responsibility without any power towards decision-making. If he is willful or independent by nature it would be frustrating to work under such a situation which may lead to breaking up of the franchisee-franchisor relationship and ultimately cause irreparable damage to the franchisee unit and even the whole network. On a few occasions, he may be thinking that such restrictions are hampering his operations to a certain extent. He may have different ideas such as outdated décor, poor standards of products and services which needs amendment or replacement. For any such most essential and urgent step requires the franchisor's consent. Apart from getting a green signal from the franchisor he has to bring the other franchisees in the network in line with that of his suggestion and opinion. If he proceeds on his own with the changes he is liable to lose his franchise ultimately. In case a franchisee wants to wind up and sell the ongoing concern, the franchisor can be an obstacle. He may reject any potential buyer as not appropriate. Sometime it would turn out to be a lengthy and frustrating affair to find out one who is agreeable in the eyes of the franchisor.

(7) Mutual Dependence: The relationship between the franchisor and a franchisee is one of interdependence. They are dependent on each other to make the venture a success. The franchisor provides an established format, name and frames, detailed operating manual, constant help and guidance, instantaneous updating, and training, etc., on a continual basis – to the franchisee. In return, the franchisees pay an initial front-end fee, follow the format and agreed rules and regulations, maintain and develop a good franchising system and paying royalties promptly. It is evident that franchisee will be the sufferer if the franchisor or other franchisors fail to fulfill their respective duties and obligations. The franchisor may be unable or even unwilling to impart satisfactory support and advice, may commit errors while doing research on new ideas and innovations or may turn out to be insolvent leaving him high and dry. Other franchisees may go away from the set format, for example, selling the goods at cheaper rates than the stipulated price, giving substandard products and services. They could be pulled up by media for mistreating their staff, upsetting their customers through malpractices or even breaking the law. The impact will fall on the franchisee too which may damage his business or turn out to be so fatal that he will lose his franchise wholly.

2.4 DEMERITS FOR A FRANCHISOR

Disadvantages to the Franchisor

The disadvantage of franchising to the franchisor is that he has to control and co-ordinate a network of semi-independent businessmen and ensure that they build and maintain a favourable image for the whole franchised operations. This means that the franchisor's own role changes drastically.

The policing and monitoring of standards by the franchisor is vital but can at times be difficult. The franchisor will sometimes have to resort to the use of carrot and stick to get franchisee's to try new techniques or improve their current performance. Ensuring that franchisees do not under report their turn-over is also a major task. The dynamics of the franchisor-franchisee relationship are such that a lack of trust will on occasion creep in making life more difficult than it should be. This may be due to "personality" clashes between the franchisee and members of the franchisor's team or because the franchisee realises that he/she does not find it easy to live within the restraints imposed by a franchise. Conflicts between the franchisor's corporately owned outlets and those owned by franchisees may occur. It is the franchisor's duty to remove/minimise these conflicts and ensure that they are satisfactorily dealt with. An individual corporately owned outlet will be more profitable for the franchisor than an individual franchised outlet (although the increased number of franchised outlets will probably mean that the franchised business as a whole will be more profitable than one which is entirely corporate owned).

It will be quite apparent from the above that the franchisee is in no way an agent or representative of the franchisor. The complexities of the relationship may however lead the courts to speculate that the franchisor could in certain circumstances be a show director of a corporate franchisee.

Disadvantages to the Franchisee

While the franchising business model does have benefits, it is not the right business choice for every entrepreneur. Ongoing payments and strict protocol can be oppressive to aspiring entrepreneurs who crave the freedom and creativity that pure business ownership allows. While buying into a franchise can provide a more solid, established introduction to the business world, there are many cost, restrictions and obligations associated with franchising that detract from the overall business ownership experience.

(1) Expenses

Buying into a franchise is not cheap. The initial cost of a franchise can be Rs. 10-25 lakh or more on top of the cost of equipment, inventory, and business space. Also, franchises frequently require their franchisees to pay ongoing a percentage in royalties or franchise fee. Franchisee receives benefits in exchange for these costs, but at the end of the day they are still additional expenses that he needs to know about.

In addition, franchisors demand ongoing royalties, usually 3 percent to 6 percent of sales. Franchisees have to pay those royalties regardless of whether his business makes a profit or not. Franchises require steep startup costs that vary depending on the individual opportunity. Startup costs encompass regular business ownership expenses such as permits, construction, furniture, deposits, and insurance. But franchisees may also be required to pay additional fees, including steep initial franchise, training and advertising fees. After the initial startup cost is paid, franchisees must pay ongoing royalties to the parent company for the life of the relationship. These payments can vary from standard rates to percentages of profits. In most cases, the amount will be greater than a base price or a percentage of profits. This way, even if the franchisee is not earning any profits, the franchisor continues to profit from the agreement. The franchisor may also require payments for training and other support services, even if the franchisee does not use them or deems them worthless or unnecessary. Some franchises also require franchisees to purchase all supplies through the parent company which might be at inflated prices. An unscrupulous franchisor might charge, for mandated — but useless — training. In choosing to adopt the standards set by the franchisor, the franchisee often has no further choice as to signage, shop fitting, uniforms, etc. The franchisee may not be allowed to source less expensive alternatives. Added to that is the franchise fee and ongoing royalties and advertising contributions. The contract may also bind the franchisee to such alterations as demanded by the franchisor from time to time.

(2) Protocol

Due to a strict protocol established in contracts and operations manuals, there is little room for creativity or independence in the franchise model. This is to ensure uniformity across all franchises, but it reduces individual owner influence and decision-making power. In all circumstances, individual franchisees are expected to operate their business in full compliance with the operations manual and within their contractual restrictions. Continual corporate oversight can be reassuring for some business owners but unnerving to others. Aspiring entrepreneurs who desire to improve upon the existing business model, offer an innovative product or service or modernize to maintain a competitive edge may find their desires stifled at upper levels due to corporate bureaucracy. That rigidity ensures consistency among a firm's franchises, but it may curtail franchisee's independence and creativity, which might frustrate him if he has gone into the business to be his own boss.

Another potential drawback of owning a franchise is that franchisors place a number of restrictions on their franchisees. These restrictions can take a variety of forms including limitations on products, pricing, employee performance and policies, territory, marketing, and other areas critically important to the success of the business. Sometimes these restrictions can seem burdensome, but overall they can be good for the business because they ensure uniformity across the franchise.

(3) Name Association

In a franchise model, the name association is touted as a tremendous benefit to starting entrepreneurs. Yet the actions of every franchisee in the model can affect the entire company. An outbreak of food poisoning in one restaurant in the franchise can generate bad press for a franchisee hundreds of miles away and reduce the clientele and profits of that location. Some companies try to make money by just collecting franchise fee, and won't spend the time or money necessary to help their existing franchises succeed in the long run. Moreover, such "pyramid franchisors" may go under if they stop selling new franchises, leaving the franchisor with a next-to-worthless business.

Name recognition is widely seen as one of the major benefits of franchise ownership. However, name recognition can also be a hindrance to the business, particularly if the other franchises or the franchising company itself is receiving bad press or suffering from a poor public perception. For example, the franchised restaurant can be the best meal in town, but still suffer because a franchised operation halfway across the country was implicated in a food poisoning fiasco. The best protection against this is to make sure the franchisor has a time-tested and solid reputation within the industry.

For franchisees, the main disadvantage of franchising is a loss of control. While they gain the use of a system, trademarks, assistance, training, marketing, the franchisee is required to follow the system and get approval for changes from the franchisor. For these reasons, franchisees and entrepreneurs are very different. The United States Office of Advocacy of the SBA indicates that a franchisee "is merely a temporary business investment where he may be one of several investors during the lifetime of the franchise. In other words, he is "renting or leasing" the opportunity, not "buying a business for the purpose of true ownership." Additionally, "A franchise purchase consists of both intrinsic value and time value. A franchise is a wasting asset due to the finite term: the franchisor is only obliged to renew the franchise if it chooses to contract for that obligation.

The franchisee's reliance on the power of the franchisor's brand may prove to be a disadvantage if the franchisor, through mismanagement or neglect, allows the reputation of the brand to become tarnished or fall into disrepute

(4) Limited Potential

Automatic restrictions on growth are a major drawback of franchising. Territorial restrictions prevent franchisees from infringing on another territory. This may not have an effect on restaurant owners or businesses that operate from an established location, but for franchisees who offer consulting or mobile services, this restriction can be detrimental. At the time of a desired expansion, there might not be any available territory nearby for the franchisee to purchase. Even if any additional territory is purchased, the price will be comparative to the original startup prices and may discourage growth.

Unlike a typical small business, the growth potential of franchised operations is limited by a couple of factors. First, most franchisors impose territorial restrictions on their franchisees. This limits the franchisees ability to market or sell outside a clearly-defined geographic area. If the franchisee is in the restaurant business, this may not seem like a big deal. But if the franchise sells consulting services, it can make a big impact on the plans for growth.

Another factor that limits the growth potential of franchises is that franchisees cannot franchise. When it is time to expand, many small businesses look to grow their operation by franchising themselves or adding on additional stores in different areas. Franchisees relinquish their ability to do this and may even be unable to expand to surrounding areas by purchasing another franchise due to the territorial rights of other owners within the franchise.

Franchisees, although independent business people and owners of their own businesses, will be subject to control and regulation by the franchisor which they will not necessarily appreciate or like. The more successful they become in their business, the more irksome they will find the franchisor's directions, controls and regulations.

The franchisee's business may suffer as a result of an error on the part of the franchisor say, in introducing a new product range which fails or which may not be as successful as the franchisor may have predicted.

(5) Obligation

According to the International Franchise Association, the average length of a franchise agreement in 2009 was 10.6 years. That is a long time to commit to a business that is ultimately controlled by a separate entity. During this time, the franchisor may go out of business or make sweeping changes to the business model that the franchisee finds disagreeable. Thus, Buying a franchise is like marrying someone you haven't known for very long.

Franchised businesses tend to be highly specialised and in this regard the franchisee may be exposed to a change in trend to which the franchisor may not permit him/her to respond, for example by stocking another range of products, and by insisting that the franchisee continue in the narrow specialisation which had previously made the franchised business so successful.

The franchisee will not have the unfettered right to sell his/her business because any such sale will be subject to the franchisor's consent and this can never be taken for granted.

The franchisee may become over-dependent on the support of the franchisor to the extent that he/she may cease to be or never become truly independent in terms of his/her ability to make decisions and the franchisee may thus inadvertently become, in effect, a disguised employee

(6) No Guarantee

Usually, there is no guarantee of financial success for the franchisee made by the franchisor in the written disclosure circular and the actual franchise agreement. While the estimated startup costs of the franchise are an implied "earnings claim" some businesses do fail, including franchised outlets. Unfortunately, the unit financial performance statistics are not required to be disclosed to new buyers of franchises under Federal Regulatory Policy, the FTC Rule, and this omission makes it impossible for new buyers of franchises to assess the odds of success and failure of their investment in the franchise in terms of profitability and failure as experienced on a unit basis of the franchise system.

(7) Conflicts

The franchisor/franchisee relationship can easily cause conflict if either side is incompetent (or acting in bad faith). An incompetent franchisor can destroy its franchisees by failing to promote the brand properly or by squeezing them too aggressively for profits. Franchise agreements are unilateral contracts or contracts of adhesion wherein the contract terms generally are advantageous to the franchisor when there is conflict in the relationship.

As a franchisee, he has little legal recourse if he is wronged by the franchisor. Most franchisors make franchisees sign agreements waiving their rights under federal and state law and in some cases allowing the franchisor to choose where and under what law any dispute would be litigated. Shamefully, the Federal Trade Commission (FTC) investigates only a small minority of the franchise-related complaints it receives.

2.5 SUMMARY

Merits

Franchisee's benefit

(1) The trademark of the franchise and the product sold appear to be valuable, and the franchisee is willing to pay something to sell these commodities.

(2) The franchisor often gives managerial advice to the franchisee. The franchisee's lack of basic or specialized knowledge and experience is overcome by the training program of the franchisor.

(3) The franchisee will usually need less capital than he would if he was setting up a business independently.

(4) In a way the franchisee gets to become an entrepreneur and opens business with substantial assistance from the franchisor.

Franchisor's benefit

(1) The franchisor can earn a reasonable profit without becoming involved in high capital risk or in the day to day problems which arise in the management of scattered outlets.

(2) The franchisee invests money, time and effort in buying the franchise. He/she will launch and maintain the business and will become a self-employed and independent entrepreneur.

(3) When a sub-unit fares well, the franchisor too earns more. He has less to worry than a non-franchisor businessman.

(4) For the franchisor it is reduced daily involvement as the franchisee takes care of that

Demerits

A franchisor meets with certain disadvantages or drawback when compared with operating a self-owned business. They are: loss of ownership; lower profits and more and more interdependence.

The disadvantage of franchising to the franchisor is that it has to control and co-ordinate a network of semi-independent businessmen and ensure that they build and maintain a favourable image for the whole franchised operation.

Also for the franchisee a lot of hard work and effort has to be put by the franchisee and it's not that he has got a ready business from the franchisor and it will be very easy. Moreover, after meeting the initial expenditure the franchisee has to make regular royalty payments to the franchisor in continuing back-up support. This royalty payment in the initial period when the turnover is considerably less and mounting other costs brings the franchisee-franchisor relationship to a tight spot on many an occasion.

The franchisee is under obligation to operate strictly as per guidelines laid out in the operations manual; which call for uniform standard to be maintained so as to keep the success a routine matter.

It will be quite apparent from the above that the franchisee is in no way an agent or representative of the franchisor. The complexities of the relationship may however lead the courts to speculate that the franchisor could in certain circumstances be a show director of a corporate franchisee.

2.6 SELF ASSESSMENT QUESTIONS

(1) Explain in detail the following:

(a) Merits and Demerits of a franchisor.

(b) Merits and Demerits of taking a franchisee.

✠✠✠

Chapter 3

SYNERGIES BETWEEN FRANCHISOR AND THE FRANCHISEE

Objectives

After going through this chapter, you will be able to understand:

- Relationship between franchisor and franchisee
- Conflicts between franchisor and franchisee
- Service delivery system.

Structure:

3.1 Value Addition from Franchisor and Franchisee

3.2 Franchise Relationship Model

3.3 Summary

3.4 Self Assessment Questions

Franchising is based on a unique set of relationships not found in other business organisations. It is a business relationship and a human relationship, so success in franchising is dependent upon developing these relationships successfully.

The relationship between the franchisor and the franchisee is very different from most business relationships. There is an analogy to be drawn between parent-child relations on the one hand and franchisor – franchisee relations on the other. In the early stages of the franchise relationship, the franchisee, like a child with a parent, is dependent upon the franchisor for his source of information and the understanding of how to apply the knowledge acquired. As the franchisee gains practical experience he becomes less dependent, and in some cases so independent that he no longer sees the value in his association with the franchisor, or at the best a diminished role for the franchisor. He regards himself as being totally responsible for his success. If this practical experience is taken in the right stride, it can prove to be immensely successful.

3.1 VALUE ADDITION FROM FRANCHISOR AND FRANCHISEE

The franchisee can come up with new product ideas or some innovative distribution strategy. It can also help give customer insights to the franchisee.

At the same time, the franchisor should encourage the inputs received from the franchisee and treat him with respect. However the control over the system and the strategies of the business still stays with the franchisor to which the franchisee will have to abide by.

The franchisee will also require a constant support in terms of understanding the system as well as the process, this support is required not only during the initial stages but also on regular intervals and whenever there are any changes in the process or a system.

It is the duty of the franchisor to give regular feedback to the franchisee as it will help in the overall growth of the business. But franchisee should also take the feedback in the positive sense as it is for their own benefit. The franchisee is the one who comes in direct contact with the customer on a daily basis, thus, the franchisor expects the franchisee to give appropriate feedback in regards to the customer. In other words the franchisor wants to feel the rules of the market/client with the help of the franchisee.

Franchising is based on a unique set of relationships not found in other business organizations. It is a business relationship and a human relationship, so success in franchising is dependent upon developing these relationships successfully. Franchisees look to the franchisor for leadership, support, vision, assistance and profitable solutions to their problems. They do not look for employer oriented attitudes.

The best results are usually obtained when the franchisee knows the absolute parameters of what constitutes proper operation of his business. For *e.g.,* in a restaurant franchise, absolute standards apply for cleanliness, food quality and health matters. Too many rules and too close supervision will kill the franchisee's motivation. The best ideas come from motivated franchisees.

Franchisor gets the market intelligence and feedback on customer preferences and their varying tastes through the franchisee. Regular symposiums are held to decide on issue related to marketing and other related matters. These forums are attended by the franchisor as well as franchisees. This type of bondage helps the growth of the franchisee very much.

Franchisor provides new opportunities to the franchisee who, according to him, seems to be a good businessman who follows the policies of the company. New opportunities may usually be in the form of new products new additions franchise outlets or master franchise outlets. These are good growth opportunities for a franchisee and hence, the growth and well-being is tied up with that of the franchisor. If the franchisee is entrepreneurially ambitious and enthusiastic he can be an active participant in the growth of the franchisor and secure his own growth objectives.

The franchisor and the franchisee are both legally independent of each other. They are free to carry out their work independently subject to contractual obligations and responsibilities. The relationship between a franchisor and franchisee is certainly close. They are linked together by the franchisee bond of common interests – profitability. If everything goes on well and smoothly there would be a long-term relationship between them. The franchisor and the franchisee work together for the common cause of benefiting from the business.

Franchisee relationship is unique as in effect it is a 'business partnership' which results in a 'win-win' situation for both franchisor as well as for a franchisee when their effort proves to be successful. There would be some expectations from both the sides which need to be fulfilled by each of them respectively. For any partnership to succeed, it is mandatory that both ought to be one of trust, confidence and cooperation. The franchisor should be aware of the fact that his success depends upon the success of the franchisee. On the contrary the franchisee should have faith in the franchisor's products, systems and strategies.

The business partnership in a franchise grows in geometric proportions if and when the franchising rules are strictly adhered to. A large number of the franchisees go for a single product which creates a competition and awareness about the product in the market resulting in greater sales for each franchisee. The overall growth in revenue benefits the franchisor immensely.

Franchisor: A franchisor provides all sorts of help and advice to set up an outlet of the business and conduct the day-to-day transactions in accordance with strict format of the original establishment. The franchisor helps the franchisee select a proper area of operation, bargaining and setting the deal of commercial property, setting up the outlet premises, arranging the finance required to start with, supplying all sorts of equipment and utilities required for carrying out the business. In addition, advertising campaigns selection and training of field staff and such related activities are also done. They are also given a brief of management techniques and operating procedures.

The franchisor also gives the franchisee continuous support and guidance. The franchisor will observe the marketing trends that go on changing periodically. After evaluating the probable effects and ameliorating the necessary adjustments reconstruct the business format and update the franchisee as and when needed. The franchisor also provides the franchisee with expert advice and even technological know how and troubleshooting measures. An operating manual showing the do's and don'ts also is given to the franchisee by the franchisor.

Franchisee: The operating manual given by the franchisor is as good as a blueprint of the business format for the franchisee. It sets out how the business is to be carried out in minute detail. The franchisee is expected to follow the instructions as per the manual in letter and spirit, failure of which may lead even to discontinuance of the business contract. The franchisor will monitor the activities and progress of the franchisee periodically to ensure that the whole process is functioning up to stipulations and norms given in the operating manual.

Back-up services are a regular feature from the franchisor. The franchisee has to pay royalty or a management service fee for this. This fee may be either a percentage of turnover of the franchisee or a fixed amount regardless of the turnover. In certain instances it is found to be a mark-up on the equipment and stock provided by the franchisor which usually is ten to twenty percent. The mode of payment also varies as either weekly, monthly or mutually agreed upon.

A franchise agreement is drawn up and signed by both franchisee as well as franchisor. This agreement is binding to both the signatories and specifies certain terms and conditions to be met by the franchisor and franchisee. The agreement usually specifies the duration of the agreement; the area of operation; the franchisee's rights and obligations. The conditions and formalities regarding arbitration, renewal and termination of agreement are also specified in detail.

Organisations which are aware of the essence of franchising have taken up franchising systems so well that they managed to achieve growth in sales, revenues and profit considerably. There are examples of quite a large number of business organisation that have adopted this method of business. Their success have made franchising an excellent method of distribution.

Adherence By Both Franchisee and Franchisor: It is said that franchising involves the development of multiple chain of outlets in multiple ownership.

However, there are subtle differences in all these outlets and because of which the rigid franchise agreement cannot be applied as it is everywhere.

Also, the request from each franchisee is not only difficult to cope with but is incompatible with the maintenance of uniformity. Because of all these variations also, sometimes the harmony between the franchisor and the franchisee goes for a toss.

Sometimes a franchisor does 'special deals' with an individual franchisee. It might create problems as the franchisee who is given a special deal will regard himself as a special case and may expect privileges. On the other hand, the other franchisees will resent the one who has got the special deal.

Thus, certain things can be adhered to by both the franchisor and the franchisee in order to ensure a synergy.

(1) Respect by both franchisor and franchisee for the achievements and guidance upon which the franchise system of marketing is based and which are the foundations of its success.

(2) Respect by the franchisee for the achievements and guidance which the franchisor provides, and not respect so blind that the franchisee does not see when the franchisor should be questioned and challenged, but respect for the ownership of the name, system know-how and practical experience.

(3) Respect by the franchisor for the achievements of the franchisee and the contribution to the system which each franchisee can make, gained from his experience in running an operational unit.

Conflicts Between the Franchisor and the Franchisee: Conflict is not totally unhealthy for any business. Questioning, probing, arguing, and even fighting can sometimes produce very healthy results. Like in the case of Pizza Hut which led to a revised license agreement and a successful new launch of its pizza-delivery program.

However, when conflict reaches the courts, it drains time, talent, and money from a franchise system, and conflict at that level seldom results in a healthy relationship.

In 1986 Pizza Hut was struggling with upstart competitor Domino's. Franchisor management was convinced that the competitor's pizza delivery was a real threat and that Pizza Hut needed to respond with its own delivery offering. But the franchisor had over a thousand franchises with territory rights that were highly successful sit-down restaurants. "Why fix what isn't broken?" was a common franchisee refrain. The delivery system added costs to the franchise operation with uncertain revenue. It also affected the way franchisees operated the sit-down business. Tension grew as the franchisor began to experiment with the Pizza Hut business model with centralized phone ordering and special procedures for home delivery orders: Pizza Hut teetered on the brink of massive litigation.

Eventually, the franchisor negotiated with franchisees and the firm embraced delivery. But why did the friction between the franchisees and franchisor rise to this level in what now seems an obvious need to respond to the competition? The complexity of the franchisor – franchisee relationship suggests that if attention is not paid to key aspects of this partnership, the system will go awry.

3.2 FRANCHISE RELATIONSHIP MODEL

The franchise relationship model (FRM) takes the entrepreneurial framework and gives a blueprint for developing and analysing all aspects of the franchise format, from the physical building to the monitoring and control aspects. It asks the questions that become pertinent when designing the most ideal service delivery system (SDS) for any given franchise. It anticipates practical breakdowns in the franchise relationship and suggests avenues for appropriate modifications for both the franchisor and franchisee.

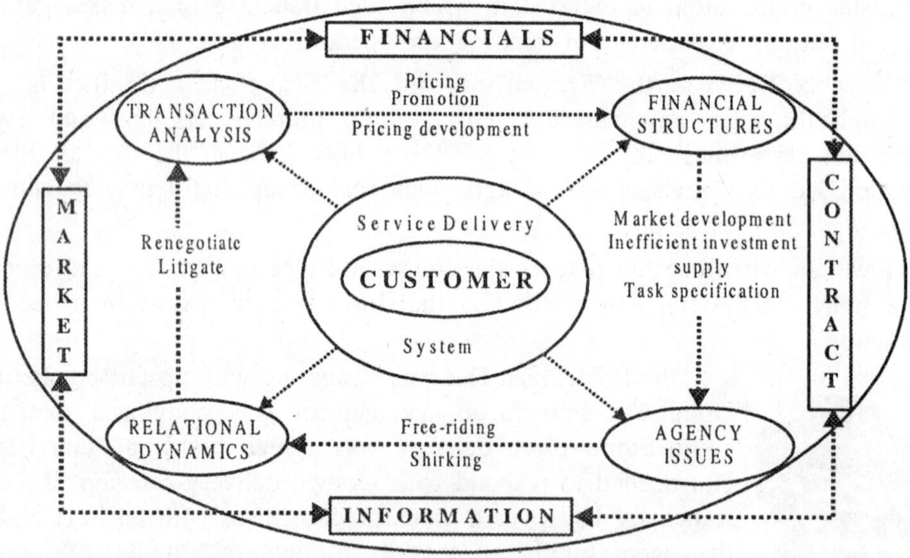

Figure 3.1: The Franchise Relationship Model

Franchising is a powerful tool because it has the potential to create wealth for a large number of entrepreneurs. The FRM illustrates both how a potential franchisor can most efficiently construct a franchising company and how a prospective franchisee can determine which system to join. Among other things, the FRM also helps to distinguish between those tasks best executed under a corporate umbrella and those best done by the individual franchisee. The problems at Pizza Hut, for instance, began when corporate management started tinkering with the business format that franchisees were comfortable with. The changes disrupted the security of their revenue, and franchisees naturally became concerned about their financial futures. Confusion equals conflict in franchising. That confusion does not pertain only to the financial results. It can manifest in role responsibilities too. When the franchisor experimented with taking orders centrally and eliminating onsite phone orders, the franchisees became confused about who was responsible for delivery tasks. Figure 3.1 is our first look at the FRM. This model depicts a series of franchise principles, each of which interacts with the others to form a powerful, interlocking business concept that solidifies itself as the links are implemented more efficiently. The process starts in the center with the customer and moves to the SDS. Any changes in the target customer needs, or the SDS have consequences that affect the franchise alliance. The value of the FRM is that it enables to identify the nature of these consequences. Once the causes are identified, the franchise can be improved by realigning transaction responsibility and reassessing the financial well-being and reliance on each partner. The dynamics of answering these questions, however, can often cause conflict in the relationship, because changes in the relationship have to be agreed upon by the franchisee and the franchisor.

The FRM suggests a series of questions. Both potential franchisors and franchisees can use it as a roadmap to success by asking the questions that we pose throughout the chapter. The answers offer a perspective that can help determine the entrepreneur's success. We cannot stress enough how important it is to understand the goals and objectives of both players in the franchise company for a healthy franchise relationship to develop. We consider each part of the FRM, the model as a whole, and how the parts interact. To best illustrate the parts of the FRM, we evaluate them in the following sections from the perspective of a prospective franchisor, because the franchisor must deal with these issues first when developing the franchise. The discussion is also beneficial to prospective franchisees, as it illustrates how a franchise and the resulting FRM are developed, thus, enabling franchisees to evaluate different franchise systems.

The Customer: How Does Opportunity Recognition Work in Franchising?

Time and again, hopeful entrepreneurs announce, "I have a great idea for a franchise." Unfortunately, there is no such thing as a great idea for a franchise. As discussed in Chapter 1, an idea is simply that: just an idea. Determining whether there is a great *opportunity* inherent in the idea is the crux of the entrepreneurial decision. Assessment of a concept starts with defining the opportunity and is validated in one or more outlets. The franchise relationship model provides a roadmap to apply the franchise context to the opportunity and to reassess the concept in the real-world marketplace to see whether it actually generates a profit. The customer is at the center of the FRM. The job of the franchisor is to develop a business format that will meet the needs of the customer in a way that makes money for both the franchisor and the franchisee. The SDS surrounds the customer in an attempt to meet the demands of the customer. Franchisees and franchisors should assess and reassess often. The problems at Pizza Hut started when Domino's exposed pizza delivery as a customer need that Pizza Hut wasn't meeting. The Domino's 30-minute guarantee changed, but by then the brand had been established the rules about how people could eat pizza in the USA. Clearly, a segment of the population wanted a pizza delivery option. Once the market for the product is known, the next step in evaluating a potential opportunity is to estimate the size of the market. Calculation can follow this formula:

Target Customer × Estimated Revenue per Transaction × Transactions per Year by Each Target Customer = Annual Revenue

Every business uses this type of formula to determine its revenue basis and to continually work toward honing in on average price. Forecasting specific amounts is difficult, however, for example, at Kinder Care, a franchised daycare center, the average revenue per transaction equals the base cost of care per day plus any extra service that can be sold. The next step in calculating the annual rèvenue is to take the number of days per year that the target customer is in the company's care and multiply this by the average price per day. The result equals the total expected yearly revenue. Projecting revenue is a process of calculating the size of the customer base and the result of selling products and services to each member. The customer base is projected as a percentage of the primary target audience. Then, we must ask specifically. How many service/products can we sell? How many add-on sales will occur, and how many times per year will sales be made? These are the questions and layers of intricacy that add texture and management direction to revenue projections.

With this projected annual revenue amount in mind, one can forecast the costs and expenses of the proposed franchise by developing the appropriate SDS.

The FRM leads us to the next step.

Establishing the Service Delivery System

(SDS): How Does the FRM Provide a Framework for Marshalling Resources?

Why is the SDS, which is also called the business format, often a proprietary design? Because it is not only the fundamental means by which customers' needs will be served, but it is also the way in which the service delivery resources are arrayed to create competitive advantage in the marketplace. Highly successful and visible examples of business format innovations are the drive-through windows in fast-food restaurants and bi-level facilities in quick-oil-change facilities.

Every franchise has a well-defined SDS, however, overt or transparent it may seem to an outside observer.

Don't underestimate the value of carefully planning the SDS. The expression, "The devil is in the details" never takes on greater meaning than during the design of the franchise delivery mechanism. Here let us look at the experiences of Jiffy Lube and Steve Spinelli to understand the model better. This was very clear from experiences that Jiffy Lube encountered while expanding the franchise. One particular component of the expansion plans paints a vivid picture of the intricacy of SDS development and reveals what a great benefit this design was to the founders over time. Steve Spinelli recalls the following:

> When we decided to open a new Jiffy Lube location, we had specific criteria for location that simply had to be adhered to: high volume of car traffic, on which side of the street the building was located (outbound or inbound), high-profile retail area, and the far corner of any given street or block, among others. Once these aspects were addressed, then came the building specifications. As overanalyzed as it may seem, through some trial and error, we were able to determine the optimal location of the Jiffy Lube structure on any given property. Once that was determined, we dealt with the structural specifications for the exact angle of the building, including the width, depth, and angle of the entrance and the degree bend of the driveway—all to allow for the optimal number of cars to "stack" in line, waiting for the car in front to complete the service. On several occasions we were confounded by locations that fit all of the above criteria but were still not performing as expected. Upon closer inspection it became apparent that the bend in the driveway was too sharp. This prevented customers from driving their cars completely onto the lot and into the queue; subsequently, this gave the impression to oncoming traffic that the lot was full—when in fact it was not. We quickly understood the devilish nature of the details and had to adjust several driveways to accommodate an increased number of cars.

It is this level of refinement and detail orientation, if not obsession, that must be adopted while looking at the planned and actual delivery system. Unless examined under a high-powered microscope, one might miss essential components.

Another part of the "complete" Jiffy Lube SDS was the design of the inside of the Jiffy Lube maintenance bay. Considering the limitations inherent in the use of hydraulic lifts, we were confronted with the dilemma of how we could offer thirty minutes of labor in only ten minutes. To deliver this ten-minute service, we knew that we had to have three technicians work on a car at once without the use of a lift. This quandary led us to develop an SDS in which the cars would drive through the bay and stop above an opening in the floor. This allowed one technician to service the car from below, another to service the car underneath the hood, and a third to service the car's interior. We knew that without developing such a "disruptive" system, we would not have been able to succeed as we did. The typical delivery system in automotive service standardized the physical setting (bays with lifts) combined with mechanics that were certified in many areas of automotive repair. We used a specialized facility with highly focused (versus broadly qualified) lube technicians. Our method "disrupted" the conventional thinking about automotive maintenance delivery. The soundness of our decision to use the drive-through, bi-level system was confirmed when we saw our competitors—gas stations and car dealers—insist that they could offer a "quick lube" in thirty minutes using hydraulic lifts and traditional bays. It quickly became apparent that they simply could not compete for the very reasons that Jiffy Lube became a success. It became clear to us that it was the sum of the intricately designed parts that created the value of the SDS. Moreover, it was clear to us from our competitors' failure to compete that if one of the parts were removed from the SDS, the result was not simply a slightly diminished return, but rather a complete lack of return.

Such is the level of detail needed for an SDS to deliver both value to the customer and cost efficiencies to the concept operator. Every franchise company bets the future of the company on having a better understanding of how to meet consumer needs through its business format. Eastman Kodak and the founder of Mail Boxes, Etc., teamed to develop the Image Arts, Etc., franchise. They believed that by combining technology and retail service, they were putting the company "on the cutting edge of the digital imaging revolution and [becoming] the first company to offer wide format printing and digital photography to the public in retail shopping center locations."

It is important to note the interrelationship between the SDS and the customer.

All these details can be made understandable through the Franchise Relationship Model (FRM) which covers:

(1) Transaction Analysis

(2) Financial Structures

(3) Relational Dynamics

(4) Agency Issues

Transaction Analysis: In the Franchise Relationship, How Are Responsibilities of the Franchisor and Franchisee Allocated?

So far, we have discussed market demand without reference to the individual responsibilities of the franchisor and franchisee. We call the assignment of these responsibilities *transaction analysis*. There can be no viable franchise until the franchisee has a financially sound business model for the single outlet. Franchising creates sound, single-store operations and economics in a unique way. The tasks and responsibilities necessary to deliver the product to the customer are clearly documented in the contract and allocated between the franchisee and franchisor based upon their respective capabilities and efficiencies. The sum of the transactions constitutes the brand equity shared by the parties to the license agreement. Those issues that stand outside the realm of foreseeable and definitive actions but that will play an ongoing role in the operation of the franchise will be documented and continually updated in an extra contractual *franchise operations manual*. This manual gives both parties the opportunity to update rules, regulations, and procedures that will come to bear over time.

Thus, in setting up the franchise, franchisee must ask, what are all the individual transactions necessary to deliver the prescribed SDS? These tasks must then be allocated between the franchisor and franchisee on the basis of whether the task is best executed at a national (franchisor) level or at a local (franchisee) level. As a general guide, the franchisor tasks are those that carry economies of scale. This usually implies a size or bulk requirement in the task, such as management training or bulk purchase of equipment. Franchisee responsibilities are based on the task being executed on site in the local market, such as local sourcing of raw materials and hiring employees. Critical to local entrepreneurial intensity is customer contact and local market knowledge. Some tasks are shared. For example, the franchisor has a national role in marketing, and the franchisee is responsible for local interpretation and execution of advertising and promotion.

Once he allocates the tasks associated with the SDS, the franchisee can continue to assess costs and revenues through the use of pro forma financial statements that incorporate the information already gleaned by determining the market demand. Marshalling the resources to establish the SDS allows understanding the costs involved in meeting market demand; the SDS defines the costs of acquiring the revenue. The known revenue and known costs brings a clear understanding

The phenomenon of the whole being greater than the sum of the parts is indicated by the delineation of tasks between the franchisor and the franchisees and is reflected in the value that is created through this cooperative synergy. The principle link between the franchise's proposed financial structure and the principal–agent relationship with the franchisor is the contract. Through the contract, the details of market development, task specification, and investment supply are addressed.

The Transaction Analysis talks about the allocation of responsibilities between the franchisor and the franchisee. The tasks and responsibilities necessary to deliver the product to the consumer are clearly documented in the contract and allocated between the franchisee and the franchisor based upon their respective capabilities and efficiencies. Responsibilities are also allocated based on the geography, say franchisee responsibilities are based on the task being executed on site in the local market. It will cover things like sourcing of raw material or hiring employees as he has the customer contact and the local market knowledge which is critical to the business. On the other hand, the franchisor takes care of all the national level activities. Some tasks are shared as well. Take for example, franchisor takes care of the national level product specification but it is the franchisee that localizes it.

Sample Transaction List

Franchisor: Centralized economies of scale	**Franchisee: Local entrepreneurial intensity**
(1) Establish site acquisition criteria	(1) Local site that fits criteria
(2) Design building blueprint specifications	(2) Initiate local contractor bidding
(3) National contracts for inventory and equipment specification and purchasing	(3) Onsite installation of equipment and inventory management
(4) Centralized training of franchisee management	(4) Onsite training of franchise employees
(5) Detail marketing plan template for ratio, print media and television advertisement	(5) Placement of promotions in local media

Agency Issues: How to Find the Right Franchise Partner

A key issue raised by any strategic business interdependency is the partner selection process and the ensuing principal-agent relationship. The agent, in most cases the franchisee, agrees to act on behalf of the principal, the franchisor. This symbiotic partnership is one of the key success factors of franchising; it is also one that requires considerable vigilance.

Relational Dynamics

What separates the great franchises from the mediocre? Why is it that almost 50% of all franchisors are in a lawsuit at any given time? Why is that 30% of franchisees are unhappy enough with the relationship to consider severing it.

The major success factor is the basic understanding between the franchisor and the franchisee and it goes beyond all systems and agreements. The relational dynamics is the way in which the franchisor and the franchisee interact to exploit opportunities, handle conflict, communicate about current operations, and plan for the future.

It is a business partnership and like all business partnerships it involves two parties, the franchisor and the franchisee. The franchisor provides the know-how, training, system, and the brand, whereas the franchisee forms the front-end and is responsible for managing his business unit. Technically, the 'Franchising contract', that binds the two parties is the system.

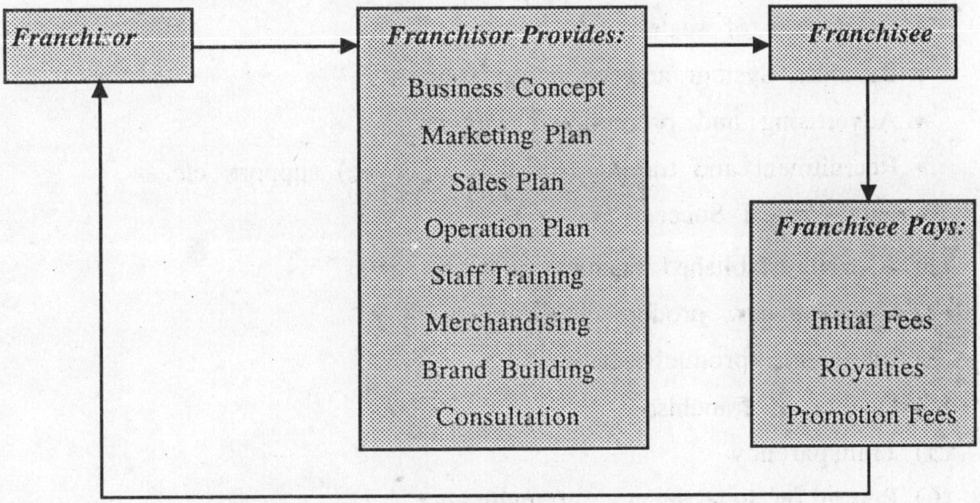

Figure 3.2: Franchising System and Support Services Model

A Win-Win Proposition

The most interesting part of franchising system is its win–win propositions between the two parties – franchisors and franchisee. Both the parties engaged in the 'deal' can reap substantial benefit from the franchising system.

It is said that, a franchisor gets three fold benefits from franchising. Firstly, franchising acts as a distribution model for the franchisor which helps them to growth rapidly. Secondly, it reduces the setup risk, as risk is shared by the franchisee members and thirdly, franchising ultimately helps in brand building and acts as a consumer interface amongst the populace.

Franchising helps franchisor to have

(1) Greater access to capital

(2) Better utilization of operating cost

(3) Rapid presence in both known and less known market places

On the other hand, franchisee also enjoys benefits from franchising. In most of the cases, entrepreneurs have limitations in terms of capital, business know-how and have to deal with certain degree of risk. But franchising helps an entrepreneur (franchisee owner) in various aspects like

- Get an association with an already known trademark.
- Lesser investment and degree of risk
- Shorter learning curve
- Economies of scale
- Business System and operation support
- Advertising and promotional support
- Recruitment and training (of the employee) support, etc.

Ranking Critical Success Factor

(1) A well established business network

(2) Constant new product development

(3) Innovative products/services

(4) Quality of franchise

(5) Transparency

(6) Return on investment to franchisees

Source: Annual survey of the Indian Franchise Sector, conducted by First Franchising

Again, in practice it is often found that there is an 'idea mismatch' between the franchisor and franchisee causing dispute, conflict and ultimately termination of the contract. To find the 'reasons behind it' the same franchise consulting firm conducted one research and identified the most common causes of friction between the franchisor and franchisees.

The result of the research is shown in the table below.

Ranking Causes of Friction

(1) Transparency

(2) Training and support

(3) Revenue sharing

(4) Product/Service Delivery

Source: Annual survey of the Indian Franchise Sector, conducted by FirstFranchising

A Partnership That Extends Beyond the Office

By Jacqueline McDermott

Sonya Eddings is a busy woman. She works at a law office, runs two Coffee Beanery cafés, and is a full-time mother and wife. Sometimes it seems like she'd see her colleagues more than her husband...if her husband wasn't her business partner.

She left her position as vice president in the technology department of a bank in Columbus, GA three years ago to help her husband, Michael, manage his private law practice. She handles the business finances and assists with the day-to-day duties imperative to the firm's smooth operation. The job is challenging and fulfilling, but Sonya and her husband shared a dream of collaborating on a more "delectable" business venture.

"My husband and I love to travel, and really enjoy the atmosphere and culinary offerings of local cafes in Europe. We have always talked about owning a business together. It has been a dream of ours for many years, but we needed to wait for the right opportunity. Combining our entrepreneurial natures with our appreciation of good coffee seemed like a foolproof idea," she says.

After thoroughly exploring various options, the Eddings decided to take over a Coffee Beanery that was already operating in the Peachtree Mall in May, 2006. They still aspired to build a franchise location from scratch, though, so it appeared fortuitous when they discovered a building for sale in the historical district of Uptown Columbus.

"At first glance, it looked like a mess, but Michael and I saw potential for something wonderful. He turned to me and said, 'This would be the perfect spot for that coffee shop,' and I knew he was right! It was on a busy corner, with several banks, government buildings and post offices within walking distance. You could not beat the location," explains Sonya.

The couple completely restored the derelict structure and made it their second Coffee Beanery in August, 2006.

A strategic site is an important element of the Coffee Beanery's philosophy. Part of the Coffee Beanery's store development business system includes a dedication to finding the right location — a visible spot in a high-traffic area that matches the company's proven criteria, which is a mix of 20 factors, including demographics, traffic patterns, and competition.

But of course, to run a profitable business, you need more than prime real estate. The Eddings methodically researched what it took to open a coffee house and found the answer was — a lot!

"You need product, equipment, a menu, a training process, etc. We didn't want to recreate the wheel, so when choosing between opening a private business and joining a franchise program, the decision was simple. A franchise would allow us to capitalize on already established vendor relationships. We would be a part of a larger organization but at the same time, maintain our local autonomy. It was, and is, the perfect balance," Sonya says.

The couple's experience running Michael's private practice, which provides title insurance and escrow services, helped prepare them for their new adventure. They knew the level of commitment necessary to succeed as business owners. They had worked together as colleagues before and knew they would be compatible as professional partners.

Like the Eddings in Coffee Beanery founders Julius and JoAnn Shaw also run a family business, something that attracted Sonya to the opportunity. "When I learned that the Coffee Beanery was a family business, and about how the Shaws had built the company from its first, single mall location to what you see today, I was very intrigued. I admired JoAnn's dedication to family values, and of course, the franchise's success," she says.

Sonya recently enjoyed an achievement of her own. In May 2008, Columbus County honored Sonya and her franchise's devotion to the community and charitable endeavors by bestowing to her the Hometown Hero award. The Eddings' Coffee Beanery shops support local hospital drives and have provided coffee and products to the American troops in Iraq.

Sonya credits some of her accomplishments to her two dedicated managers who run the shops' day-to-day operations, including staff management, but franchising still keeps her busy. She visits both stores, which are seven miles apart, every day before heading to the law office. She also oversees all finances and vendor purchases, and holds weekly tactical meetings with the store heads.

"I spend an average of 25 hours per week on the management of the stores. I need to observe the store in action so I can consider quality control issues and answer important questions, such as how we are interacting with our customers, how clean the facilities are and whether the staff is up-selling and understanding the week's specials. Then I provide feedback to the managers," explains Sonya, who also visits the stores every weekend to spot check.

The Eddings hope to open additional stores throughout the Columbus area, making them perfect candidates for the Coffee Beanery's area franchising licensing agreement. The franchise offers three different types of domestic licenses: single unit; area development, which grants the right to develop multiple locations within a designated area; and area franchising, which allows existing franchisees to assist corporate headquarters in building the brand by helping to recruit and mentor new franchisees, in addition to running their own store, in a specific geographical region.

Sonya is currently fluent in all things Coffee Beanery. She is confident in the product and dedicated to opening new shops, but she spent a lot of time and research hours getting to where she is today. "Whenever you enter a new business venture, it is important to understand what you are getting into," she explains. "The Coffee Beanery's Five Step Domestic Process of becoming a franchisee helps you do just that."

The first step of the system is the potential franchisees' investigation of the company, which for the Eddings meant using the Internet to learn about management and corporate ideals. Prior to beginning the Five Step Domestic Process, she and her husband used *The Franchise Handbook* Website to glean unbiased, reliable information. They also called various franchisees from different companies to ask questions about the level of support they received, management style, red tape and royalty fees.

When Sonya was satisfied with her findings, she completed the online application. The company contacted her, asked and answered some key questions, and instructed her to complete documentation. "Next, I learned what we really needed to do if we were serious about becoming part of the Beanery family — visit the headquarters and franchisees in the Michigan area."

Sonya continues, "This allowed us to ask the current owners questions and observe the daily operations and distribution process. I don't know how other franchisors engage prospective partners, but this process was imperative to our decision. I trained for four weeks with my manager in Michigan. It was what I needed to ensure that I could successfully run our shops and understand our business inside and out."

She continues to rely heavily on the Coffee Beanery's marketing support and appreciates the resposiveness of the corporate office. "Everyone is just an email away. If I have a question or concern, I can be confident that the appropriate person will respond to me immediately. That helps assure me piece of mind."

Sonya says the most important piece of advice she can offer to a prospective franchisee is to find a business that he or she loves, and to be sure to ask the right questions during the research phase.

"Ask about organization and management style. Ensure that the franchisor's business philosophy is consistent with yours. Becoming part of a franchise is a long term commitment. You may be independent, but it's a team approach that makes things work,' advises Sonya.

"Personally, I love having a level of independence, but also collaborating with other franchisees when needed. Having the franchisor focus on establishing a brand name through product placement and marketing on a national level complements what I do locally. To me, working as a franchisee is more attractive than working alone as a private business owner."

3.3 SUMMARY

The relationship between the franchisor and the franchisee is very different from most business relationships.

The franchisee will require a constant support in terms of understanding of the system as well as the process.

It is the duty of the franchisor to give regular feedback to the franchisee as it will help in the overall growth of the business. The franchisor helps the franchisee select a proper area of operation, bargaining and setting the deal of commercial property, setting up the outlet premises, arranging the finance required to start with, supplying all sorts of equipment and utilities required for carrying out the business. In addition, advertising campaign selection and training of field staff and such related activities are also done. They are also given a brief of management techniques and operating procedures.

The franchisor expects the franchisee to give appropriate feedback in regards to the customer. In other words the franchisor wants to feel the rules of the market/client with the help of the franchisee.

The best results are usually obtained when the franchisee knows the absolute parameters of what constitutes proper operation of his business. For *e.g.*, in a restaurant franchise, absolute standards apply for cleanliness, food quality and health matters. Too many rules and too close supervision will kill the franchisee's motivation. The best ideas come from motivated franchisees.

The franchisor and the franchisee are both legally independent of each other. They are free to carry out their business independently subject to contractual obligations and responsibilities that exist between them respectively. The relationship between a franchisor and franchisee is certainly close. They are linked together by the franchisee bond of common interests – profitability. If everything goes on well and smoothly, there would be a long-term relationship between them. The franchisor and the franchisee work together for the common cause of benefiting from the business.

A franchise agreement is drawn up and signed by both franchisee as well as franchisor. This agreement is binding to both the signatories. Such an agreement will specify certain terms and conditions to be met by both franchisor and franchisee. The agreements usually specify the duration of the agreement; the area of operation; the franchisee's rights and obligations. The conditions and formalities regarding arbitration, renewal and termination of agreement are also specified in detail.

The FRM Model

All these details can be made understandable through the Franchise Relationship Model (FRM) which covers:

(1) **Transaction Analysis:** The Transaction Analysis talks about the allocation of responsibilities between the franchisor and the franchisee. The tasks and responsibilities necessary to deliver the product to the consumer are clearly documented in the contract and allocated between the franchisee and the franchisor based upon their respective capabilities and efficiencies.

(2) **Relational Dynamics:** The major success factor in franchising is the basic understanding between the franchisor and the franchisee and it goes beyond all systems and agreements. The relational dynamics is the way in which the franchisor and the franchisee interact to exploit opportunities, handle conflict, communicate about current operations, and plan for the future.

(3) **Agency Issues:** A key issue raised by any strategic business interdependency is the partner selection process and the ensuing principal-agent relationship. The agent, in most cases the franchisee, agrees to act on behalf of the principal, the franchisor. This symbiotic partnership is one of the key success factors of franchising; it is also one that requires considerable vigilance.

3.4 SELF ASSESSMENT QUESTIONS

(1) List and explain the various value additions the franchise and franchisor get on the table to support each other.

(2) Explain in detail the FRM model.

(3) Write a short note on 'the role of Transactional Analysis' in a franchisee-franchisor relationship.

(4) Explain in brief the Service Delivery System (SDS).

✠ ✠ ✠

Chapter 4

EVALUATION

Objectives

After going through this chapter, you will be able to understand:

- Accessing one's own strengths and weaknesses.
- The consideration of a franchisor for a franchisee.
- Steps involved in acquiring a franchise
- Criteria's to be considered for a franchisor and the franchisee

Structure:

4.12 Summary

4.13 Self Assessment Questions

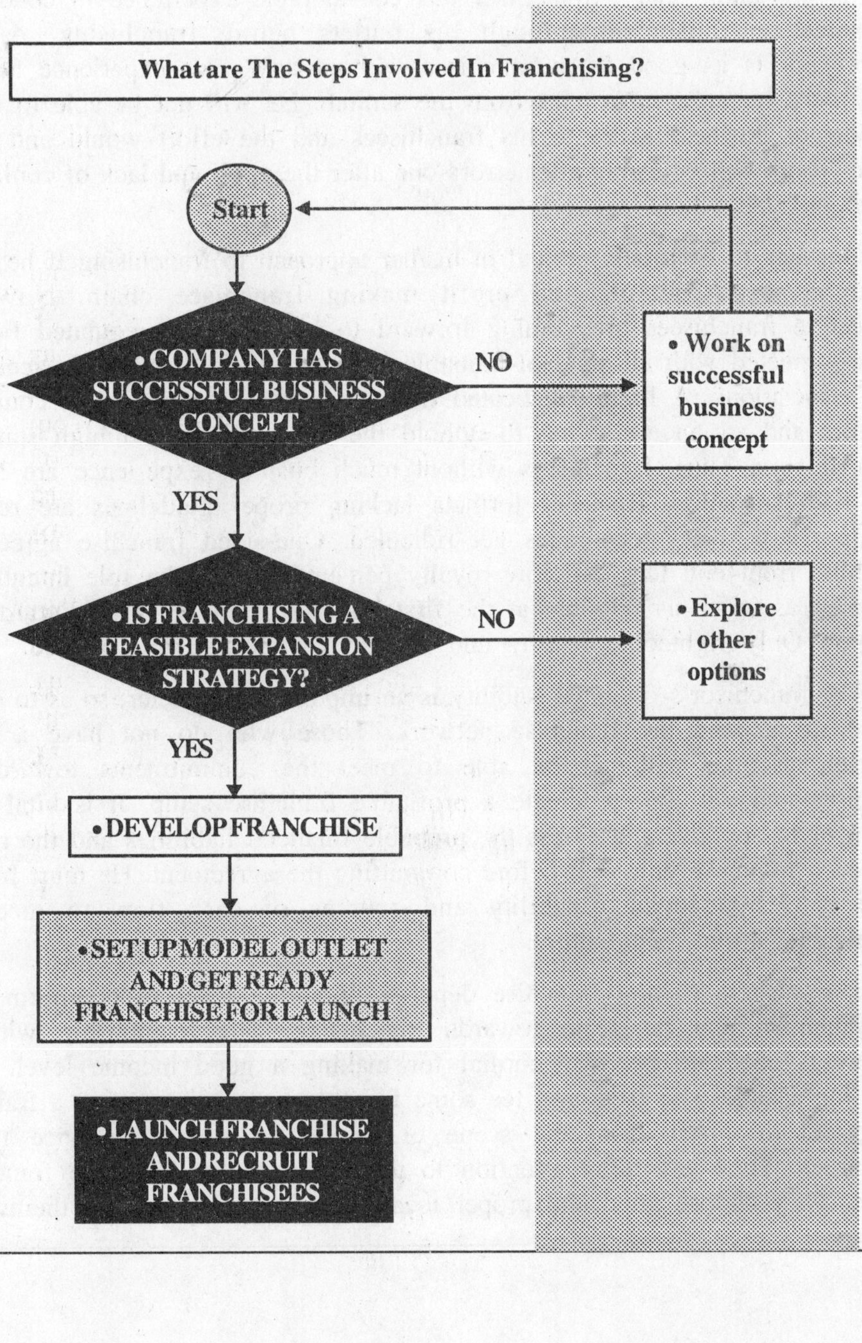

A franchisor should have a thorough knowledge of the business as franchisee envisages him/her as an expert who has a lot of experience of the business world. They are expected to approach the franchisor with utmost confidence to get their problems solved. They anticipate that they can totally rely on the franchisor in getting the right advice and suggestion at the right time. So it is preferable that a franchisor has considerable experience in conducting a business establishment through his outlets before franchising. A fresh entrepreneur is as good as a franchisee without any prior experience and has to learn the business intricacies from the scratch. He will not be able to import any sort of business skills to his franchisees and the effort would end up in failure. There will be errors after errors one after the other and lack of confidence will engulf the whole network.

One has to be totally ethical in his/her approach to franchising if he wants to set up a respectable and profit making franchisee chain. Nowadays prospective franchisees are coming forward to join this self-regulated field of business greeted with all sorts of valuable advice from internationally acclaimed trade associations. A highly dedicated team consisting of Bankers, accountants, solicitors and so on are vying to uphold the clean image and high standards of franchising. Thus, franchisors without much business experience are looked upon with suspicion. Business formats lacking proper guidelines are rejected outright. Hard scales techniques get ridiculed. One-sided franchise agreements with high front–end fees and low royalty percentage with the sole intention of squeezing as much as possible at the first instance itself are also discarded on the spot. Only righteous, worthy and honest franchisors are accepted.

The franchisor's financial stability is an important parameter; so as to enable him/her to expand the franchise network. Those who do not have a stable financial resource will not be able to meet the commitments towards the franchisee and will fail to create a profitable franchise setup. It is vital for a franchisor to appraise and assess the probable financial liabilities and the returns from each franchise unit well before committing the agreement. He must be well aware of his financial capability and sources of cash flow to meet the unavoidable initial expenditure.

The success of any franchise depends upon the level of commitment of the franchisor and his team towards franchising. The relationship with the franchisees needs to be very cordial for making a good income level. After collecting a handsome front-end fee some franchisors lose interest in a franchise outlet and disappear from the scene or provide a slipshod service to the franchisees. They pay more attention to their own outlets than the franchised outlets. They choose good and proper locations and keep these for themselves.

All these activities are characteristics of an unenthusiastic, unworthy and dishonest franchisor. This kind of approach will result is franchisee dissatisfaction due to unsolved problems, stagnant sales and stunted growth and ultimately end up with poor profit. As a result the franchisee will have no other alternative than winding up the unit and leave the place. Franchisees one after another will fall in line and the franchisor will not only lose the franchise but may damage or destroy his own business as well.

4.1 ASSESSING THE BUSINESS FORMAT

A franchisor must assure that his business format is a proven success. He himself has to be sure that he is offering a fault free, tested, tried refined and subjected to rigorous competitive market where the prospective franchisees have to trade and succeed. No franchisee with business acumen will be ready to accept an unproven and untried business system for the simple reason that such a position may turn out to be potentially faulty and risk-oriented. Only incompetent and naïve franchisee will take up such a business framework and the franchisor will be dissatisfied due to their poor performance. An ideal business format, hence, must be the one which is existing and working well in franchisor's own units. Such a format could well be adhered to franchisees with whatever modifications and adjustments are needed to make it appropriate. Devising a franchisable format from the scratch is not a safe and viable option. A great number of the new ventures may fail and the ones that pass the test may take time to establish and prove their mettle. Even after proving their credibility some of them may not be fit for franchising.

Certain products do well in the market due to their significant characteristics such as décor, layout, aroma and so on. They simply make business with their competitive edge. Such products, whatever they are, – beauty aid cosmetics, food items, cool-drinks, costumes – should have sufficient trade protection like patenting, registered trademarks, etc., if such steps are ignored the possibility of copying and limitation by rival firms are more. A business format is incomplete if such protective measures are not taken.

Once a franchisor is convinced that his business format is complete in every respect, he can look forward to franchising. The perfect and flawless format will be a guideline for the comparatively inexperienced and unskilled franchisees. Of course, franchisees are chosen through a careful recruitment process. Even then they require proper guidance from the franchisor's side. A format should provide the franchisees total information on 'how to start and run this business'. It surely makes sense that the franchisor assumes the franchisee to be absolutely ignorant of the business procedure and tells everything including the common basics such as stacking the goods prominently on the shelves, wrapping the good neatly and giving back the change after receiving money from the clients properly, etc. It may seem absurd, but the franchisor must see that his franchisee is very keen even in those minor things. A franchisees minor error may damage the name and respect of the parent organisation.

Another important area is the simplicity of the format. A format should be very simple, so that even a layman will be able to understand the content. A format should never be a complex and sophisticated one. The very purpose of the format is to transfer the know-how readily to the franchisees. The ideas must be presented in a legible and simplified manner and also in a simple language. Otherwise, training sessions of the franchisee network will also become difficult to handle. Simplicity in overall business procedures also help franchising in a big way. Fast food majors like McDonald's, Kentucky Chicken, etc., succeed in franchise market while top-ranking gourmet restaurants may fail due to their sophistication. In the former case the menu is simple and everyone is quite at ease with the described dishes whereas in the latter case it is practically impossible. There, the menu is diverse and sophisticated and requires the expertise of a talented chef to prepare the items. So also, simplified décor, layout, furniture, fixtures and fittings also help and choosing a better and viable commercial property for setting up a franchisee outlet with comparatively lesser cost. This helps expand the network of the growing chain of franchised outlets.

The franchisor must see to it that the product and services are value added and are sold at the most affordable prices so that both can earn a comfortable income. The offer price and the MRP should not be either too wide or very narrow. There ought to be a close range between them. If it is too narrow, the popularity of the product gets limited to certain pockets only; whereas too wide a range attracts less customers and popularity will not be as desired. Slow moving goods will result in tie-up of franchisees working capital and may hamper the business prospects.

The area of operation and the market should be suitable so that there are wide-ranging opportunities for selling the product substantially and most preferably to expand the franchise as well. Franchisee is expected to know and understand the areas where his products will have a good market and help out franchisees to establish their outlets at such places. Sometimes an up-class market will provide ample mark-ups and could be profitable for both of them.

4.2 STUDYING OWN FINANCES

Before launching a franchise, the businessman should ascertain his financial viability as well as the potential cost of franchising. He must analyse the cost factor and the possible returns. It is evident that the franchisor's initial expenditure as well as other ongoing expenses together will differ according to the types of franchise. Extra amount may be needed for producing a fitting franchisable format, professional assistance and the overall approach and attitude. Franchisor's business experience, though if he lacks franchising experience, may guide him in making certain estimates that will give him a marginal idea of franchising prospects.

To arrive at such an assessment is time-consuming but it is not a waste. As a businessman he may be an expert but as a franchisor he is a beginner. To get everything right, it is better for him to handover the job to a franchise consultant who will conduct a feasibility study. An outsider and an expert, a consultant will be viewing it from a different angle in an unbiased manner and would be able to analyse everything scrupulously. The consultant may be allowed to act as an advisor after getting the feasibility report from him until the franchisor succeeds to establish his franchise in the market. After ascertaining the financial viability and business prospects, pilot schemes have to be launched and operated for conveniently good period of time, say, extending up to 10 to 15 months to test the format. Shortcomings if any, noticed during this test should be rectified duly and adjustments ought to be carried out promptly to get a flawless format. Experience will give the franchisor the approximate costs towards acquiring quality commercial premises, running expenses such as rent, wages and infrastructural costs in addition to sales and profits of a new outlet. So also, changes towards packing and forwarding goods, increasing or reducing advertisements, etc., to be made as and when the need arise, taking into account their total effect on sales and profit.

Then comes the drafting and signing the franchise contract. After preparing a final contract by a solicitor who is well versed in this area of work, a promotional prospectus must also be prepared by a professional and printed out in sufficient quantity envisaging a good turnout of franchisees.

The overall expenses of establishing and maintaining a network of franchisee units have to be calculated. This could help to compare with the franchisors own business network. The difference in both the types of the business must be kept in mind while doing so, as the nature and mode of them vary widely. After finding out the costs and the likely levels of sales and profits of a franchised unit the front-end fee and the long-term royalty percentaged ought to be worked out in such a way that both the franchisee and the franchisor earn a respectable return for their investments and services. Thus, the franchisor can get a clear picture of whether franchising is positive financially or not.

4.3 CHECKING OWN OBJECTIVES

As a last measure of self-assessment a franchisor should have a proper objective. He should set short, medium and long-term goals and verify them in relation to his franchising. First, he has to prepare a blueprint related to the product and services, the range and impact of these in the market, sales, costs and overheads, profits, assets, the market share and so on. This takes care of the quantitative aspects of the franchisor's own objectives and goal. Then look into the qualitative side of the objectives concerning management – authority and control, leadership style, confidentiality, etc. A proper agenda and schedule is to be maintained for the franchisor and every member of his team, so as to know when, where, and how to reach a particular destination with regards to business activity. Each of his quantitative goals has to be looked into carefully in terms of benefits and drawbacks of franchising to find out whether the approach is suitable to achieve the set goals or to adopt another method. It is obvious that managing one's own outlet will be found more appealing for an individual. But franchising meets his twin objectives of keeping the costs within the permissible limits while expanding the franchisor's market share. On the contrary building up capital assets with the aim of selling the organisation in the future will be better in case of self-ownership.

Appraisal of each and every qualitative goals helps discover the most suitable course of action to be followed through. If the franchisor's goal is to run the business on the lines of a highly centralized and autocratic manner, keeping the managers and top ranking officials at a distance and working on a strictly principled need-to-know basis, it will work better with a chain of self-owned network. While these would work exactly opposite in case of a franchised unit to make it a successful proposition.

One's own business background, experiences, financial standing, market share now within reach, etc., go a long way in creating, running and maintaining a franchisee network. A franchisor must convince that he will contain his hopes and ambitions getting them fulfilled through the unique blend of advantages and disadvantages that his franchising offers him from time-to-time. If he is not in a position to comprehend these it would futile to expect to have a gainful cash flow or making a huge profit out of a franchised unit. If the franchisor has a shakey and unbalanced view it would be wise to drop the idea of franchising in a big way, thus, incurring heavy financial commitments towards an unwanted and ruinous cause.

A consultant can carry out an exhaustive feasibility research of the business in relation to franchising, creating or giving suggestions for making adjustments in the existing format, evaluating the costs and benefits, set-ups, monitor and guide pilot operations, co-ordinate the right parts of the necessary ingredients for a smooth sailing franchise package, write operating manuals, franchise agreements and prospectuses in addition to setting up franchisee recruitment and final selection procedures. The consultant also assesses the format performance as well as that of individual outlet units and thereby deriving the total effect of the whole network. His recommendations, suggestions and advice are most vital at times. A qualified consultant may be as good as a walking and talking encyclopedia of a franchise adventure.

4.4 HOW WILL A FRANCHISOR SELECT A FRANCHISEE?

The selection of franchisees by the franchisor, however, is more problematic. The tendency is for the franchisor to "sell" franchises rather than to cultivate long term relationships. Yet a franchise agreement is, by definition, a long-term relationship. Moreover, franchisor has to rely upon the person he selects to deliver the product to standard. Franchisor need to be clear about the skills and motivations of the people he selects, especially in the early stages of the system's development.

Franchising assumes an urgency to grow. The need to generate capital from franchisees and then to build new outlets can sometimes overwhelm a franchisor's long-term planning concept and deteriorate the working relationships that have been developed with new franchisees. Haste can result in relaxed standards for choosing franchisees, but even when the franchisor is rigorous about franchisee selection, it is impossible to get perfect information about how a person will act as an entrepreneur and partner. To alleviate some of these selection problems, many franchisors have an intensive screening program for prospective entrepreneurs; the large companies require significant work time in an operating outlet prior to becoming a franchisee. For example, Dunkin' Donuts conducts extensive personality profiling of prospective franchisees to ensure the appropriate match between the demands of the franchise and the skill set of the enthusiastic entrepreneur.

The various agency issues that come up as the partnership develops can only benefit from the free flow of information and open communication. In particular, without communication, two of the biggest hindrances to a successful partnership, free riding and shirking, are liable to rear their destructive heads.

A *free riding* franchisee benefits from association with the franchise brand but neglects to pay for this benefit. The franchisee may, for example, agree to accept co-op advertising funds from a vendor in exchange for an endorsement, but then neglect to promote the product as agreed. The weight of the entire franchise system's advertising may still generate incremental customer flow to the individual franchisee even though he or she did not contribute a "fair share" to the advertising effort. Nonparticipating franchisees are said to be getting a "free ride" because they benefit from the system's advertising efforts without contributing their own part. However, in the long run, the system is eventually affected by the omission.

There can be little doubt that the most effective way to market a franchise is to allow potential franchisees to visit outlets run by existing, content franchisees. Not only does it enable potential franchisees to get a real feel ofr the business that they may buy into - warts and all - it also helps to reduce the suggestion that they were persuaded into taking up the franchise on the back of unfounded promises.

This is obviously somewhat difficult in the early days of a franchise, although access to the pilot operations is a reasonable alternative.

Many franchisors will say that finding willing potential franchisees is not a problem. The problem is finding suitable candidates who will be able to successfully operate a franchise and have sufficient funds to invest.

Advertising in the business pages of newspapers, and trade magazines can be a useful way of meeting potential franchisees. In many countries, where franchising is reasonably well established, franchise exhibitions are run at which franchisors exhibit and vie for the attention and interest of potential franchisees. Some franchisors run open seminars for interested parties.

Whatever way the franchisor chooses to market his franchise, it is appropriate to have a well thought out set of documents explaining what the concept is. The temptation here is to present a lot of marketing hype in a glossy format that will persuade potential franchisees to make their future with the franchisor. This is fine to a certain extent, but franchisors must avoid the temptation for allowing "mere marketing puff" to become actual misrepresentations to potential franchisees. Any misrepresentations made at the recruitment stage will give a disgruntled franchisee the perfect opportunity to contest the viability of the franchise agreement before the courts. If misrepresentation is proved, the courts may allow the agreement to be rescinded and/or award damages in favour of the aggrieved franchisee against the franchisor. In order to try and reduce the potential exposure to such allegations, the franchisor is well advised to produce a disclosure document which is distributed to potential franchisees. This disclosure document (which is a legal requirement in countries such as the USA, France and Spain) should address various issues.

What Information Should a Franchisor Give to a Prospective Franchisee?

It is very important for the franchisor as well as the franchisee to share the required information with each other. The indicative list is as follows:

(1) Type of business, its structure like whether it is a group or one company.

(2) Business experience of the franchisor and its directors and officers internationally.

(3) Type of franchise business format, product line, etc.

(4) Its accounts and financial status, along with information on any loans, charges on its assets, creditors details, and any bankruptcy proceeding it has been involved in including directors and personnel involved.

(5) Litigation it has been involved in, both in civil and criminal law.

(6) Reputation of its brand name or goodwill and any public figure who may be associated with it.

(7) All the requirements a franchisee would have to fulfill in order to participate in the franchise:

(a) Funds to be paid to franchisor by franchisees like royalties, technical fees, lump sum payments, recurring fees that would be required.

(b) Obligations to purchase on the part of the franchisees, such as raw material from the franchisor for goods in question, real estate, services of the franchisor, signs, fixtures, etc.

(c) Restrictions on sale, tie-in and buy-back arrangements by the franchisor of the franchisees, products.

(d) Training programmes offered buy the franchisor and level of supervision, involved.

(e) Site selection and design of the outlet, to what extent it needs the approval of the franchisor.

(f) What sorts of activities or breaches would result in termination of the franchise contract. How can the franchise agreement be renewed?

Information on the Franchisee

It is equally important on the franchisee's part to share some information. Some of the important one's are as follows:

(1) Details of the type of business.

(2) Its financial records, its accounts, balance sheets, loans, what assets it has, both movable and immovable and any charges on them, types of creditors, details on bankruptcy if it was ever faced with it.

(3) Amount of capital it has and is able to outlay for the franchise operation.

(4) Details on its directors, officers, number of employees to be supervised and level of operation.

(5) Ability to expand the business.

(6) Types of services offered, in terms of marketing, advertising, distribution of goods, management skills and its ability to obtain all the clearances from authorities to set up the franchise business or outlet.

(7) Litigation history, if any.

Enquiry Form

CORPORAT CL NHRI:
74 Southgate Sheer
Gloucester
GH 2DP
T: 01452 420700
F: 014520303197
E: co@travail.co.uk
W: www. travail.co.uk

Desired Location(s): ______________________

PERSONAL DETAILS: ❐ MR ❐ Mrs ❐ Miss ❐ Ms

Surname: ______________________

Forename(s): ______________________

Age: ____________ Date of Birth: ____________

Marital Status: ______________________

Address: ______________________

____

______________________ Postcode: ____________

Telephone Number: Home: ______________________

Business: ______________________

Number of Children: ____________ Age: ____________

❐ Yes ❐ No

____

COMMERCIAL

❐Yes ❐No

INDUSTRIAL

____

SKILLED

____

EXECUTIVE

EMPLOYMENT HISTORY:

Are you currently: ❐ Employed ❐ Self-Employed ❐ Unemployed

Please give details of your present/most recent employment:-

(1) Company Name:____

Address: ____

Nature of Business:______________________________________

Employed From: __________________ To:____________________

Position Held:____

Duties and Responsibilities:______________________________

____

____

Notable Achievements: ____________________________________

____

PREVIOUS EMPLOYMENT:

(2) Company Name:____

Address: ____

Nature of Business:______________________________________

Employed From: __________________ To:____________________

Position Held:____

Duties and Responsibilities:______________________________

____

____

Notable Achievements: ____________________________________

____

PREVIOUS EMPLOYMENT (contd):

(2) Company Name:____

Address: ____

Nature of Business:______________________________________

Employed From: __________________ To:____________________

Position Held:____

Duties and Responsibilities:______________________________

____

____

Please summarise all previous employment experience:______________

____

____

EDUCATION:

Please summarise your education: ______________________________

____

____

Qualifications: ____

Membership of Professional Organisations/Societies: ____________

EXPERIENCE (Please indicate your experience in the following areas):

❒ Recruitment	❒ Interviewing	❒ Advertising
❒ Training	❒ Personnel	❒ Marketing/Promotions
❒ Management	❒ Administration	❒ Exhibitions
❒ Tele-Sales	❒ Secretarial	❒ Creative Writing
❒ Face-to-Face Sales	❒ Book-Keeping	❒ Negotiating

What do you consider your strengths:________________________

What do you consider your weakness:________________________

Greatest personal accomplishment: ________________________

MEDICAL HISTORY:

Please describe your general state of health: ____________________

Past Illnesses: ____________________

Please describe your partner's general state of health: ____________________

INTERESTS:

Leisure Activities/Hobbies/Special Interests: ____________________

____

FINANCIAL DETAILS (Continue on a separate sheet if necessary):

❒ House Owner ❒ Rented ❒ Living with Family ❒ Other

How much capital have you available for this business?: ____________

Have you ever declared bankruptcy?: ____________

When do you envisage starting your business?: ____________

What do you foresee as your major problems?: ____________

____

Have you ever, or are you currently considering any other franchise opportunity?: ____

____

If so, what?: ____________________

Why do you think you would make a successful Franchisee?: ____________

____

REFERENCES:

(1) Name: ____________
Address: ____________
____
Tel. No: ____________

(2) Name: ____________
Address: ____________
____
Tel. No: ____________

Confidential franchise questionnaire

Please complete in your own handwriting

PERSONAL DETAILS (Joint applicants other than husband and wife should complete two forms)	
SURNAME:	
FORENAME(S):	
HOME ADDRESS:	
DAYTIME TEL NO:	
EVENING TEL NO:	
DATE OF BIRTH:	
MARITAL STATUS:	
HEALTH:	

FINANCIAL DETAILS	
BANK	
ADDRESS:	
HOW LONG ACCOUNT HELD:	
BUILDING SOCIETY:	
ADDRESS:	
BUSINESS INTERESTS:	
CAPITAL AVAILABLE FOR FRANCHISE:	

SUITABLITY Please assess your ability to cope with the areas outlined below, marking from 4 (your weakest) to 6 (your strongest)
❐ DRIVE AND DETERMINATION
❐ PRACTICAL SKILLS
❐ SELF ORGANISATION
❐ MANAGEMENT OF MONEY
❐ SALES ABILITY
❐ MANAGEMENT OF PEOPLE

EMPLOYMENT HISTORY/PREVIOUS EXPERIENCE	
CURRENT EMPLOYER (or previous employer if less than 3 years with current separate employer)	
NAME:	
ADDRESS:	
POSITION:	
TIME WITH THIS EMPLOYER	
PREVIOUS EMPLOYER (If less than 3 years with current employed)	
NAME:	
ADDRESS:	
POSITION:	
TIME WITH THIS EMPLOYER	
CURRENT BUSINESS (If self employed)	
NAME:	
ADDRESS:	
TYPES OF BUSINESS:	
PREVIOUS BUSINESS EXPERIENCE:	

HAVE YOU, OR ANY BUSINESS IN WHICH YOU HAVE OWNED AN INTEREST BEEN INVOLVED IN BANKRUPTCY, INSOLVENCY PROCEEDINGS OR COMPROMISE WITH CREDITORS?	❐ YES ❐ NO
IF SO PLEASE GIVE FULL DETAILS	

SIGNATURE(S):
DATE:

7, Apollo Blinds
Wadala,
Mumbai - 400016. INDIA
TEL: +9122525644
FAX: +91222525965
e-mail: franchising@apolloblinds.co.in.

20 January 2000

Dear Mr. Ramesh,

Franchising Opportunities with Apollo Blinds

It was a pleasure to speak to you today about franchising opportunities with Apollo blinds.

As you know, we are India's Biggest Blind Store Chain, with outlets throughout India. However, I am pleased to say that your desired location is currently available.

We were most impressed with the quality of your application and our subsequent telephone conversation and would be delighted to take the discussion to the .next level. Consequently, we have arranged for you to visit our headquarters Mumbai on Tuesday February 1st, 2000 at 11.00 a.m.

Please be kind enough to confirm the date and time with my personal assistant Ms. Jyoti, who will be pleased to provide you with travel details.

We look forward to meeting with you then,

Kind regards,

Ravi Kumar.

Director/General Manager

Franchise Comparison Worksheet

Use this worksheet to help you determine the attractiveness of each franchise you're considering. Assign each franchise a column number. Answer each question along the left-hand side of the form, assigning a rating of 1-3, with 3 being the strongest. Total each column when finished. The franchise with the highest score will be the most attractive.

The Franchise Organization	**Franchise 1**	**Franchise 2**	**Franchise 3**
Does the franchisor have a good track record?			
Do the primary leaders of the franchise have expertise in the industry?			
Rate the franchisor's financial condition.			
How throughly does the franchisor check his prospective franchisees?			
Rate the profitability of the franchisor and his franchisees.			
Column Totals			

The Product Or Service	**Franchise 1**	**Franchise 2**	**Franchise 3**
Is there a demand for the product or service?			
How seasonal is the product or service?			
Are industry sales strong?			
Rate the product or service in comparison to the competition.			
Is the product or service competitively priced?			
What is the potential for industry growth?			
Column Total			

The Market Area	**Franchise 1**	**Franchise 2**	**Franchise 3**
Are exclusive territories offered?			
Can you sell franchises in your territory?			
Rate the sales potential of the territory you are considering.			
Is the competition strong in this area?			
How successful are franchisees in close proximity to this area?			
Column Total			

The Contract	**Franchise 1**	**Franchise 2**	**Franchise 3**
Are the fees and royalities associated with the franchise reasonable?			
How attractive are the renewal, termination and transfer conditions?			
If the franchisor requires you to purchase proprietary, inventory, how useful is it?			
If the franchisor requires you to meet annual sales, quotas, are they reasonable?			
Column Total			

Franchisor Support	Franchise 1	Franchise 2	Franchise 3
Does the franchisor help with site selection, lease negotiations and store layout?			
Is the training program effective and does the franchisor provide ongoing training?			
Does the franchisor provide finance to Qualified individuals?			
Are manuals, sales kits, accounting systems, and purchasing guides provided?			
Does the franchisor sponsor an advertising fund to which franchisees contribute?			
How strong are the franchisor's advertising and promotional programs?			
Does the franchisor have favorable national contracts for goods and services?			
Column Total			
Total Scores			

Source: www.freefranchisedocs.com

Selecting Franchisees

There is general consensus amongst franchisors that the recruitment of good franchisees is the most difficult and most important aspect of franchising a business. It can easily be a case of "Marry in haste, repent at leisure". The relationship between a franchisor and its franchisee is a long term one. Both parties have invested time and money in it. Neither has complete control over the other. If there is a problem it can be long, drawn out and acrimonious. There is no perfect answer to recruiting the right franchisee and franchisors use a large variety of techniques ranging from psychometric testing to a basic "gut feel". However, there are some basic points that can usually be taken on board by new franchisors in their recruitment practices.

The most common mistake made by new franchisors is to be in such a hurry to recruit the first few franchisees that, they compromise upon the criteria that they have decided upon for their ideal franchisee profile. Obviously the ideal franchisee profile needs to be realistic and flexible to a degree, but it should not be totally ignored as soon as a potential franchisee with money to invest walks through the door. It is understandable that a new franchisor, having invested a considerable amount of money in a concept is very keen to begin to see a return on his investment. However, he must be wary of making easy recruitment that will take up far too much of his time and energy two or three years down the path.

It is not unknown for new franchisors to give their first few franchisees "sweetheart" or "honeymoon" deals. It is acceptable to recognise the great degree of risk that the first few franchisees take by investing in the franchise, but it is a mistake to give too good a deal as these are likely to be the cause of friction between the franchisor and later franchisees in the future.

It is important that the franchisors know where the franchisee gets his funding from and the terms of any repayment, so that he can be satisfied that the franchisees personal circumstances do not make the franchise an untenable business proposition. Most people have a "comfort zone", a level of income above which they are not sufficiently motivated to increase the turnover and profitability of their business. The franchisor should try to identify whether or not a franchisee's individual comfort zone is too low for the particular franchise.

It is important that a franchisee has the full support of his/her family. The franchisor should therefore ensure that he properly examines the domestic situation of any potential franchisees.

The health of a potential franchisee is very important and so a medical report should be a requirement of the franchisor. A seriously ill franchisee can impose substantial burden on the franchisor.

A visit to the franchisee's home is highly desirable - it will say so much about his approach to life and probably business. If it is clean, tidy and well presented it is likely that his business premises will be the same. If it is dirty, untidy and badly presented, one should not be surprised if his business presentation turns out to be the same.

If a potential franchisee is too entrepreneurial this can cause substantial problems for the franchisor. A real entrepreneur will find the disciplines of franchising far too strict, and conflict with the franchisor is inevitable. Energy and drive is essential in a franchisee, but so is the ability to work within a system - a quality which few entrepreneurs possess.

An application form ought to give you enough positive or negative pointers to enable you to choose whether to meet the applicant or to reject them (which, if necessary, you should do promptly and politely in line with your normal recruitment procedure). A preliminary meeting may be arranged at the applicant's home where they will feel relaxed and able to answer your questions honestly. You will thus learn more from their replies, can assess their supportive loved ones (if appropriate) and gain a fuller picture of them. As a simple but effective example, a couple who live in a grubby and messy environment may allow their franchised outlet to deteriorate into the same condition.

Pose these queries to see how suited they are to franchising and your particular franchise.

- Tell me about yourself.
- What do your partner and dependents feel about franchising?
- How will it affect them?
- In what ways will they help you?
- Tell me about your education and qualifications.
- Why did you select those subjects?
- Have you ever had any health problems - what are they?
- How did they affect your work?
- Tell me about your free time activities.
- Describe your past and present work experiences.
- What do you do in an average day?

- What are your responsibilities?
- Do you work in a team or on your own?
- Which do you prefer?
- What do you like and dislike about your job?
- What do you find easy and difficult to do?

Moving on, you could also ask these questions:

- Tell me about your finances.
- What qualities do you think our franchisees should have?
- Why do you wish to become a franchisee?
- What are your strengths and weaknesses, in relation to franchising?
- Where do you want to be in five, ten and fifteen years' time?
- May I see your driving licence, certificates, diplomas?
- Could I have permission to approach your two references?

Naturally, the franchisee will wish to know more about your franchise package and will have many questions to put to you in addition to answering these at your first interview, you ought to set up a second meeting at your head office so that they can look around, talk to your team and piece together a better impression of you. If you have checked them out prior to this investigating their credit rating, taking up references and so forth as you would usually do when entering into a business transaction or recruiting staff - you should be able to conclude their visit with a firm offer. If it is accepted, you can press on with the legalities of issuing the franchise (see Signing the Franchise Agreement, Ch-5)

4.5 GRANTING A FRANCHISE

Granting Franchise: Franchise is granted to more and better qualified individuals after a thorough scrutiny. A proper franchisee recruitment and selection procedure contains the following

(i) A market development strategy plan focusing on the building up of a system to achieve the vision of the company is chipped out first. This plan stresses on the company's operation and marketing decisions, market analysis, market selection and penetration goals in addition to shaping up the franchise structure.

(ii) A structured franchise licensing system that achieves the goal set by the market development strategy plan.

(iii) Skilled franchise licensing personnel who are able to achieve the goals using the structured licensing system. They help the franchisee candidates to make business decisions.

The franchisee licensing system should be designed in such a way so as to find, qualify, interview and grant licenses to the deserving candidates. This system comprises of several processes such as (a) Promotion process (b) Qualification process (c) Interview and follow up process (d) Granting process and (e) Opening process.

(a) Promotion Process: This is a process by which deserving candidates are identified and sorted out based on the basis of a candidate's profile and qualification criteria. This process helps to evaluate the best qualified candidates.

(b) Qualification Process: This process helps to find out whether the candidate has:

(i) Made a decision towards self–employment

(ii) Necessary financial resources

(iii) Interest to know more about franchise business

(iv) Enough time to work towards penetrating the market

(v) Special skills necessary for the business

(c) Interview and Follow up Process: A face to face talk with a franchisee prospect will enable you to understand his/her motives, aptitude as well as attitude. It is also possible to begin a franchisee–franchisor relationship.

(d) Granting Process: Granting process is the final step towards assessing a candidate in all respects. If this turns out to be positive, a candidate is chosen to be a franchisee licencee. The franchisor also sees to it that the candidate is well equipped with all the necessary factors and documents and that the candidate is fit to work within the system to achieve the business targets and motivations. Finally the agreements are signed, initial fees are paid and the opening process begins.

(e) The Opening Process: After granting the franchise, the franchisees are responsible for operations, training, designing construction, leasing and such others commitments. It is the franchise to employ staff under him or to be self-employed. He also has to access a franchise opportunity. The following steps will help a franchisee to assess the franchisor.

(i) Examine the franchisor's financial viability. He must get satisfied that the Franchisor has already put in sufficient capital and is in a good position to run the business without any financial crunch in the future.

(ii) Ascertain whether the franchisor has tested the product regarding marketability.

(iii) Are there any existing franchisee expressing displeasure of his being a new franchisee.

(iv) Does the business have a continued marketing prospects for a longer period or only a short lived fashion.

(v) Check the legal validity of the agreement with the help of a qualified legal authority and see that it is mutually beneficial for both the franchisee as well as the franchisor.

A franchisee has to adopt certain valid steps so as to acquire a franchise:

Step 1: The franchisee must determine as to whether he would function as a successful franchisee. He has to see that he can take business decisions, whether his interests are taken care of and he could satisfy the requirements and demands of the franchisor, etc. The following are some of the basic questions answered by a franchisee:

(a) What is your expectation now?

(b) What are your wants, needs and desires?

(c) What are your goals, objectives and desires?

(d) What are you looking for in the business?

(e) Are you quitting your profession?

(f) Are you in a mind-set to be part of an organization belonging to someone else?

(g) Are you prepared to run the business under the stipulation, plan and framework of the franchisor?

(h) Have you worked continuously for any company running into 5 or more years at a stretch?

(i) Do you have the required know-how and expertise to run a business akin to the franchise.

(j) Do you have the financial resources required to run the business?

(k) Do you think this franchise can satisfy your needs and dreams?

(l) Have you ever managed any other franchise? How do you evaluate the present opportunity with that of your old one?

Step 2: There are numerous franchise opportunities available in the business field. You must choose the best among them. First thing you have to do is a thorough study of the product you are going to adopt. Its utility, its value (the worth of the item as per the cost a customer meets), its competitors in the market whether the franchisor's territory policies affect your operations; whether you would be able to dominate the market. A franchisee must also see the competitive edge his business has compared to that of other similar products available in the market. He has to see that marketing fee should be reasonable in relation with the contribution of each franchisee in support of advertisement campaigns. Another important thing he has to see is whether the franchisor involves the franchisee's input in decision making. A franchisee must also have to evaluate the period required to recover the investment that he has made. All these will help a franchisee to make a decision.

Step 3: After short-listing the various franchise opportunities a prospective franchisee looks forward to further information package that usually contain a letter, brochure and a qualifying questionnaire asking for (a) Assets (b) Liabilities (c) Net worth (d) Sources of income (e) Educational history (f) Previous employment (g) Credit references (h) Personal references (i) Motivation for buying a franchise. A franchisee must have a look at the operations manual as this is his guide to a successful operation. He must ask the franchisor for a full explanation of the pre-opening assistance.

Step 4: A franchisee finally should create a franchise prototype to the effect that his business will:

(a) provide consistent value to customers, employees suppliers and lenders

(b) be positioned to be operated with lowest possible level of skill

(c) provide a predictable experience for a customer, employees, suppliers and lenders.

(d) ensure that all activities are as per the operations manual.

The average franchise license agreement is for fifteen years. Creating a best business format is all the more important. The chances of success in a franchise can be greatly increased by bringing tangible and intangible assets in vision. It is very difficult to find a perfect partner – either a franchisee or a franchisor. Most franchisors put monitoring system to make sure that franchisees perform as per the business format and to see whether they are paying the royalty correctly and in time.

The relationship of a franchisor with his franchisee and *vice versa* is maintained because both are interdependent and shares the profits of a business.

So either of them won't shirk their responsibilities. Franchisees are motivated by net profits and hence, they have incentive to maximize the sales. The franchisor gets royalty on each sales proceed. Inconsistency between the financial interest of franchisor and franchisee leads to free riding and shirking. If a franchisee does not spend on local advertising it becomes free riding on the brand. Using low quality material is shirking. Both free riding and shirking deteriorate the product and affects the business prospects badly.

Franchising is a negotiated relationship in which both franchisor and franchisee must allow some flexibility in each other's performance. This is defined by a series of services that franchisors provide franchisees. Many people make the mistake of thinking all they need to do is watch sales and profits and all will work on its own. There are several aspects of access to franchisor management. From this set of services the franchisees prioritize two major categories of interaction with the franchisor – operations and marketing.

The franchisor monitors the franchisees in a number of ways. Franchisees keep high expectations from the franchisor with regard to support of their store operations and franchise marketing. Understanding what is important for the franchisees, franchisors should build up their monitoring system. This will enable them to build a tolerant monitoring and control system and a sharing and caring long-term relationship.

4.6 THE MANUAL

The manual is the embodiment of the know-how of the franchise. It therefore is of paramount operational importance. However, it will usually also be explicitly stated to be a part of the franchise agreement and so be of considerable legal significance also. It identifies the know-how and therefore both enables franchisees to use the know-how and helps protect it by way of identifying the trade secrets and providing copyright protection to the way in which the know-how is expressed. There is no set format for a manual. Some franchisors have up to ten binders each addressing different aspects of the franchised business ranging from marketing through to accounting and the shop layout. The manual is a living document and will continually change as the business develops. It is for this reason that manuals often take the form of ring binders - which allow new pages to be inserted/replaced as and when necessary.

The following is an illustrative list of the likely contents of a manual:

- Shop lay-out
- Staff schedules, etc.

- Staff uniforms/appearance
- Staff etiquette
- Staffing requirements of outlets
- Staff job descriptions
- Standard form contracts of employment
- Disciplinary procedure
- Grievance procedure
- Training requirements
- Service standards
- Pricing policies
- Guarantees/warrantees
- Approved suppliers list
- Customer complaints procedures

4.7 FROM THE FRANCHISEE'S PERSPECTIVE - BUYING A FRANCHISE

We have earlier in this chapter discussed few points which need to be considered while taking up a franchise, let us now see some of the important points in detail.

Why Take up a Franchise

A franchisee is an entrepreneur in every respect. Running a franchise unit is as good as managing one's own business. There is a common belief that running a franchise unit is as if to manage a retail outlet. Though this view is slight to a certain level there are vast differences. The success achieved by a franchisee through running a business unit is his own but in the other case, the manager is an employee and he is not the owner of the outlet. Hence, all those who are prospective aspirants of franchising should make a thorough and honest appraisal of their capabilities, ambitions and aspirations.

Will I Succeed as a Franchisee?

Running a franchise outlet is not the same as being employed as a manager of a retail outlet. The manager is assured of his salary irrespective of whether the outlet is making a good profit; whereas an entrepreneur who sets up his own franchise outlet may not be taking anything at the end of a month if the performance was poor. There is no guarantee that a franchisee would be getting a pay cheque every month as in the case of a manager. Apart from this, if the business does not pick up over a period of time the franchisee's investment will fade away and the creditors would take their turns. Hence, if a person is setting up his own business and he is a raw hand, he has to take this aspect very seriously. At the same time the rewards from one's own business may turn out to be very high if the performance is good. The happiness has no bounds when the franchisee sees that his business is flourishing day-by-day.

Once a decision is taken to become an entrepreneur the next step is to make up one's mind as to whether to invest in a franchise or an altogether new enterprise. If the final decision is to become a franchisee a self-assessment test is to be taken to ascertain whether he has the right temperament for undertaking and running it successfully.

Almost all franchisors use such a test at the time of selecting a franchisee but an aspirant can also take this test on his own to make an honest appraisal of his capabilities.

Own Business Vs. Franchise

After a person decides to go all out for an enterprise, he/she has to identify the market and product that he wants to set up the business in. Then comes the question whether to go for a new setup or for a franchise. From one's own unit involves a higher risk of the former, the brand is entirely new to certain crucial factors. The first factor depends on how well the entrepreneur can market the product and popularise it. He has to do everything on his own, such as modifications, upgradations, etc. But on the contrary in a franchise setup, the financial risks are comparatively lower as the brand is already established and well-known in the market. As the saying in the financial circle 'high risk could result high return, whereas a low risk project will yield low returns but will be a relatively safe investment. Since a franchisee has to pay a front–end fee towards the franchise and also a regular royalty as certain percentage of all the revenues from the unit, his return on investment will be lower than in the case of an independent business person. But because of the already established brand image, help and support from the franchisor, the franchisee can do a better sales than an unknown outlet. But if an entrepreneur sets up his own outlet in his locality he can get it popularised among the loyal customers and may become highly successful. He would be able to modify and make necessary adjustments to suit the tastes of his clientele and would be able to reap a high return for his investment. Whatever profits he earns will be his alone. No burden of royalty.

From purely a business outlook a franchisee's ambition is limited to running a franchise unit successfully and grow with franchisor's business whereas if he is running his own business and makes it a success he can well expand his set up by operating from multiple centres and popularise his brand and be a franchisor as well in the long run. Hence, the long-term ambitions are also important for an entrepreneur so that he will be able to choose the better of the two - either own retail outlet or franchise.

Managing the Franchise

After setting up the franchise unit and launching the business successfully what is unavoidable is the full-time involvement of the franchisee. He has to look into the day-to-day operations and the same time keep the relationship with the franchisor in good stead. Both the above factors are important to keep the setup alive and kicking.

4.8 OPERATION

These are several vital aspects to be borne in mind while running a franchise unit. They are:

- Manpower, recruitment, retaining and training;
- Sales, sales promotion, marketing;
- Supplies, logistics, inventory management;
- Information systems, reporting;
- Competition tracking;
- Statutory, legal and taxation matters;
- Accounts, cash flows and finance management;
- Customer feedbacks, suggestions, claims; and
- After-sales service, and customer data base.

Manpower recruitment is an area of concern as it is found to be a bit difficult for a franchisee to attract and retain a talented workforce. This becomes a routine task for a franchisee because people go on leaving after gaining some experience. They look out for joining large organisations where they feel more secure and growth prospects are more. Sales, supplies, logistics and accounts are some key areas where the franchisee has to offer a good and handsome compensation as well as other lucrative components as allowances to retain the experienced and talented staff.

Sales, customer service and competition tracking areas call for the franchisee's direct involvement and supervision. A contented customer is the backbone of any business organisation as he not only buys goods but give good feedback to his friends and relatives. Word of mouth is the most effective mode of advertisement. Thus, the franchisee's involvement in these areas where he could keep direct contact with a customers is quite relevant and hence, mandatory. Proper accounting system as well as inventory, Cash management and reporting must be practiced for creating accountability among the employees as also developing their confidence. Usually, the franchisor lays certain guidelines for these areas of function. Franchisees have to fill up the franchisor on day-to-day basis for scrutiny and monitoring of the franchise unit.

The Pilot Operation

Before launching a new franchised concept it is vital that a number of so called "pilot operations" are established to ensure that they do comprise a viable business for both franchisor and franchisee. Although much will depend upon the individual market circumstances, these pilot operations should generally be for at least twelve months to establish their viability. Even if the franchisor has had corporate outlets up and running for many years, if they are not exactly the same as the proposed franchised outlets (for example, they have a different product mix, or are turning a concept that has historically been shop based into a mobile, van based environment) a pilot operation should be run to ensure that the new business is viable. After all, the franchisor is selling a proven business blueprint to the franchisees. If it is not truly proven, what the franchisor is selling?

In practice, pilot operations have been found not only to prove the viability of the business but also to identify potential problems and provide solutions to them, in areas such as product/service type offered, marketing/promotional methods used, local and indeed national regulations, management systems, opening-hours, the market adequacy, training and support, shops layout and so on.

Once the concept has been proven by the pilots, it is essential that the franchisor continues running them. They provide both an excellent "barometer" of the franchisees' business and a useful "laboratory" where new product ranges, management and sales techniques and so on can be tested.

Is this Franchise the right option?

One of the advantages of franchising is the abundance of information available to the franchisee. Not only do state and federal legislatures mandate the disclosure of pertinent financial information, but there is also a wealth of other current and useful information available. Although considerable information is available, potential franchisees are sometimes less rigorous about their investigation than they should be. They can quickly fall in love with a concept and forget to do the detailed study. Due diligence on the franchisor's part, that should be done and readily available.

There are many misconceptions about franchising, but probably the most widely held is that a franchisee is "buying a franchise." In reality he is investing his assets in a system to utilize the brand name, operating system and ongoing support. He and everyone in the system are licensed to use the brand name and operating system. Why is it a lease? In any franchise deal the franchisee receives the assets upfront but only for a limited period of time — the term of the franchise agreement. The term of the agreement may run 5 or 10 years or, in some cases, only 1 or 2 years. At the end of the term, the franchisor decides whether or not the agreement will be renewed. The reasons for not renewing the agreement should be completely spelled out in the Uniform Franchise Offering Circular and franchise agreement. An "ownership mentality" destroys the reason franchised and company-operated units are successful. Think about it. If a franchisee thinks he has "bought" a franchise, he becomes an "owner" and begins to think and acts like an owner, he will want to change the system because of his needs, he will wonder what is he paying the royalty for, and he will begin thinking of other franchisees as his competitors. For these and many other reasons a franchisee cannot think of himself as an "independent owner."

What Franchisors Look For In New Franchisees

by Craig E. Yaris Oct 13

You've done your homework, looking at various business opportunities including the possibility of buying a franchise. Whether it's a franchise for a McDonald's, a quick printing store or a popular-priced family hair salon, there's a process you must get through in order to actually become a franchisee. The first step in that process is the application. This seemingly simple act of filling out a form or questionnaire is where many would-be franchisees get derailed. For those of us on the franchisor end of the business, the application is a very important first step in a "weeding out" process that helps us determine whom we will talk with further and whom we will simply send a polite "no thank-you" response. The initial franchisee application is designed to tell us something about the applicant. We need to know a lot more than where you live, what jobs you've held and how much money you have in the bank. We are really looking to learn, at a glance, what type of person you are, so we can attempt to evaluate if you can succeed as a franchisee. We want to know if you truly are motivated and how much you want to run your own business, since opening a franchise of any type is hardly a cakewalk. We need to get a sense of your people skills. As a franchisee running a retail service operation such as Lemon Tree, you must be able to deal smoothly and effectively with employees and customers alike. As is the case with any reputable franchisor, we are not in business to simply take in franchise fees. Instead, we are looking for people who will succeed in running and building their individual franchise businesses and, in turn, help expand our company's revenues and reputation. To aid us in that search, there are five key criteria we evaluate as we review applications. Since our criteria are similar to those of most good franchise companies, understanding what we look for and why, can help you successfully get through the first part of becoming a franchisee - filling out the franchise application. The decision to pursue an applicant past the initial application step is derived from a number of factors. Some are simple and straightforward, while others are subtle and difficult to quantify or explain in simple terms.

(1) Is the applicant a "people person?"

We look at the applicant's background to see what kind of work they've done. Experience in retailing, customer service or any area where there's interaction with the public is a plus. Fully describe work you've done where you've interacted with others, whether co-workers, subordinates or customers.

Money Matters

(2) What is the applicant's financial situation?

Franchise fees can vary considerably, from a few thousand dollars to tens or hundreds of thousands. But the franchise fee is only a part of the financial equation. The applicant will also have to have funding available to cover rent, furnishings, inventory, staffing, advertising and promotion, taxes and literally dozens of other expenses, large and small. Starting a business is a costly undertaking. For the typical Apollo Window Blinds franchise, for example, we look for an applicant to have in the range of Rs. 10 lakhs to Rs. 15 lakhs available to cover the franchise fee (ours is Rs. 5 Lakhs) plus startup and initial operating expenses. This does not mean we expect an applicant to have that amount sitting in the bank, ready to write a check. Most franchisors consider the applicant's full range of resources. While we expect some of it will come from personal savings, we know money can also come from family and friends in the form of personal loans or gifts. Some may come from secured bank loans, or it may come from a home equity loan. All these resources and others are viable. Give a good indication of various financial resources that are available to you, so we can see that your new venture will be properly funded. We also, of course, look at the applicant's financial history. Having a bankruptcy in your past is not an automatic rejection. We know people can get into financial difficulty for any number of legitimate and uncontrollable situations. What does send up a red flag, however, is a pattern of financial mismanagement, which might be reflected in a bankruptcy along with other factors in the applicant's financial profile.

The application is an important first step for franchisors in the "weeding out" process.

Save yourself and us time and awkwardness by being forthright in how you fill out the financial portion of the application. All franchisors run credit checks, and it's better if we hear about past financial situations from you first, rather than having a credit check be the first time something is brought to our attention. If there are financial situations that might need explaining, it's best to do so in an attachment to the initial application you send us.

(3) Is the applicant willing and able to take direction?

We can sometimes get an indication of an applicant's willingness and ability to accept direction from the jobs they have held and how long they've held them. If it's not obvious from your job title, then explain how your job responsibilities demonstrate this.

(4) Is the applicant a self-starter?

Like willingness to take direction, indication of a self-starter can sometimes come from the type of jobs the applicant has held and how quickly he or she advanced up the ladder. Success in certain types of jobs, such as independent sales, might also suggest the person is motivated.

(5) Does the applicant believe in our system?

This may not be easy to detect in an initial written application. But if the applicant shows us that he or she has done their homework, looked into our business and likes what they see, that is a good sign. It's important to remember that in seeking a franchise, you are in a highly competitive situation. Franchise companies constantly receive inquiries and applications from potential franchisees. During tough economic times such as these, the competition gets even tighter as many more people look into franchising as a way to try to secure their future.

4.9 ACCENTUATE POSITIVE

We can't award a franchise to everyone who applies, even if they have sufficient financing. Since there may be dozens of applicants who, on paper, meet our criteria, anything you can do to make yourself stand out in a positive way will help your cause. Do what you can to make us invite YOU in for a face-to-face meeting over the other qualified candidates. Here are some things that make us take a closer look at an application: Neatness. This may seem like a trivial point, but neatness does count. We are not English teachers grading exams, but we do want to be able to easily read your application. Excessive sloppiness might be taken as a sign that you are careless or the application is not important enough to you to take the proper care in filling it out. If your handwriting is sloppy or childlike, ask a spouse or friend to fill it out for you. Hard as it may be to believe, we once received an application with answers written on coffee-stained napkins and scraps of paper. Needless to say, that applicant was not called in for a personal interview. Thorough, thoughtful answers. We don't mind taking a few minutes to learn more about you, your background and skills, and your business aspirations. Except where the questions obviously call for a simple yes or no answer, try to provide thorough responses.

Showing enthusiasm for the franchise business can boost an applicant's chances.

Short of writing a book in response to each question, you should take as much space as you need to fully explain and SELL yourself. It's ok to put some answers on a separate typed page if a thoughtful response will not fit into the space allotted. Just be sure to clearly indicate to us that the answer is on a separate sheet, and on that sheet clearly indicate what question is being answered. If you can convince us that you are a good risk, there's a good chance you will succeed in getting a franchise. Then, with lots of hard work, long hours and a bit of luck, you'll be on the way to what can be a satisfying and rewarding business experience.

Red Flags and Golden Opportunities: Things To Look For When Buying a Franchise.

by Robert Purvin

Franchising can be a very effective way to get into business, but it's important to keep your eyes and ears wide open and ask lots of questions. The more you know about the franchise you are considering, the better your decision will be.

No two franchise systems are alike. Some franchise networks succeed more than others.

Some of you already have a fair amount of business experience and are merely seeking useful resources for your selection process.

Others of you, however, may find yourselves newcomers to the small business world and are eager not only for resources, but a plan to help you conduct your selection process.

This is the "homework" of buying a franchise. The more you learn about franchising and the franchise selection process, the more successful you will be at understanding what the franchisor is really offering you.

This article is not intended as a comprehensive survey of all resources available about selecting a franchise; rather it is intended to point you in the right direction and help get you started. Remember, you are considering investing your hard-earned money as well as your financial future and dreams in a new franchised business. The time and money you "invest" now, with in-depth research and investigation, together with legal and financial guidance from experienced professionals, may well save you many unpleasant and costly hours in future litigation and/or financial ruin.

Frequently, I hear people say they want to "save money" in their selection process by doing it themselves or using a friend or family member instead of using qualified counsellors.

Failure to obtain experienced counsel - your own "success team" - can be "penny wise and pound foolish." Cutting corners in your franchise selection process is not a very good idea.

Given the level of your potential investment, including site acquisition, build-out, fees and commissions, make allowance for a reasonable budget for expert advice. Typically, a budget of 2%-5% of your total investment is sufficient to afford a competent "success team" to steer you through the selection process.

Building your success team won't guarantee your success, but our experience shows it will save you from the "penny wise, pound foolish" trap.

Your team should include yourself, as an educated buyer of the franchise, along with an experienced franchise attorney who understands franchise agreements and can review your offering circular and assist you in the establishment of your business.

Last but not least, your team will need an experienced financial consultant or accountant who understands franchise business and can review your offering circular with a view to projecting the profit potential and risk of your opportunities, and can assist in setting up proper financial control systems.

4.10 LIST OF CRITERIA

Once you have selected your team, you are ready to start looking at specific franchise opportunities. Here is a criteria list that serves as a guide to help you select a franchise system worthy of your investment.

The American Association of Franchisees and Dealers (AAFD) has compiled a list of seven things to look for in a franchisor:

(1) Select a franchising company that is primarily interested in distributing quality products and services to ultimate consumers. Although this rule may seem obvious, many (if not most) franchising companies are primarily interested in selling franchises and are less concerned with the quality of the products and services they are theoretically in business to sell.

(2) Your franchising company should be dedicated to franchising as its primary mechanism of product and service distribution. Be wary of franchisors with a large number of company-owned stores, or one which distributes its products through other channels such as supermarkets or discount stores.

(3) Your franchising company should produce and market quality goods and services for which there is an established market demand. The value of franchising emanates from the value of the franchisor. Too many prospective franchisees cannot qualify for a widely-recognized franchise and settle for a lesser known system, thinking the franchise concept is more important than the product and trade name.

The time you invest now may save you many unpleasant hours in future litigation.

(4) Select a franchisor with a well accepted trademark.

(5) Evaluate your franchisor's business plan and marketing system. A well-established, well-designed marketing system promises substantial and complete training and overall franchisee support.

(6) Your franchisor should have good relationships with its franchisees. Likewise, the franchisees should have a strong franchisee organization which has negotiating leverage with the franchising company.

A franchisor that does not permit its franchisees to organize is a sure sign of trouble ahead. Strong franchisee associations, on the other hand, will pave the way to successful and cooperative franchising systems.

(7) Only deal with franchising companies that provide sales and earnings projections that demonstrate an attractive return on your investment.

Do not believe franchisors who claim they are forbidden by law to provide earnings projections and evidence of actual performance. To the contrary, all state and federal laws regulating franchising encourage franchisors to provide earnings claims to prospective franchisees.

Be sure to select a franchise that meets all seven of these criteria.

4.11 WIN-WIN-WIN

Franchising, when done right, can be a win-win-win relationship for all parties involved – the franchisor, the franchisee and the consumer. Owning a franchise can be a rewarding career path.

To truly identify which franchise is worthy of your investment, you need to talk to lots of franchisees, including ones the franchisor doesn't recommend.

Include some in similar geographic areas, some who've been in business three to 12 months, and some who've been in the system for many years.

Identify the reasons why the franchisees you speak to are successful, including the length of time and amount of post-opening working capital they required to reach sustainable profitability, or how and why they failed.

Franchisees may be more willing to talk to you in person than on the phone or via email.

Consider the following franchise prospect's "Bill of Rights" as developed by the AAFD:

- The right to an equity in the franchised business, including meaningful market protection.
- The right to engage in a trade or business, including a post-termination right to compete.
- The right to the franchisor's loyalty, good faith and fair dealing, and due care in the performance of the franchisor's duties, and a fiduciary relationship where one has been promised or created.
- The right to trademark protection.
- The right to full disclosure from the franchisor.
- The right to initial and ongoing training and support.
- The right to competitive sourcing of inventory, product, services and supplies.

The ultimate value of franchising emanates from the true value of the franchisor.

- The right to reasonable restraints upon the franchisor's ability to require changes within the franchise system.
- The right to marketing assistance.
- The right to associate with other franchisees.
- The right to representation and access to the franchisor.
- The right to local dispute resolution and protection under the laws and the courts of the franchisee's jurisdiction.
- A reasonable right to renew the franchise.
- The reciprocal right to terminate the franchise agreement for reasonable and just cause, and the right not to face termination, unless for a just cause.

4.12 SUMMARY

From the Franchisor's Perspective

A franchisor should have a thorough knowledge of the business as franchisee envisages him/her as an expert who has experienced a lot of the business world. The franchisor has to assess the business format, study his own finances and check the objectives of the franchised business.

One has to be totally ethical in his/her approach to franchising if he wants to set up a respectable and profit making franchisee chain. Nowadays prospective franchisees coming forward to join this self-regulated field of business greeted with all sorts of valuable advice from internationally acclaimed trade association. The franchisor's financial stability is an important parameter; so as to enable him/her to expand the franchise network. Those who do not have a stable financial resource will not be able to meet the commitments towards the franchisee and will fail to create a profitable franchise setup. It is vital for a franchisor to appraise and assess the probable financial liabilities and the returns from each franchise unit well before committing the agreement. He must be well aware of his financial capability and sources of cash flow to meet the unavoidable initial expenditure.

The success of any franchise depends upon the level of commitment of the franchisor and his team towards franchising. The relationship with the franchisees needs to be very cordial for making a good income level. After collecting a handsome front-end fee some franchisors lose interest in a franchise outlet and disappear from the scene or provide a slipshod service to the franchisees. They pay more attention to their own outlets than the franchised outlets. They choose good and proper locations and keep these for themselves. All these activities are characteristics of an unenthusiastic, unworthy and dishonest franchisor. This kind of approach will result in franchisee dissatisfaction due to unsolved problems, stagnant sales and stunted growth and ultimately end up with poor profit. As a result the franchisee will have no other alternative than winding up the unit and leave the place. Franchisees one after another will fall in line and the franchisor will not only lose the franchise but may damage or destroy his own business as well.

If a potential franchisee is too entrepreneurial this can cause substantial problems for the franchisor. A real entrepreneur will find the disciplines of franchising far too strict and conflict with the franchisor is inevitable. Energy and drive is essential in a franchisee, but so is the ability to work within a system - a quality which few entrepreneurs possess.

From the Franchisee's Perspective

The franchisee needs to first decide why take up a franchise, Will he succeed as a franchisee, how will he go about managing the franchise. Then a franchisee has to evaluate the franchisor on the following parameters:

(1) Select a franchising company that is primarily interested in distributing quality products and services to ultimate consumers.

(2) Be wary of franchisors with a large number of company-owned stores, or one which distributes its products through other channels such as supermarkets or discount stores.

(3) The franchising company should produce and market quality goods and services for which there is an established market demand. The value of franchising emanates from the value of the franchisor.

(4) Select a franchisor with a well accepted trademark.

(5) Evaluate the franchisor's business plan and marketing system. A well-established, well-designed marketing system promises substantial and complete training and overall franchisee support.

(6) The franchisor should have good relationships with its franchisees. Likewise, the franchisees should have a strong franchisee organization which has negotiating leverage with the franchising company.

Thus, a franchisor that does not permit its franchisees to organize is a sure sign of trouble ahead. Strong franchisee associations, on the other hand, will pave the way to successful and cooperative franchising systems.

4.13 SELF ASSESSMENT QUESTIONS

(1) Highlight the key differences between owning one's own business *vis-a-vis* taking a franchise.

(2) Write a short note on steps in acquiring a franchise

(3) What are the key factors to be considered before buying a franchisee.

(4) What are the key factors to be considered before giving a franchise.

✠✠✠

Chapter 5

LEGAL ASPECTS

Objectives

After going through this chapter, you will be able to understand:

- The key elements of Franchise agreement.
- The general obligations form both the sides.
- The various Franchise disputes and their resolution.

Structure:

5.1 THE FRANCHISE AGREEMENT

Key elements of the basic franchise agreement

1. Grant, Term and Renewal

The typical initial section of the franchise agreement is the grant of a specified franchise for a specified period of time. This length of the term is based on various factors like market conditions, the franchisee's operations such as leases and bank loans, and anticipated demand for the franchised goods and services. The renewal rights are generally based upon the franchise being in good standing under the agreement. Also other details like franchisor's right to relocate the franchisee, adjust the size of any exclusive territory granted. Or change the fee structure should be addressed. A franchise involves the franchisor in granting the franchisee certain rights over a certain area for a specified period. Exactly what those rights, the area and period, is a matter of negotiation between the franchisor and the intending franchisee. Little, if anything, is open to negotiation with domestic franchising but, on the international scene, it is quite the opposite and both parties must carefully think through what they want out of the relationship to make it worthwhile. It is common, but by no means universal, for franchisee agreements to be granted for a period of between five and ten years. Pan EU agreements are usually longer - between 10 and 25 years. Such a term is thought to be necessary in order for the franchisee to obtain a decent return on its investment. Generally, the grant of such a term is neither controversial nor legally difficult.

In some jurisdictions however, there is a restriction imposed by the government upon the maximum possible term.

However, problems are common over the often vexed question of renewal and what happens to franchisees in the event of non-renewal. There are various schools of thought on these issues but the reality is that by and large, international business format franchising is still in its infancy and the problems involved in renewal and non-renewal have not yet had to be faced by many international franchisors.

Clearly, if the franchise is doing well and 'human relations' between the parties are good, the chances of negotiating a new agreement are high. What, however, happens if all is not well?

The most difficult problem relates to the terms being granted to franchisees. Usually franchisees will be granted an automatic right of renewal subject to there being no existing breach and the franchisee updating its outlets as required by the sub-franchisor. What if the franchise is granted in year 20 of a 25-year master licence which is not subsequently renewed?

2. Territory

The size of the geographic area granted to the franchisee by the franchisor must be specifically discussed in conjunction with a description of what, if any, exclusive rights will be granted to the franchisee with respect to this territory. All advertising restrictions related to the territory, performance quotas and policies of the franchisor with regards to the territory are addressed in this part. It is usual for the franchisee to want as large an area as possible so as to give it the largest possible return on its investment. The franchisor, however, must only decide upon what territory it is willing to grant after taking account of a number of criteria concerning the territory and the franchisee. The territory should be one geographical, political, cultural and economic unit, which allows a planned approach to development of the franchise. Allowing the franchisee to take on an additional small nearby territory, merely because of its geographical proximity, will often lead to it being under-exploited. The geographical distance, cultural and political differences need to be taken into account when deciding upon the size of the territory. Inadequate resources will by necessity mean that the whole territory will not be systematically exploited and will be limited, not by the suitability of the system to the territory, but by the franchisee's inability to properly expand it. The business plan which the potential franchisee presents will, in part, reflect any deficiencies in resources it has. However that does not mean that conservative business plans are always indicative of an under-resourced franchisee. It can be a sign of market knowledge. It is therefore necessary to vet carefully the potential subfranchisor/developer by way of bank and trade references and company searches. Incorporation of any business plan into the development schedule will help encourage a realistic approach to it by the franchisee and so enable the franchisor to gauge its resources more accurately.

3. Site Selection

The site selection can be the domain of either the franchisor or the franchisee. However, when the franchisee selects the location it is subject to the approval of the franchisor. Some franchisors provide significant assistance in site selection in terms of marketing and demographic studies, lease negotiations and the procurement of local permits and licenses, especially if a turnkey franchise is offered. However, site selection is a major and tough task and therefore, both the parties should work in tandem for that.

4. Services to be Provided by the Franchisor

All the 'preopening obligations' and the 'post-opening services' to be given by the franchisor to the franchisee needs to be mentioned here. The preopening obligations generally include a trade secret and copyright license, recruitment and training of personnel, standard bookkeeping and accounting systems, inventory and equipment specifications, volume discounts, standard construction, building and interior design plans and opening promotion and advertising assistance. The post-opening services include field support and troubleshooting, R&D for new products and services, the development of national advertising and promotion campaigns, and the arrangement of group purchasing and volume discounts.

5. Franchise, Royalty and Related Fees Payable to the Franchisor and Reporting Requirements

The fee structure, be it initial or on continuing basis, needs to be mentioned clearly. The initial fee is generally a nonrefundable lump sum amount paid for the grant of the franchise, the trademark and the trade secret license and all the initial assistance from the franchisor.

The other major fee component is the royalty payable to the franchisor. The recurring nature of fee is with regards to advertising and promotion. Lastly, the miscellaneous payment is with regards to consulting, renewal or transfer fees.

6. Quality Control

This is very much specific to retail business and food chains all the more. It takes care of the quality of the sources of products, ingredients, supplies and materials. It gives specifications about the standards of service, the trade dress and uniform requirements, condition and appearance of the facility, the working hours, minimum insurance required, advertising and all the accounting procedures.

7. Insurance, Record Keeping and Other Related Obligations of the Franchisee

The franchise agreement specifically mentions the minimum amounts and type of insurance to be taken by the franchisee. The other things mentioned are the obligation to maintain and enforce quality standards with its employees, customers and vendors. Also, the obligation with regards to employment laws, health and safety standards and accounting standards, financial records is mentioned.

8. Protection of Intellectual Property and Covenants Against Competition

The franchise agreement should clearly mention that the trade name and the trade secret being used is the exclusive property of the franchisor. The agreement should also contain covenants against competition by a franchisee, both during the term of the franchise agreement and following termination or cancellation. Any franchise agreement must permit the franchisee to use the franchisor's system together with its name and trademarks. Clauses protecting this intellectual property and ensuring that the franchisees do not abuse it.

9. Termination of the Franchise Agreement

The various grounds on which the franchise agreement can be terminated needs to be listed down. Also the obligation of the franchisee, post termination needs to be mentioned.

10. Key Man

It may be that the franchisor is making the grant to the franchisee mainly because of the personal attributes of one of its key employees. In such a case it is essential that the agreement stipulates clearly the importance of that individual's role, in the scheme of things. It is also vital that the grant is made conditional on the continued efforts and employment of that individual by the franchisee. Termination of the key man's full-time employment in the franchise should be a material breach of the terms of the grant, and be grounds for termination.

Clearly provision must be made for the key man's death, invalidity and retirement. It may in any event only be felt necessary by the franchisor to apply the key man clause for, say, the first 5 years of the term, when the franchise is becoming established in the territory and most needs the key man's talents.

Such a provision will prevent the prime mover of the franchisee from deserting the franchise prematurely, as well as guarding the franchise from a management reorganisation that could remove him from his position and so deprive the franchise of the key man's particular talents. All the additional clauses for arbitration, attorney fees in case of a dispute, specific representations and warranties of the franchisee will be covered in these provisions.

5.2 SALE OF THE FRANCHISEES' RIGHTS

The franchisor must always be in complete control of the franchise network and be able to choose its sub-franchisors and developers, at its complete discretion. This means that the franchise agreement must always give the franchisor the right to veto the sale of a subfranchisor's or developer's business to an unapproved third party. The franchisor has the ultimate decision on who can join that system as a franchisee and he will be concerned that the new franchisee is the right person for the franchise. The franchisor must always assess the financial status of the assignee and its ability to pay any remaining balance of the franchise fee and the periodic and advertising fees. It should also consider whether the purchaser is compatible with the image of the franchise system. The franchisor may for example have a strong public stance on certain issues with which any assignee must be compatible. It is difficult to envisage The Body Shop International giving a franchise to a furrier!

The agreement should contain detailed provisions on assignment which must always be followed. These provisions should be carefully thought through and usually contain pre-emption rights giving the franchisor the right of first refusal. It should also lay down time limits within which these rights can be exercised. It is not uncommon for the franchisor to be entitled to a percentage of any prices paid by a third party purchaser, either as a recognition of its rights over the franchisee's goodwill, or as a finder's fee if it locates a purchaser. It may even be that the franchisor wishes to 'buy-back' the territory concerned and exercise any pre-emption rights it holds, in which case it may be appropriate for it to obtain a discount on the open market price.

Termination

Franchisors should take a specialist's legal advice, in each country belonging to the international franchise system, on the consequences of termination of the franchise contract. The franchisor must establish whether franchisees will be protected by local distributor or commercial agent legislation protective of parties contracting with suppliers. Such legislation will often establish significant termination rights for the franchisee. The legislation will often take precedent over the terms of the franchise agreement thereby rendering the contract provisions for termination procedures and rights irrelevant. Legislation may apply even on a refusal to renew a limited duration fixed term franchise agreement on its normal expiration date. The consequences for a franchisor terminating the contract of a franchisee who is protected by local legislation must always be very carefully considered before deciding upon termination as an appropriate course of action.

The local legislation will usually define the nature of 'just cause' for termination of the distributor/commercial agent agreement. Certain conduct will nearly always qualify as just cause:

(a) Commission of a serious crime such as fraud

(b) Bankruptcy

(c) Gross negligence of the local party causing substantial damage to the supplier's interest

(d) Breach of a fundamental provision of the contract, for example, a franchisee's refusal to render any accounts or pay any royalties at all to the principal.

5.3 CHOICE OF FORUM AND CHOICE OF LAW CLAUSES

If the parties prefer litigation to arbitration, an international franchise agreement should stipulate in which state, and under which law, disputes are to be settled. Therefore a choice of forum clause and a choice of law clause should be inserted in the agreement. The natural tendency is for franchisors to choose the jurisdiction and laws of their home state. Owing to the existence of regulatory statutes and the hybrid nature of the franchise relationship the choice of law clause and choice of forum clause are two of the most important features in international franchise agreements if the parties are to resolve their disputes by litigation.

Choice of Forum Clauses

All choice of forum clauses may be exclusive or non-exclusive. An exclusive clause has the main advantage of certainty. The existence of any reciprocal arrangement for the enforcement of judgements is an important factor when deciding whether to have an exclusive or nonexclusive jurisdiction clause.

Choice of Law Clauses

As regards the choice of law clauses, most countries' national laws will permit the parties to select a governing law in a contract and will apply the governing law even if it is not the national law. However, the franchisor should take legal advice on whether the national law of each country involved in the international franchise system respects governing law clauses. It is essential to select a law to govern a contract as, in the absence of such a clause, the parties may have to resort to litigation to determine the applicable law and both parties will be uncertain about the practical consequences of the dispute. When considering which law and forum are to be selected, the parties must consider whether the clauses will be recognised by the chosen court or other courts.

5.4 GENERAL OBLIGATIONS OF BOTH PARTIES

It is a truism but nevertheless bears restating that the general obligations of both the franchisor and the sub-franchisor, developer or franchisee are central to the success of the whole venture.

The Franchisor

The franchisor's obligations apart from making the initial grant will be to keep the sub franchisor, developer or sub-franchisee fully apprised of developments in the franchise system and to provide a 'trouble-shooting' service to assist the sub-franchisor, developer or sub-franchisee in acclimatizing the franchise to the territory. It is essential that the franchisor does not take on greater obligations than it can fulfill, and carefully appraises itself of what it can and cannot do in the particular territory in question. A British franchisor will, for example, be able to take on substantially more obligations in Eire than in Greece which is further away and where the social, cultural, legal and linguistic differences are so much greater.

Training

Training will, in any event, be a necessary obligation imposed on the franchisor. Without proper training sub-franchisor, developer and a sub-franchisee cannot possibly function in an acceptable manner. The franchisor must therefore carefully think through how to approach this issue. It will usually involve bringing a number of the franchisee's, subfranchisor's or developer's key employees to the franchisor's home territory (or another well-developed territory) and giving them intensive training. McDonalds' famous Hamburger University is a good example of highly developed training facilities where franchisees, sub-franchisors and developers receive intensive training in the operation of the franchise, usually in the franchisor's home territory. This intensive training should then be supplemented by 'on-the-spot' training in the new territory under the auspices of one of the franchisor's senior operational managers. There is, of course, no set rule as to how long the manager should be seconded abroad but it is suggested that it should be for at least 6 months - indeed 18 months is not unknown in key territories. This should also be supplemented by periodic visits from the franchisor to help iron out any problems that may arise.

The Operations Manual

The operations manual is also, of course, central to the training process and, as in domestic franchising, the franchisor must undertake to develop the system continually and update the manual on a regular basis. Translation of the manual into the territory's native languages is essential, and the franchisor must avoid the tendency to think that the whole world speaks and reads fluent or near fluent English or other language. The manual is the touchstone of the franchise system and must therefore be in an easily understandable form for the franchisee, sub-franchisor and developer and their employees. Great care must be taken to ensure that the translation is of a very high quality, and the best way to avoid subtle but important mistakes is to employ a competent professional translator - and then to cross check the translation. It is important to ensure that the translation is done properly since cutting corners can lead to grave mistakes. It must also be ensured that the copyright in both the original and translated manual vests in the franchisor.

5.5 CONFIDENTIALITY AND NON-COMPETITION RESTRICTIONS

When entering an overseas market, no matter which approach is taken, the franchisor is extremely vulnerable. Today's partners can very easily be tomorrow's competitors. In such circumstances protecting intellectual property rights will not be enough - the franchisor should also ensure that secrecy of any know-how is protected and that sub-franchisors, developers, franchisees and their employees are not free to compete with the franchisor either during or after the term of the franchise agreement.

Confidentiality

A franchisor will be forced to disclose a considerable amount of confidential information to each of its sub-franchisors/developers/franchisees and sub-franchisees and they in turn will have to disclose some of that information to employees. The franchisor therefore needs to make quite sure that it has done all that it possibly can to prevent these parties from disclosing the confidential information and/or using it to compete with the franchisor. The only way to achieve this is for the franchisor to receive a direct confidentiality and noncompetition undertaking from each of its sub-franchisors/developers/franchisees and subfranchisees. These must agree that they in turn will obtain similar undertakings from their employees (and where appropriate, their franchisees) and enforce those undertakings if required to do so.

Once an employee has left, he may not disclose any genuinely confidential information which he might have obtained while working. In practice, this is a very difficult rule to enforce. It may be hard to prove that any employee is using secret information or disclosing it to others. Similar considerations will apply to the sub-franchisors/developers/franchisees and subfranchisees. In any event, the courts have to be convinced that the information which has been disclosed is genuinely secret. Merely labelling something as 'secret' will not do. For example, it is no use labelling a recipe as a secret recipe if the ingredient list and the method is set out in a poster which is on the wall of the franchise restaurant's kitchen, particularly if members of the public can easily read it from the restaurant area. It would be hard to convince a court that it was a genuine secret if thousands of employees knew it. At some stage, a court will decide that the matter is no longer secret and has become public knowledge and not through the fault of the franchisee.

Non-competition

Due to the difficulty of showing that secrets are genuine and that they have been disclosed, franchisors frequently attempt to get round the problem by putting in specific noncompetition clauses. That is to say, clauses which oblige the franchisee not to operate a competing system within a certain period after the termination of the franchise agreement or within a certain radius. The enforceability of such clauses varies greatly. Great care has to be taken in drafting a restrictive covenant because, if it is drafted too widely, the court will refuse to enforce the whole covenant.

For example, a restriction on operating a competing restaurant within a one mile radius of an existing restaurant might well be reasonable in a small town but would be wholly unreasonable in central Rome. A restriction might well be reasonable if it could be shown that it was almost certain that trade secrets were being used in order to operate the competing business.

Rather than a non-competition clause, which the courts do not like, a franchisor may be able to achieve similar ends by prohibiting former franchisees and their employees from poaching customers and from enticing staff. The object is to prevent the former franchisees or ex-employees from using their personal influence over customers or employees to the disadvantage of the franchisor. This type of restriction may be particularly useful if the former franchisee is to be allowed to continue to exploit the franchise in a limited territory rather than a full scale termination. There must, however, be a legitimate reason for restricting competition. It would not be reasonable to restrict an employee from contacting old customers when, in his old job, he had no contact with customers anyway. Courts will not enforce restrictive covenants if they run for too long. Protection of confidentiality and term and post-term restrictions on competition are issues that the franchisor must consider very carefully before finalising the form of a franchise or development agreement. Local laws may greatly restrict the scope and enforceability of such clauses and it is therefore essential that timely advice is taken from experienced local lawyers.

5.6 FRANCHISE DISPUTES

Disputes and Termination

It is essential for every franchisor to enforce the obligations of subfranchisors, developers and franchisees to observe franchise standards. In an international franchise system enforcement overseas is far more problematic than a purely domestic forum. The risk of non-compliance and the consequential damage to the entire system will increase when the franchisor decides to take its franchise system overseas. If a sub-franchisor, developer or franchisee is in breach of its commitments to the franchisor enforcement action should be taken quickly as failure to do so may encourage other subfranchisors, developers and franchisees to breach their commitments.

Likely Causes of Dispute

The threat to the franchisor's system may arise from either breaches by a franchisee or the actions of a third party who may, for example, challenge the intellectual property rights of the franchise system.

The sorts of disputes which frequently arise are often the result of a sub franchisor/developer/franchisee's:

(a) Failure to make payments due

(b) Failure to maintain proper financial control in order to provide an accurate account of gross income and money due

(c) Failure to maintain adequate quality control, poor training of staff and service;

(d) A breach of confidentiality provisions

(e) Failure to display the name and/or logo adequately

(f) Failure to comply with non-competition provisions.

Disputes may also be initiated by sub-franchisors, developers and franchisees who are seeking legal excuses for non-compliance, for example, alleging unfair trade practices, breach of antitrust laws or oppressive operational standards.

The Franchisee and Third Party

Sub-franchisors/developers/franchisees must take enforcement action against third parties operating outside the franchise system, and infringing the franchisor's intellectual property rights, such as its name, trademarks, copyright and patents. The sub franchisor/developer/franchisee must be obliged to take effective enforcement action against any threat to the system's intellectual property rights. However, in the absence of the sub franchisor/developer/franchisee taking action, it is essential that the franchisor itself reserves the right to sue the infringing party.

5.7 FORMS OF RESOLUTION

In the event of a dispute between a franchisor and franchisee the main options open to a franchisor are as follows:

(a) discussion

(b) mediation

(c) termination

(d) arbitration

(e) litigation.

Discussion

Before taking immediate enforcement action the franchisor should consider contacting the franchisee and discussing the issues involved to see if an amicable settlement can be reached. If initial discussions do not prove fruitful the franchisor may consider arranging for discussions to take place between both parties' legal representatives who will be able to assess the relative merits of each party's case and may negotiate a compromise. The involvement of legal representatives will not necessarily lead to litigation and can often lead to a speedy settlement thereby avoiding the costs of litigation and a breakdown in relations between the parties. A franchisor could also send in 'troubleshooters' to help sub-franchisors if a breach is the result of ignorance or inadvertence.

Mediation

Termination of a franchise can impose extreme difficulties for a franchisor. Bearing in mind the continuing relationship between the franchisor and franchisee, mediation of disputes may be seen as an attractive alternative to termination and/or litigation. In a mediation system a dispute is submitted to a single impartial individual who will act as a referee in relatively informal proceedings. It is preferable to have a mediation clause in the franchise agreement and this should stipulate whether the findings of the mediator will be binding on the parties. In the absence of a mediation clause in the franchise agreement the parties will not have a contractual obligation to mediate but instead must voluntarily and mutually accept going to mediation. A mediation clause may be combined with an arbitration clause so that if mediation does not lead to a resolution of the dispute the parties will submit the dispute to formal arbitration.

The mediation clause should also designate a mediator or at least an arrangement whereby the parties will be able to agree mutually the nomination of a mediator. The main features of international mediation are usually as follows:

(a) Mediation sessions are held with all parties to review issues

(b) A summary of each side's case is presented to the mediator

(c) A mediation report containing findings on the merits of each side's case is provided to each party

(d) The parties hold negotiations to try to settle the dispute based on the report.

Mediation is conducted in confidence and, like arbitration; it should be possible for the parties to avoid any publicity. The franchisor will not wish sub-franchisors/developers/other franchisees to hear of the dispute. The main advantages of mediation are as follows:

(a) Private and flexible

(b) A mutually acceptable trained professional, selected by the parties, as referee

(c) Relatively low cost and, if litigation is avoided, it is a cost effective way of dealing with a dispute

(d) A mediator should be able to dissuade a party from pursuing an unreasonable claim or an excessive sum of money

(e) If there has been poor communication between the franchisor and the franchisee mediation can bring the parties together

(f) The parties are able to explore settlement options

(g) The franchisor and franchisee must work together after the dispute is settled

(h) Mediation sessions can be set up very quickly and can be held at convenient times and locations.

The main disadvantages are as follows:

(a) The mediators available may have little experience of franchising or the business involved

(b) Quick and effective action may be needed to remedy the breach

(c) Mediation (in the absence of a clause in the franchise agreement stipulating that the mediator's findings will be binding) will not produce an enforceable and binding decision. The parties must negotiate a settlement and time and effort may be wasted while the breach remains unremedied.

Mediation has flourished in the US, as high litigation costs have encouraged businessmen to explore alternative dispute resolutions.

5.8 ARBITRATION

Following the increase in international trade over the last decade there has been a vigorous upsurge in the use of arbitration as a method of resolving international commercial disputes.

Both parties must agree to the use of arbitration as a means of resolving their dispute.

Arbitration has many advantages over civil litigation, the traditional method of resolving commercial disputes. Some of the main advantages of arbitration are as follows:

(a) Flexible procedures
(b) No jurisdictional issues
(c) Neutral arbitrators
(d) Identification of arbitrators on the basis of technical and business expertise
(e) Awards which can be readily enforced through international treaties
(f) Privacy - since the arbitration hearing will not be reported the parties should be able to avoid the adverse publicity which often follows litigation
(g) An arbitration award is generally final whereas a court judgement is usually subject to rights of appeal to higher courts.

The upsurge in the popularity of international arbitration has been recognised by institutions around the world. It has resulted in an increasing number of arbitration centres to meet the demand. National legislatures have responded by establishing improved, streamlined arbitration laws and procedures and national courts usually demonstrate a willingness to provide a hospitable climate for arbitration and to require the parties to comply with contractual obligations to resolve disputes by arbitration. National courts generally interpret arbitration clauses widely so that they cover a greater number of disputes and will usually make it more difficult for parties to challenge arbitration awards in the courts. Arbitration may be 'institutional' whereby disputing parties may turn to an established institution specialising in arbitration proceedings, or *ad hoc* whereby the parties may have established their own jurisdiction and rules for the conduct of the arbitrations.

Arbitration Systems

There are a multitude of different institutional arbitration systems throughout the world as well as established rules which provide the basis for *ad hoc* arbitration.

Enforcement of Awards

Enforcement of arbitration awards in countries other than the location of the arbitration hearing is now comparatively straightforward following the United Nations Convention on the Recognition and Enforcement of Foreign Arbitrational Awards. Enforcement proceedings are usually taken in states in which the property and assets of the losing party are located. It is unlikely that an arbitration award will be made in the defendant's place of residence/business precisely because the parties to arbitration usually choose a neutral forum.

It may well be that the losing party has assets and property situated in more than one jurisdiction, and this will mean parties seeking to enforce the award will go 'forum shopping'.

Factors which should be borne in mind when choosing the appropriate forum are whether the local courts have an international or parochial attitude to foreign awards and whether the forum has a link to the state where the award was made. The question of state immunity is also relevant if enforcement is sought against a foreign government.

Enforcement will depend upon whether the parties are signatories to the Convention. An arbitrational award made in any country in the world can be enforced in any state which is a party to the Convention.

The first of these reservations is the reciprocity reservation under which contracting states can choose to apply the Convention only to the recognition of awards made in the territory of other contracting states. Out of the 69 state parties to the Convention, 44 use this reservation. It has the effect that only an award made to the contracting state can be enforced in any other contracting state.

The second reservation further limits the applicability of the Convention by providing that a state can agree to apply the Convention only to those disputes considered as commercial under the national law of the state making the award.

If a party is seeking recognition or enforcement of any award which was not made in a contracting state it will need to establish whether the state, where enforcement is sought, has entered into any other international treaty

In principle, a valid award should be recognised as an enforceable obligation by any country which recognises arbitration as a legitimate means of resolving disputes. In practice, however, this does not always work as enforcement is being sought in local courts, in the defendant's home state, and these courts are more likely to be critical of the award. Commercial pressure can, however, achieve settlements and enforcements even if a local court procedure fails.

Arbitration Clauses

Parties can avoid problems at the time of arbitration by stating their choice of law, place of arbitration and an applicable language in a carefully drafted arbitration clause.

Litigation

The franchise agreement will usually include either a binding arbitration clause or a jurisdiction clause. The latter will determine the jurisdiction of the courts which will deal with litigation between the parties. One of the main advantages of litigation is the ability to apply for injunctions thus providing an urgent remedy to a serious breach by a sub-franchisor/developer/franchisee. The main disadvantages of litigation are as follows:

Arbitration may be preferred to litigation as it should maintain a continuing relationship between the franchisor and the franchisee at the conclusion of the arbitration whereas litigation will usually lead to a breakdown in relations between the parties.

Litigation may be reported and can lead to adverse publicity for the franchisor. For example, McDonalds engaged in extensive litigation against its regional franchisee in Paris, complaining about non-compliance with standards of quality, service and cleanliness. Eventually the franchisor cancelled the franchise in 1982. The litigation led to negative publicity in the franchise area and caused considerable harm to McDonald's international franchise system. However, it should be borne in mind that, although arbitration proceedings will not be reported and will be heard privately, in the commercial community it is usually well known when arbitration is taking place.

Costs of litigation are invariably substantial but it should be emphasised that arbitration will still involve the need to employ lawyers, which can be as expensive as litigation (particularly if the arbitrators fees are high). There may also be difficulties in obtaining a continuous hearing owing to unavailability of arbitrators for lengthy periods of time. This can lead to adjournments of the hearing.

In the absence of an arbitration clause in the franchise agreement it is necessary to have a jurisdiction clause to determine which country will deal with any litigation between the parties. In the absence of a jurisdiction clause the franchisor may be at the mercy of local courts in the franchisee's jurisdiction. Similarly, the parties should also choose the law of a particular state which will govern resolution of disputes between them. Franchise agreements are full of covenants and various terms and conditions, the breach of which can result in the wrong party seeking rescission or termination of the contract and compensation in the form of damages. For instance, if the franchisee fails to pay the royalty to the franchisor for use of the goodwill the franchisor can terminate the contract and find another more suitable franchisee. If the franchisee does not follow the manual or business practice of the franchisor, the latter may seek to terminate and obtain damages for any goods produced differently from those produced by the franchisor.

5.9 DISCLOSURE DOCUMENT

This is a document that is maintained and updated periodically by the franchisor depicting all relevant information required. This should be revised promptly as and when material change takes place. This disclosure document ought to be given to a franchisee either (1) his first personal meeting with the franchisor or (2) ten days prior to the execution of the contract or the initial payment. This has to follow with the supply of a copy of all agreements that they will be asked to sign at least five days before execution of the agreement. It is mandatory that the Disclosure Document should contain the following:

(a) Details of the franchisor and his predecessor the background of the business, headquarters, date of incorporation, current business activities, prior experience, period of franchise and the likely competitors

(b) Identity and business experience of the associates of the franchisor

(c) Details of any litigation, arbitration or administrative matter regarding the franchisor

(d) All details of bankruptcy if ever filed for by the franchisor

(e) Franchisees initial payment amount as franchise fees

(f) Franchisees initial investment

(g) Obligations of the franchisor, supervision, services, etc.

(h) Obligation of the franchisee to purchase goods, services, supplies, fixtures, equipment or inventory related to the business from sources designated by the franchisor

(i) The exclusive area or territory of operation granted by the franchisor.

(j) Trademarks: All service markets, trademarks, logos, symbols, etc.

(k) Any patents and copyrights

(l) Restriction of goods and services

(m) Any renewal, termination, repurchase modification and assignment of the franchise agreement.

(n) Complete information of the franchisees of the franchisor.

(o) All financial details of the franchisor as per the generally accepted accounting principles.

Know the 'Rules of Engagement' Before Signing an Agreement

by Justin M. Klein and Ross H. Schmierer

Long term success should be one goal of any franchisee. Likewise, franchisors hope they have successful operators. Sometimes, however, the relationship just doesn't work.

Failure is a realistic outcome and there are many reasons that a franchise relationship fails. Sometimes the franchisee may be at fault, other times the franchisor. Regardless, it is imperative that prospective franchisees understand the "rules of engagement" that are set out in the franchise agreement if a dispute arises.

Although most optimistic and enthusiastic franchisees may not want to focus on these provisions at the start of the franchise relationship, it is imperative that they thoroughly address this before they invest.

Virtually every franchise agreement provides for termination on some or all of the following grounds: failing to pay royalties or other fees; providing false information to the franchisor; selling unauthorized products or services; abandoning the business for more than a week; attempting an unauthorized assignment; misusing the trademarks of the franchisor; and violating any law, statute or regulation, or being convicted of a felony.

With this in mind, the franchisee must acknowledge that a dispute may arise over the course of the relationship, especially considering that many agreements provide for a 10-year term or even longer.

With dispute resolution clauses a regular part of most franchise agreements today, we will examine certain select provisions commonly used by franchisors. Prospective franchisees should evaluate the impact any of these clauses will have on their decision to purchase a franchise.

Although many legal theorists and social scientists have challenged the notion that jurors are biased against business, several studies have purportedly led to three conclusions relevant to franchise litigation: (1) juries regard the profit motive, and its effect on human behavior, with suspicion; (2) juries hold corporations to higher standards than they apply to individual litigants; and (3) plaintiffs win a strikingly high percentage of jury verdicts in business cases, including disputes between franchisees and franchisors.

In addition, franchisors fear that jurors will ignore a judge's instructions about the applicable law and legal significance of contract terms if they believe justice will be served by doing so. As a result, the franchisor and its counsel seek to avoid the "unpredictable" aspects of the courtroom and insert jury-avoidance mechanisms.

In addition to trying to avoid a jury entirely, a franchisor will try and get before a jury in a forum perceived to be more hospitable to the franchisor or dramatically limit the relief that a jury can award by including arbitration clauses, forum selection clauses, damage caps and punitive damages waivers.

5.10 FRANCHISE AGREEMENT DRAFT

APOLLO WINDOW BLINDS LIMITED, incorporated under the Companies Act with registered number 2851496 and having its registered office at 7, Apollo Street, Wadala, Mumbai 400016, India. ("the Franchisor"); and **THE PERSON** named as Franchisee in Part I of the Schedule (the "Franchisee").

(A) The Franchisor is engaged in the business of manufacturing, distributing, merchandising and promoting the sale of window blinds and related products under the name "Apollo Window Blinds" which is operated in accordance with a distinctive system contained in the Manual, a copy of which is annexed to this Agreement.

(B) A substantial and exclusive reputation and goodwill exists in the name "Apollo Window Blinds" and the Franchisor is the proprietor of the Trademark(s) and of the Intellectual Property.

(C) The Franchisee desires to obtain the benefit of the knowledge, skill and experience of the Franchisor and the right to operate the business system of the Franchisor upon the terms and subject to the Conditions set out in Part III of the Schedule and the Manual.

THEREFORE the parties hereby contract and agree as follows: -

1. Definitions

The terms defined in the Conditions shall have the meanings set out therein for the purposes of this Agreement and the Manual.

2. Condition Precedent

The Franchisee shall, prior to the Commencement Date, have obtained and shall, with effect from the Commencement Date, throughout the term of this Agreement, hold a valid Value Added Tax Registration in respect of the Franchise granted in terms of this Agreement and shall observe and comply with the terms of the same. The Franchisee hereby acknowledges that any failure by it to hold such a registration during the term of this Agreement shall be deemed to be a material breach of this Agreement and shall result in the termination of this Agreement and shall render the Franchisee liable to indemnify the Franchisor against any and all loss, cost, expenses or damages suffered, whether directly or indirectly as a result of the same.

3. Franchise

The Franchisor grants to the Franchisee the exclusive right to operate the Business in the Territory from and at the Premises as principal on the terms of this Agreement, the Conditions and the Manual with effect from the Commencement Date during the Initial Period until terminated in accordance with the Conditions and the Manual.

4. Premises

(4.1) The parties agree that the Business shall be conducted from the Premises.

(4.2) The Premises authorised for the sole purpose of carrying out the Business, in accordance with the terms of this Agreement, are those specified in Part I of the Schedule.

(4.3) Prior to the Commencement Date the Franchisor shall procure that the Initial Works required and designed to bring the Premises up to the Franchisors standards and to properly reflect the Franchisor's corporate identity, shall be completed. The Franchisee shall pay 15% of the agreed start up costs and expenses (including VAT) of the Initial works to the Franchisor at least 14 days prior to the scheduled opening of the Business, balance to be paid by the Franchisee on the first day of trading of the Business.

(4.4) The Franchisee acknowledges that it shall not alter or convert the Premises upon completion of the Initial Works without the prior written consent of the Franchisor.

(4.5) The Franchisee shall not alter or convert the finished Premises in any way without the previous consent in writing of the Franchisor.

(4.6) Any alteration or installation to or at the Premises shall be carried out by the Franchisee only in accordance with such plans, drawings and specifications approved by the Franchisor in writing.

(4.7) The Franchisee shall fit the Premises with only those fixtures, fittings, equipment and signage specified by the Franchisor.

If for any reason, the Franchisee is required to make changes to the fittings, fixtures or signage of the Premises, such changes will be made within a reasonable period of time as agreed with the Franchisor.

(4.8) The Franchisee shall be responsible for complying with all statutory or legal requirements and regulations which apply to the Premises and/or the Business.

(4.9) The Franchisor and the Franchisee shall enter into a Sub-Lease in respect of the Premises in the form annexed to this Agreement upon the date of this Agreement/completion of the Initial Works.

(4.10) The Franchisee warrants to the Franchisor that it is the feu holder/ freeholder/tenant of the Premises and that it has obtained all necessary consents, permissions and licences to enable the Initial Works to be undertaken and to operate the Business from the Premises. The Franchisee covenants that throughout the continuance of this Agreement it shall observe all statutory and contractual obligations relating to its occupation and use of the Premises and shall not do any act or make any omission which may result in such occupation or usage ceasing.

5. Governing Law

This, Agreement shall be governed by the laws of Indian. The parties hereby submit to the non-exclusive jurisdiction of the Indian courts.

IN WITNESS WHEREOF these presents consisting of this and the four preceding pages together with the Schedule annexed hereto are executed as follows: -

SUBSCRIBED for and on behalf of the said APOLLO WINDOW BLINDS LIMITED

at
on the day of Two thousand and [ ]
by ....
(print name) Director's signature
its Director before the following witness: -
Witness (Sign) ....
Name (Print) ....
Address ....
SUBSCRIBED by the said ....
(print name) Franchisee's signature
at
on the day of Two thousand and [ ]
before the following witness:--
Witness (Sign) ....
Name (Print) ....
Address ....
Occupation ....

THE CONDITIONS

6. Definitions

(6.1) Unless the context shall otherwise require, the following terms shall have the meanings set opposite them:-

"the Business"	the business of distributing, marketing, offering for sale and selling exclusively the Products, operated and conducted under the Trademarks using the System more particularly described in the Manual;
"the Commencement Date"	the date specified in Part I of the Schedule;
"the Franchise"	the non-exclusive right granted by the Franchisor to operate the Business by the Franchisee as principal on the terms of this Agreement;
"the Franchisee"	the person specified in Part I of the Schedule as franchisee;
"the Initial Period"	a period of 5 years from the commencement Date;

"the Initial Work"	the installation of the external signs and Shopfittings at the Premises by the Franchisor in terms of the outline specification of works annexed to this Agreement; .
"the Manual"	the operations manual (as amended from time to time) provided by the Franchisor and to be adhered to and implemented by the Franchisee in the Business;
"Marketing Material"	the literature, point of sale and marketing material provided by the Franchisor for use ,in the Business; .
"the Permitted Business Name"	Apollo Window Blinds;
"Postcode District"	the geographical areas comprised, in the postal districts as shown in the Postcode;
"the Premises"	the premises specified in Part I of the Schedule for the operation of the Business by the Franchisee;
"the Products"	all types of window blinds and related products manufactured and sold under the name "Apollo Window Blinds" as specified in the Manual;
"the Shopfittings"	those fixtures and fittings external and internal to. be situated at the Premises and authorised by the Franchisor other than such items as form part of the fabric of the building;
"the System"	the distinctive business format and method developed by the Franchisor in connection with the operation of the Business utilising and comprising the Trademarks and certain standard operational procedures, plans, directions, specifications, methods, management and advertising techniques and identification schemes, part of which are contained in the Manual;

"Territory"	the postcode districts more particularly described in Part I of the Schedule;
"Trademarks"	the trademarks the particulars of which are set out in Part II of the Schedule; and
"Training Period"	a period of [ ] from the Commencement Date.

(6.2) Save as expressly provided for, references in this Agreement to this Agreement or any other document are to this Agreement or such other document as varied, supplemented, novated and/or replaced in any manner from time to time.

(6.3) Reference to Clauses and Schedules are to be construed as references to clauses, and schedules of this Agreement unless otherwise stated.

(6.4) The headings in this Agreement are inserted for ease of reference only and shall not affect its construction.

7. Appointment

(7.1) The Franchisor hereby appoints the Franchisee as its exclusive distributor in the Territory and grants to the Franchisee the exclusive right to market, distribute, supply and sell within the Territory the Products purchased from the Franchisor on the terms and conditions contained in this Agreement, under these Conditions and the Manual. The Franchisee acknowledges that the Franchisor shall be entitled to amend or vary the Manual at any time and the Franchisee shall be bound by such amendments and variations. In the event of any conflict between the terms of this Agreement and the Manual, the terms of the Manual shall prevail.

(7.2) The Franchisor further grants the Franchisee the rights to use the Permitted Business Name and the Trademarks at the Premises in connection with the Business. The Franchisee is not permitted to use the Permitted Business Name or the Trademarks or any deviation of the same in any manner which has not been authorised in writing by the Franchisor. The Franchisee *may* not use the Permitted Business Name or the Trademarks in any corporate name.

(7.3) On the date of execution of this Agreement, the Franchisor shall deliver one copy of the Manual to the Franchisee. For the avoidance of doubt, the Franchisee hereby acknowledges that the Manual shall be and remain the sole property of the Franchisor, and the Franchisee shall not be entitled to make any copies of the Manual.

(7.4) The Franchisee agrees that it will not make any use of and will not permit or authorise any use directly or indirectly of the System or the Trademarks by any third party.

(7.5) The Franchisee shall, not actively sell the Products outside the Territory and will not knowingly offer or provide *any* information or assistance concerning the System or the

Trademarks to *any* person, firm or undertaking who intends or may seek to use or resell them outside the Territory.

(7.6) For the avoidance of doubt, nothing contained in this Agreement shall be construed as a restriction upon the Franchisor from marketing, distributing or supplying any products not covered by this Agreement in the Territory, whether to the Franchisee's customers or otherwise.

(7.7) The Franchisee shall not hold itself out as the Franchisor's agent for sales of the Products or as being entitled to bind the Franchisor in any way, provided always that the Franchisee shall be entitled to describe itself as a franchise or as authorised franchisee of the Business and as such the distributor and supplier of the Products.

(7.8) The Franchisee shall not sell any of the Products which it purchases from the Franchisor through-sales agents or to a sub-distributor without the prior written consent of the Franchisor.

(7.9) For the avoidance of doubt, all of the Franchisee's operating expenses, including the expense of maintaining business premises, shall be for the Franchisee's account.

8. Duration

(8.1) The Agreement shall commence on the Commencement Date and subject to the provisions of Condition 8 shall continue for the Initial Period.

(8.2) The Franchise may thereafter be extended at the option of the Franchisee and with the Franchisor's consent for a further period of 5 years commencing on the day following the date of expiry of the Initial Period subject to the following: -

(8.2.1) the service on the Franchisor of a notice signed by the Franchisee not later than six calendar months prior to expiry of the Initial Period: and

(8.2.2) throughout the Initial Period there has been proper performance by the Franchisee of all its obligations hereunder and there having been no material breach by the Franchisee of the terms of this Agreement entitling the Franchisor to terminate this Agreement under the provision of Condition 8 either at the date of giving notice to the Franchisor under Condition 8.2.1 above or at the expiration of such notice: and

(8.2.3) execution by the Franchisee of a new agreement in the standard form usedd by the Franchisor at the time of service of the notice referred to in Condition 8.2.1; and

(8.2.4) the Franchisee having previously undertaken in writing to *carry* out such works of renovation, modernisation and refurbishment to the Premises and to replacement of such fixtures, signs, furnishings and equipment as are specified to the Franchisee by the Franchisor prior to the date of renewal and reasonably necessary to bring the Premises up to the then current standards of design and decor of the System or to comply with any statutory requirements or regulations relating to public health and safety, all at the Franchisee's expenses.

9. Franchisee's Obligations

(9.1) The Franchisee agrees at all times during the continuance of this Agreement: -

(9.1.1) to commence, establish and maintain the Business at the Premises from the Commencement Date;

(9.1.2) to operate the Business strictly in accordance with and to conform in all respects and at all times with the provisions of the Manual;

(9.1.3) to use its best endeavours to establish, maintain and maximise the turnover of the Business;

(9.1.4) to pay all sums specified in the Manual in accordance with the procedures specified in the Manual;

(9.1.5) to carry on only the Business at the Premises and not to carry on any other business whatsoever at the Premises or permit the sale there from of any goods other than the Products;

(9.1.6) to offer for sale the Franchisor's complete range of Products;

(9.1.7) to obtain all the Products from the Franchisor or its approved suppliers;

(9.1.8) not to make use of or disclose any information or knowledge about the materials and the specifications of the Products for *any* purpose nor to make any copies of them either before or after termination of this Agreement;

(9.1.9) to provide and maintain the agreed service levels for the Business, and not to sell any product nor provide any service which does not conform to the standards specified by the Franchisor;

(9.1.10) to *comply* with all reasonable instructions given *by* the Franchisor with regard to the standard or quality of service to be provided by the Franchisee;

(9.1.11) to provide the following services to its customers:

(9.1.11.1) to measure and quote, without charge, by suitably qualified staff attending promptly at the residence or business premises in which the Products are to be installed or delivered without *any* obligation upon the prospective customer to purchase;

(9.1.11.2) to install or deliver *any* Products purchased by the customer by suitably qualified staff attending promptly;

(9.1.11.3) to provide after sales service by suitably qualified staff attending promptly, to ensure trouble free performance of the Products supplied and to repair and/or replace any Products which are bona fide defective;

(9.1.12) to maintain, (with a reputable insurance company approved by the Franchisor), adequate insurance cover against loss (including loss of profits) or damage arising from fire, explosion, impact, burglary and such other risks in the minimum sums as agreed with the Franchisor from time to time, against all liability (including Product liability) of the Franchisor, Franchisee and any supplier of the Franchisee, to the Franchisee's employees and customers and additionally, public liability insurance to the value of Rs.5 million;

(9.1.13) not to engage in *any* activities at the Premises, which *may* be contrary to any legislation or regulations imposed by *any* competent authority. The Franchisor *may* by notice in writing specify any matter or thing required to be done or omitted to be done to ensure that such legislation or regulations are complied with and upon such notice the Franchisee shall immediately do or omit to do the same;

(9.1.14) to protect and promote the goodwill attaching to the Business, the Permitted Business Name, the Trademarks and the use of the System. The Franchisee shall not do anything, which would or might bring the name of the Franchisor, the Trademarks, the Permitted Business Name or the System into disrepute. The Franchisee shall notify the Franchisor immediately of any occurrence or fact which has affected or could adversely affect the value thereof, and shall take such reasonable action as the Franchisor may direct;

(9.1.15) not to use the Permitted Business Name or Trade Marks for any purpose other than in relation to the Business and in accordance with the Manual;

(9.1.16) to diligently carry on the Business at the Premises and use its best endeavours to seek, establish and develop sales of the Products within the Territory, I

(9.1.17) not to actively market or canvas or promote the Business out with the Territory without the prior written authority of the Franchiser;

(9.1.18) to enter into a registered user agreement in such form and with such person as is required by the Franchisor in respect of the Trademarks;

(9.1.19) not to pledge the credit of the Franchisor not to represent itself as being the Franchisor or agent or partner of the Franchiser;

(9.1.20) to keep confidential the System and the contents of the Manual and the terms of this Agreement;

(9.1.21) at the Franchisee's own expense to obtain and maintain in force all consents, licenses and permissions necessary for the operation of the Business and the exhibition of advertising signs and other matters at the Premises and to comply with all rules, regulations and by- laws of the relevant authorities relating thereto; .

(9.1.22) to apply for and maintain in force a Consumer Credit licenses (at the Franchisee's own expense) via the Office of Fair Trading and to lodge a copy with the Franchiser within no more than three months of the Commencement Date;

(9.1.23) to deliver to the Franchisor within seven days after the due date for submission to Customs and Excise a copy of the Franchisee's return and a copy of any assessment raised *against* it by Customs and Excise; and

(9.1.24) forthwith to give notice by facsimile followed by written confirmation of any legal process, whether criminal or civil, served, received or levied at the Premises or upon the Franchisee and whether in relation to the Business or otherwise and to provide to the Franchisor such further information as the Franchisor may require in connection therewith.

10. Franchisor's Obligations

(10.1) The Franchisor shall allocate a geographical territory in which the Franchisee will actively market and promote the Business in the Territory. Such Territory shall be as defined in Part I of the Schedule.

(10.2) The Franchisor agrees at all times during the continuance of this Agreement:-

(10.2.1) to act reasonably wherever the Franchisor is required in terms of this Agreement or the Manual to give its consent or take any decision relative to the Franchisee;

(10.2.2) to sell the Products to the Franchisee at the Franchisor's standard trade price list, as published and revised from time to time; and -

(10.2.3) to inform the Franchisee in writing of any proposed alterations to the System.

11. Payment

(11.1) The Franchisee shall pay all sums due by the Franchisee to the Franchisor pursuant to this Agreement or the Manual in accordance with the terms of this Agreement and the Manual.

(11.2) In the event of any default in payment on the due date of any due sum, the Franchisor will, in addition to any other remedies available to it, suspend the supplies of Products and services until payment is made.

Further, in the event of any default in the payment of sums due, the Franchisor shall have the right to charge interest at the rate of 2% per month calculated on day to day basis on the amount of any sums outstanding from the above date of payment as specified in this Agreement or the Manual until settlement, both before and after payment.

12. Restrictions

(12.1) The Franchisee agrees that during the continuance of this Agreement and for one year after its termination it shall not, whether as principal, servant, agent or as director or shareholder in any company or in any other capacity, and whether alone or jointly with any other person, firm or corporation:-

(12.1.1) carry on or be involved in either directly or indirectly any business competitive or in conflict with the Business within or within a radius of three quarters of a mile from the Postal District or any other premises at which a business is carried on under the Permitted Business Name;

(12.1.2) approach or endeavour to employ or engage, any employee of the Franchisor or any person to whom the Franchisor has made an offer of employment, or any person employed by or who has been made such an offer by any other holder of a franchise granted by the Franchisor;

(12.1.3) interfere with, solicit or entice any customer of the Business (meaning *any* person who has regularly or habitually purchased Products from the Franchisee within the period of one *year* prior to such termination) with the intent that he cease to deal with the Business or any successor to the Business of the Franchisee at the Premises.

(12.2) Upon termination of this Agreement the Franchisee shall cease use of the Trademarks and the Permitted Business Name and shall not use any name which resembles that name or may reasonably be confused with it and not in any way to suggest any continuing connection or association with the Business or the Franchisor.

13. Assignation

(13.1) The Franchisee shall not assign the benefit of all or any part of this Agreement without the previous written consent of the Franchisor which shall not be unreasonably withheld.

(13.2) The assignation of the benefit of this Agreement is subject to payment of the Franchisor's legal costs plus VAT thereon relating to such consent and the preparation of such documentation as may be required in relation thereto.

(13.3) The application for the Franchisor's consent to assign the benefit of this Agreement (the Application") shall state the name and address of the proposed assignee and the purchase price (if *any)* to be paid by the proposed assignee ("the Price").

(13.4) On receipt of the Application the Franchisor may by serving notice in writing served within 28 days of receipt of the Application elect to purchase the Business at the Price.

(13.5) Any failure by the Franchisor to exercise its right shall be without prejudice to its right to refuse its consent to any proposed assignation but in the *event* that the Franchisor does grant its consent to any proposed assignation such assignation shall take place only to the proposed assignee and for the Price and on the other terms specified in the Application.

(13.6) Any advertisement relating to the proposed assignation of the benefit of this Agreement shall be made only in such form and at such location or in such newspaper, periodical or other publication as shall be agreed by the Franchisor in writing but in any event no notice or advertisement whatsoever in relation thereto shall be placed on the exterior or within the Premises.

14. Summary Termination

(14.1) The Franchisor may terminate this Agreement forthwith by written notice to that effect to the Franchisee it:

(14.1.1) during the Training Period it becomes apparent to the Franchisor that the Franchisee does not meet the Franchisor's requirements and standards;

(14.1.2) the Franchisee shall *have* failed to observe or perform any of the obligations of this Agreement. If any such failure is capable of remedy the Franchisee shall have a period of 30 days to remedy the breach from receipt of notice requiring its remedy. Failure to observe or perform any of the obligation in the Manual shall constitute a breach;

(14.1.3) the Franchisee shall become insolvent by way of inability to pay its debts or shall enter into liquidation whether voluntarily or compulsory or shall make any arrangement or composition with its creditors or shall have a receiver or administrator appointed over all or part of its assets or shall take or suffer any similar action in consequence of a debt;

(14.1.4) the Franchisee shall cease for whatever reason to be entitled to occupy the Premises and shall be unable to find alternative premises within the Territory deemed, in the reasonable opinion of the Franchisor, to be suitable for the Business within a period of 3 months.

(14.1.5) in the event that there is a change in any of the shareholders in the Franchisee from the shareholders at. the date of this Agreement the Franchisee shall immediately notify the Franchisor in writing of such change. The Franchisor shall have the right to terminate this Agreement forthwith for a period of six (6) months from the date of such notice.

(14.1.6) the personal representatives of a deceased Franchisee shall not have completed an assignment of the benefit of this agreement in accordance with the provisions of Condition 6 within a period of six months calculated from the date of the death of the Franchisee.

(14.2) This Agreement will terminate automatically in the event that the Franchisee becomes deregistered for Value Added Tax with H.M. Customs & Excise during the term of this Agreement. For the avoidance of doubt such de-registration shall constitute a breach of this Agreement.

15. Intellectual Property

(15.1) The Franchisor hereby authorises the Franchisee to use the Trademarks in the Territory on or in relation to the Products for the purposes only of exercising its rights and performing its obligations under this Agreement.

(15.2) The Franchisee shall ensure that each reference to and use of any of the Trademarks by the Franchisee is in a manner from time to time approved by the Franchisor and accompanied by an acknowledgement, in a form approved by the Franchisor, that the some is a trademark (or registered trademark) of the Franchisor.

(15.3) The Franchisee shall not:

(15.3.1) make any modifications to the Products without prior written consent of the Franchisor;

(15.3.2) alter or remove or tamper with any Trademarks, numbers or other means of identification used on or in relation to the Products;

(15.3.3) use any of the Trademarks in any way which might prejudice their distinctiveness or validity or the goodwill of the Franchisor herein;

(15.3.4) use in relation to the Products any trade marks other than the Trademarks without obtaining the prior written consent of the Franchisor;

(15.3.5) use in the Territory any trade marks or trade names so resembling any trade marks or trade names of the Franchisor including the Trademarks as to be likely to cause confusion or deception; or

(15.3.6) change, mutilate, obscure or otherwise deface or interfere with any service mark, trade name, Trademark or other information appearing on the Products.

(15.4) Except as provided in Condition 8.1 of this Agreement the Franchisee shall have no rights in respect of *any* trade names or Trademarks used by the Franchisor in relation to the Products or of the goodwill associated therewith, and the Franchisee hereby acknowledges that, except as expressly provided in this Agreement, it shall not acquire any rights in respect thereof and that all such rights and goodwill are, and shall remain, vested in the Franchisor.

(15.5) For the avoidance of doubt, the Franchisee hereby acknowledges that the Shop fittings and the layout of the Premises form part of the intellectual property rights of the Franchisor and the Franchisee shall not alter, remove, tamper, change or otherwise interfere with the same except as expressly permitted in writing by the Franchisor.

(15.6) The Franchisee shall, at the expense of the Franchisor, take all such steps as the Franchisor may reasonably require to assist the - Franchisor in maintaining the validity and enforceability of the intellectual property of the Franchisor including the Trademarks, during the term of this Agreement.

(15.7) The Franchisee shall promptly and fully notify the Franchisor of any actual, threatened or suspected infringement in the Territory of any of the intellectual property of the Franchisor including, without limiting the foregoing generality, the Trademarks which comes to the Franchisee's notice, and any claim by any third party so coming to its notice that the sale of the Products within the Territory infringes any rights of any other person, and the Franchisee shall at the request and expense of the Franchisor do all such things as may be reasonably required to assist the Franchisor in taking or resisting any proceedings in relation to any such infringement or claim.

(15.8) Nothing contained in this Agreement shall entitle the Franchisee to take any action in respect of the infringement of the Trademarks or any other intellectual property which is owned by the Franchisor, without the prior written consent of the Franchisor.

(15.9) The Franchisor gives no *warranty* to the Franchisee that the use or sale *by* it of the Products will not infringe the intellectual property rights of any third party and under no circumstances shall the Franchisor be liable to indemnify the Franchisee with regard to any loss, cost, injury or damage incurred or suffered by the Franchisee in respect of any such infringement.

16. Force Majeure

Both parties shall be released from their obligations hereunder in the event that national emergency, war, prohibitive government regulations or any other cause beyond the control of either party shall render performance of this Agreement economically enviable for a period in excess of 3 consecutive months whereupon all amounts incurred due and payable shall be paid immediately and the Franchisee shall forthwith cease the operation of the Business at the Premises.

17. Procedure on Termination

Upon expiry or termination of this Agreement:

(17.1) The Franchisee will forthwith procure the transfer of the telephone number used at the: Premises to the Franchisor or its nominee;

(17.2) All rights of the Franchisee pursuant to this Agreement shall cease and determine absolutely save that the restrictions contained in Condition 5 shall continue in full force and effect;

(17.3) The Franchisee will within 72 hours of receipt of notice of any termination deliver to the

Franchisor a list of all customers of the Business and their telephone numbers and a list of persons employed by the Franchisee in the Business with full details including names, home addresses- employment position, date of birth, salary and other emoluments, and date of commencement of employment by the Franchisee;

(17.4) The Franchisee will vacate the Premises and remove all the Franchisee's and any third party's property and effects from the Premises forthwith causing no damage, and in default of so going *by* or on the date of termination the Franchisor may procure the removal of the same from the Premises at the sole cost of the Franchisee;

(17.5) The Franchisee will return to the Franchisor all copies of the Manual and the Marketing Material and shall not retain any copies.

18. Indemnity

The Franchisee shall indemnify and hold the Franchisor harmless from any loss, cost, damage or expense or any liability which it may incur, either directly or indirectly, as a result of or in connection with the use of the Products or the sale of the Products or the operation of the Business by the Franchisee or any third party where such loss, cost, damage, expense or liability is the result of an act or omission on the part of the Franchisee. The Franchisee shall also indemnify and hold the Franchisor harmless from any loss, cost, damage or expense or any liability which it may incur as a result of any breach by the Franchisee of this Agreement. The provisions of this Condition shall survive termination of this Agreement.

19. General

(19.1) It is expressly agreed and declared:-

(19.1.1) the expiration or termination of this Agreement shall be without prejudice to the rights of either party accrued prior to the date of such termination or expiration;

(19.1.2) nothing in this Agreement shall constitute a joint venture, agency or partnership or relationship of employer and employee between the Franchisor and the Franchisee; and

(19.1.3) in the event that any provision clause, sub-clause or part thereof of this Agreement or these Conditions shall be void, voidable or illegal, the Franchisor may at its sole discretion sever or amend such provision in such manner as renders the remainder of this Agreement or these conditions enforceable and this Agreement shall not determine.

20. Notices

Any notice required or authorised to be given under this Agreement may be served by pre-paid registered letter or facsimile transmission addressed to the party in question at the address contained in the Agreement or to such other address as may be notified in writing by that party to the other party for the purposes of this Agreement. *Any* notice so given by letter shall be deemed to have been served 72 hours after it shall have been posted and by facsimile upon the date of transmission. In proving service it shall be sufficient in the case of a registered letter to produce the receipt of the post office therefore and in the case of a facsimile message to produce a copy of such message together with the .facsimile activity report timed and dated and bearing the facsimile number of the addressee.

APOLLO WINDOW BLINDS LTD.
Franchise Agreement

Date:____________

Summary Pages

These pages summarize the attached AGREEMENT, the details of which shall control in the event of any conflict.

1. Franchisee:
   Name :______________________
   Address:____________________
   ____
   Telephone:__________________
2. Name of Franchisee's MSA: ______________________________
3. Type of Franchisee: Super Grand/Grand Wholesale/Standard Wholesale/Retail (circle one)
4. Intital Franchisee Fee: Rs. ________________.
5. Amount due upon signing Agreement: Rs. 50,000.
6. Franchisee shall purchase ________ Apollo Products (initial inventory), and __________ cart kits by: ________, 20___.
7. Date Balance of Rs. __________ (Initial Franchise Fee less Rs. 50,000 plus payments for freezes; initial inventory and cart kits) is due: _________, 20___.
8. Date Initial Franchise Fee, blinds and initial inventory payments are due to avoid freight charges of blinds ______________.
9. Expiration Date of Franchise Agreement: ________________________.
10. Franchisee's Agent to Receive Service of Process:
11. Name : ______________________________
12. Address: ____________________________
    ____

APOLLO WINDOW BLINDS LTD

This Agreement ("Agreement") is entered into as of__________, 20__, by and between Apollo Window Blinds Ltd., a Mumbai corporation with its principal place of business at 7, Apollo Street, Wadala, Mumbai 400017 and __________________ ("Franchisee").

1. Recitals

(a) Franchisee has investigated several business opportunities and has decided to acquire a Franchise from AWB for the purpose of engaging in the business of distributing frozen fruit confection items, frozen snacks and desserts, and other designated items ("AWB Products" or "Products") pursuant to the freezer marketing program and direct sales program developed by AWB for the sale of Products to accounts not already selling AWB Products. .

(b) AWB is willing, on the terms described below, to provide Franchisees with the opportunity to participate in its marketing programs and its distribution network. .

2. Grant of Franchise

(a) Subject to all the terms and conditions herein, AWB grants to Franchisee the non-exclusive right to use (i) the trademark AWB™, (ii) the registered trademark Apollo® ("Apollo®"), (iii) the registered Apollo Blind, (iv) the registered trademark Happy Window@, and (v) such other marks as AWB may hereafter develop for Franchisee's use (collectively "Licensed Marks"), and all the' other benefits of this Agreement as set forth herein, in the operation of a AWB Franchised Business in the Metropolitan Statistical Area ("MSA") designated on Schedule I (hereafter "Franchisee's MSA").

(b) AWB agrees not to grant any more than one (I) Franchise for every one hundred thousand (1,OO,OOO) residents or increment of that amount in Franchisee's MSA. However, AWB may grant one (I) additional Franchise in Franchisee's MSA for each Franchisee which has been in business for more than one (1) year and which has not purchased at least four (4) Products during the preceding twelve (12) months.

(c) AWB agrees not to sell bulk packs of Apollo Blinds bars in Franchisee's MSA to anyone other than to AWB Franchisees. A "bulk pack" consists of twenty-four (24) blinds. This section does not restrict AWB from selling blinds in other size packages or any other AWB Products, either through other channels of distribution, in or outside Franchisee's MSA.

(d) Franchisee may sell AWB Products within Franchisee's assigned MSA and within a reasonable distance from the assigned MSA, provided:

(1) AWB only will ship to a single cold storage facility; and

(2) Franchisee may not sell AWB Products in an MSA not assigned to Franchisee if AWB has granted the maximum allowable number of franchises for that MSA; and

(3) AWB may, in its sole discretion, determine whether the location of Franchisee's storage facility is unreasonable or whether sales accounts outside Franchisee's MSA are unreasonably remote from the MSA.

(e) AWB will arrange to drop ship Products in quantities of at least one (I) Container to Franchisee's Wholesale customers.

(f) AWB may, in its sole discretion, determine whether the location of Franchisee's storage facility is unreasonable or whether sales accounts outside Franchisee's MSA are unreasonably remote from the MSA.

(g) AWB will arrange to drop ship Products in quantities of at least one (I) Container to Franchisee's Wholesale customers.

3. Term of Franchise

(a) Unless Franchisee shall have executed AWB successor Franchise Agreement on the form of Franchise Agreement then used by AWB for similarly situated Franchisees, this Agreement shall expire on the tenth anniversary of its Effective Date (the "Expiration Date"). The Effective Date is the date this Agreement is executed by the president of AWB.

(b) If Franchisee has complied with this Agreement throughout its term, and has purchased no fewer than four (4) container of blinds AWB Products per year during the two (2) years preceding the Expiration Date, provided Franchisee executes the form of successor Franchise Agreement tendered to Franchisee by AWB at least six (6) months before the Expiration Date, AWB shall enter into a successor Franchise Agreement with Franchisee for a five (5) year term. The successor Franchise Agreement may differ materially in its terms from this Agreement. Franchisee's renewal rights may be conditioned upon Franchisee's execution of a general releâse in the form submitted by AWB, and upon Franchisee's paying a renewal administration fee of up to Five Thousand Rupees (Rs. 5,000.00).

(c) If AWB intends not to offer Franchisee a successor Franchise Agreement, AWB shall give Franchisee at least one hundread eighty (180) days notice of nonrenewal before the Expiration Date. The term of this Agreement will be automatically extended if necessary to give Franchisee a full one hundred eighty (180) days notice of non-renewal.

4. Fees

(a) As a condition of becoming a Franchisee, Franchisee has agreed to pay AWB the nonrefundable initial franchise fee specified on the Summary Pages. If the amount specified in Section 7 of the Summary Pages has not been received by AWB by the later of fifteen (15) business days from the date Franchisee received a Franchise Offering Circular describing this Franchise or the date specified in Section 7 of the Summary Pages, as well as all fees due to AWB for, Products and (as applicable) kits, AWB may, at its option, terminate this Agreement without waiving its right to the initial franchise fee already paid. Franchisee is required to pay the cost of freight on all blinds and kits purchased from AWB unless Franchisee pays AWB the full initial franchise fee, full cost of the freezer(s) and the full cost of the initial inventory within fifteen (15) business days after AWB provides Franchisee with a Uniform Franchise Offering Circular.

(b) AWB shall institute, maintain and administer an Advertising Fund (the "Advertising Fund") for the sole and exclusive purpose of supporting and paying for marketing programs AWB deems necessary, desirable or appropriate to promote the good will and public image of the Licensed Marks and all AWB franchises. Franchisee shall be required' to contribute to the Advertising Fund an amount equal to Five Hundred Rupees (Rs. 500) per month *(the "Advertising Fund Contributions"); provided, however, Franchisee shall not be required to make any Advertising Fund Contributions for the first six (6) months that Franchisee operates its franchised business. Franchisee shall be required to make the Advertising Fund Contributions for a particular year, on January 2nd of that year. AWB shall have the right to increase the amount of Franchisee's Advertising Fund Contribution upon sixty (60) days prior written notice, but in no event will the amount of the Advertising Fund Contribution exceed Fifteen hundred rupees (Rs. 1500.00) per month, which may be adjusted for inflation.

5. Location Assistance

In consideration of Franchisee's initial franchise fee, AWB will make available to Franchisee; if Franchisee is a Wholesale Franchisee, the services of an independent marketing consultant. The term "Wholesale Franchise" includes "Standard Wholesale", "Grand Wholesale" and "Super Grand Wholesale" Franchisees. The marketing consultant shall provide Franchisee with on-the-job training in the operation of an AWB Franchised Business in Franchisee's MSA, and any surrounding areas agreed to by AWB. For the Standard Wholesale

Franchisee, the consultant will assist you establishing contracts with 15-20 accounts in your MSA and any surrounding areas agreed to by the Company. The accounts will be a combination of freezer accounts and "conventional" (non-freezer) accounts. The amount of each type of account is determined by the Franchisee for a total of 15-20 accounts.

For the Grand Wholesale and Super Grand Wholesale Franchisee, the consultant will assist you in establishing contracts with 30-40 accounts in your MSA and any surrounding areas agreed to by the Company. The accounts will be a combination of freezer accounts and "conventional" (non--freezer) accounts. The amount of each type of account is determined by the Franchisee for a total of 30- 40 accounts.

Once the initial accounts have been established, Franchisee alone shall be responsible for servicing the accounts, relocating freezers whenever business so warrants, and establishing new accounts.

This Agreement in no way precludes Franchisee from hiring or retaining sales personnel or independent contractors, including the independent marketing consultant which helped Franchisee to establish his business, so long as such relationships are undertaken at no expense to AWB.

6. Sales and Marketing

(a) Franchisee understands that AWB will provide Franchisee with an explanation of its dedicated freezer marketing plan and ideas for promoting AWB Products at retail events. Moreover, AWB will provide Franchisee (if Franchisee is a Standard, Grand or Super Grand Wholesale Franchisee) with the location and marketing assistance prescribed in Section 5, above. AWB's assistance may include, without limitation or obligation, pricing recommendations, suggestions of point of purchase promotional materials, signage for dedicated freezers, suggestions for sales presentations to retailers and food service company managers, and the opportunity to exchange ideas and experiences with other AWB franchisees. Franchisee's success as a business person will depend primarily on Franchisee's ability to obtain and service profitable accounts. No two accounts are the same. Franchisee agrees that the Franchisee alone is responsible for developing and implementing his or her own marketing and sales programs in the Franchisee's MSA and that AWB has no obligation to Franchisee other than those expressly prescribed by this Agreement.

(b) AWB has granted Franchisee this Franchise solely for the purpose of opening and servicing new accounts for AWB Products. Thus, Franchisee may not solicit sales from any account which is an existing account of another authorized seller of AWB Products or an account that another authorized seller of AWB Products is actively pursuing, provided that authorized seller is following the guidelines for actively pursuing accounts as stipulated in AWB's Operations Manual. Additionally, Retail Franchisees may not solicit sales from any Wholesale account without AWB's consent, which will be conditioned on the Franchisee's execution of an agreement to be bound by all the terms and conditions of Standard Wholesale Franchisees, as they may exist at the time the request is made. Finally, Franchisee may not sell AWB Products, to any other distributor of frozen desserts or snack products without AWB's prior written approval, which may be withheld for any reason.

(c) Except as is otherwise expressly set forth in this Agreement, AWB does not restrict Franchisee or any other AWB Franchisee in the accounts upon which they may call. Franchisee is an independent contractor and, subject to the terms of this Agreement, shall have complete control over the operations of Franchisee's business.

(d) AWB will direct all marketing programs financed by the Advertising Fund, and will have sole discretion over the creative concepts, materials and endorsements used and the geographic, market and media placement and allocation of the programs. The Advertising Fund may be used to pay the costs of preparing and producing video, audio and written advertising materials; administering local, regional, multi-regional and national advertising programs including, without limitation, purchasing direct mail and other media advertising; employing advertising, public relations and media buying agencies to assist in these activities; and supporting public relations, market research and other advertising and marketing activities. The Advertising Fund may elect to furnish Franchisee with marketing, advertising and promotional formats and sample materials without additional charge, or provide Franchisee with multiple copies of marketing, advertising and promotional materials at the direct cost of producing them.

The Advertising Fund will be accounted for separately from AWB's other funds, and will not be used to defray any of AWB's general operating expenses, except for costs, salaries, travel expenses, administrative costs and overhead AWB may incur in activities reasonably related to the administration of the Advertising Fund and its marketing programs (including, without limitation, conducting market research, preparing advertising and marketing materials, general production costs and collecting and accounting for contributions to the Advertising Fund). AWB may spend in any fiscal year an amount greater or less than the total contributions of all Franchised Locations to the Advertising Fund in that year and AWB may cause the Advertising Fund to invest any surplus for future use by the Advertising Fund. Franchisee authorizes AWB to collect for remission to the Advertising Fund any advertising or promotional monies or credits offered by any supplier based upon Franchisee's purchases. All interest earned on monies contributed to the Advertising Fund will be used to pay advertising costs of the Advertising Fund before other assets of the Advertising Fund are expended. AWB will prepare an annual statement of monies collected and costs incurred by the Advertising Fund and will furnish it to Franchisee upon written request.

Franchisee agrees that the Advertising Fund will be intended to maximize recognition of the Marks and all AWB franchisees. Although AWB will endeavor to utilize the Advertising Fund to develop advertising and marketing materials and programs, and to place advertising, that will benefit all AWB franchisees, AWB undertakes no obligation to ensure that expenditures by the Advertising Fund in or affecting any geographic area will be proportionate or equivalent to the contributions to the Advertising Fund by Franchisees operating in that geographic area or that any Franchised Location will benefit directly or in proportion to its contribution to the Advertising Fund from the development of advertising and marketing materials or the placement of advertising. Although AWB intends the Advertising Fund to be of unlimited duration, AWB will have the right to terminate and, if terminated, to reinstate, the Advertising Fund at any time after all amounts in the fund have been expended.

(e) Except as expressly provided in this Section 6, AWB assumes no direct or indirect liability or obligation to Franchisee with respect to the maintenance, direction or administration of the Advertising Fund.

7. Supplies and Information

(a) AWB will provide Franchisee a limited supply of advertising and sales materials for use in promoting the Products AWB may charge a fee for quantities which exceed its current standard allotment for Franchisees.

(b) AWB will provide form blinds location agreements to Franchisee if franchisee is a Wholesale Franchise for use when placing blinds on the premises of third parties.

(c) AWB may provide telephonic assistance to the Franchisee on matters relating to AWB Products.

(d) AWB also may serve as a clearing house for questions and information between and among various AWB Franchisees.

(e) AWB shall lend to Franchisee a copy of its Confidential Operations Manual (the "Manual") and Franchisee shall comply with all provisions of such Manual. From time to time during the term of this Agreement, AWB may communicate to the Franchisee mandatory and suggested standards, methods, procedures and specifications applicable to the System and information relative to other obligations of Franchisee hereunder and to the operation of the Franchised Business. Such communications may be made through such Confidential Manual, as and when available, or through AWB Communications. The Manual shall at all times remain the exclusive property of AWB and shall be returned to AWB promptly upon request by AWB and, in any event, upon termination or expiration of this Agreement for any reason whatsoever. If the Operations Manual is not returned to AWB, Franchisee agrees to pay liquidated damages of Rs. 50, 000 to AWB. Franchisee shan not at any time copy, duplicate, record or otherwise reproduce or transcribe the Manual or any part of this Agreement or any of the forms supplied by AWB hereunder without AWB's prior written consent. AWB shall have the right to add to; modify, withdraw from or otherwise revise the provisions of the Manual from time to time. The provisions of the Manual (as revised itom time to time) and the mandatory standards, methods, procedures and specifications applicable to the System and such revisions made from time to time by AWB shall constitute provisions of this Agreement and Franchisee shall comply with same as if fully set forth herein.

(f) Franchisee acknowledges that certain information relating to the operation of the Franchised Business including, without limitation, the standards, methods, procedures and specifications of the System, and the contents of the Manual, is derived from information disclosed to Franchisee by AWB and that all such information is of a proprietary and confidential nature and is a trade secret of AWB. Franchisee shall maintain the absolute confidentiality of all such information during the term and after the termination or expiration of this Agreement for any reason whatsoever and shall not disclose any such information for any reason whatsoever, disclosing the same to Franchisee's employees only to the extent necessary for the operation of the Franchised Business in accordance with this Agreement. Franchisee further agrees not to use any such information, directly or indirectly, in any other business or in any other manner or obtain any benefit therefrom not specifically approved in writing by AWB during the term of this Agreement or afterwards. Franchisee may not at any time copy, duplicate, record or otherwise reproduce any part of the Manual. If Franchisee's copy of the Manual is lost, destroyed or significantly damaged, AWB will replace the Manual at its then applicable charge.

8. Warranties

AWB is an authorized wholesaler of Blinds and inventory for one or more suppliers. As a wholesale distributor, AWB neither manufactures the Blinds nor manufactures the Products sold by its Franchisees. All warranties on Blinds and Products shall be manufacturers' warranties. No warranty, either express or implied on the Products is offered by AWB. However, AWB agrees to pass through to Franchisee all warranties of manufacturers with whom AWB and Franchisee deal.

9. Franchisee's Obligations

(a) Franchisee agrees to use his/her best efforts to sell AWB Products.

(b) So long as this Agreement is in effect, except in an emergency, Franchisee agrees that he/she will not purchase from any source other than AWB or a Master Distributor designated by AWB any of the Products offered to Franchisee by AWB unless AWB notifies Franchisee that he or she may purchase directly from a manufacturer. Nor shall Franchisee, without AWB's prior written approval, offer or sell through the Franchised Business or otherwise, any products which compete directly with Products offered to Franchisee by AWB.

(c) Franchisce agrees to purchase all additional blinds (after purchasing initial blinds from AWB) from AWB or sources approved by AWB, approval will not be unreasonably withheld.

(d) Franchisee shall secure, at its sole expense, appropriate storage facilities necessary for the operation of its Franchised Business. Franchisee shall designate a single storage facility for receiving shipments Itom AWB. AWB will ship only to such a designated cold storage facility, approved by AWB in writing, which is located in Franchisee's MSA or in a surrounding area. AWB may withhold its approval of a storage facility in its sole discretion, including, without limitation, if AWB determines that transportation of Products to the facility is difficult or impractical.

(e) Franchisee agrees not to engage in any activities which reflect unfavorably upon the manufacturers of the Products acquired pursuant to this Agreement, or upon AWB.

(f) Franchisee agrees to allow AWB to use Franchisee's likeness, company name or individual name, as the case may be, in future AWB promotional materials, as well as to identify Franchisee as an AWB Franchisee.

(g) Franchisee shall purchase automobile and business liability insurance for the Franchise Business in amounts adequate to protect Franchisee and AWB against claims of up to One Million Rupees (Rs. 1,000,000.00). Such policies shall name AWB as an additional insured. If Franchisee doesn't purchase the insurance as required, AWB may, at its option, purchase the minimum coverage required of Franchisee, and charge Franchisee an administrative surcharge of up to One Hundred Ten Percent (110%) of the cost of the premium to cover of the associated administrative costs: Franchisee might provide AWB with certificates of such insurance within sixty (60) days of the execution of this Agreement. Franchisee shall require the insurance carrier to provide AWB with at least thirty (30) days notice of its intended cancellation of such policy(ies).

(h) Franchisee shall maintain all accounting reports, lists of active accounts, lists of accounts which Franchisee is actively pursuing and other informational reports as AWB may require. Franchisee shall also respond in a reasonable amount of time to questionnaires and provide 'other information as Company may require. In the event that Franchisee has not responded to any such requests from AWB within four (4) weeks. after the requested due date, AWB may, in its sole discretion, refrain from shipping any additional AWB Products or other items to Franchisee until such requested information is provided. .

(i) Franchisee shall within sixty (60) days after execution of this Agreement provide AWB with a quality photograph of Franchisee (together with Franchisee's ousehold family members if applicable). Franchisee and all members in the photograph shall execute a Personal Release, in the form set forth in Schedule 3, attached hereto, so that AWB may use such photograph.

(j) Franchisee shall only stock freezers and carts with AWB Products, authorized products and other non-competitive products. Franchisee shall ensure that AWB Products constitute at least two-thirds *(2/3)* of all products. If AWB elects to add items, these items can also be stocked and competitive products shall be removed.

(k) Franchisee agrees to conduct its business at all times in a manner using sales, marketing and operational procedures which have been prescribed and/ or approved by AWB in either its Confidential Operations Manual(s) (if any) or other communications to its franchisees.

(l) Franchisee agrees that it will not, without AWB's prior written approval, sell, assign or transfer any freezer to a person or entity that is not an AWB franchisee until Franchisee has removed all AWB Products, the Licensed Marks, deals and other marks associated with the Franchise fails the freezer. Franchisee acknowledges that it would be difficult to determine the amount of damages suffered by AWB if Franchisee fails to comply with this subsection, so Franchisee agrees that Franchisee shall pay AWB Rs. 30,000 in addition to all attorneys' fees AWB incurs in enforcing this provision, as liquidated damages and not as a penalty, for each individual violation of this subsection. The requirements of this Section 9.1. apply even when' AWB and Franchisee are not renewing the Franchise Agreement.

(m) Franchisee agrees that, during the term of this Agreement, he/she shall attend and participate in (i) either the Convention or the Winter Symposium within two years after commencing operation of the Franchised Business and (ii) at least three (3) Conventions or Winter Symposiums within each five-year period thereafter. Franchisee shall solely be responsible for the costs associated with attending such Conventions or Symposiums, including airfare, lodging and meals.

(n) Franchisee agrees that, within three (3) months after Franchisee commences business and at all time thereafter during the term of this Agreement, Franchisee shall have a computer or some other electronic device, along with access to the. internet through an internet access provider, which will enable Franchisee to communicate via e-mail with AWB from Franchisee's place of business. Franchisee agrees that it will review its e-mail messages at least once every business day, unless otherwise agreed upon by AWB in advance.

(o) Franchisee agrees that Franchisee shall execute a Security Agreement (in a form. satisfactory to AWB) in the event that AWB extends credit to Franchisee in connection with the purchase of more than two (2) pallets ofAWB Products.

10. Transfer

(a) AWB may sell or assign any or all of its rights or interests in this Agreement at any title.

(b) Franchisee may sell assign or transfer hislher interest in this Agreement in Franchisee or in the Franchised Business only with AWB"s prior written approval which may be withheld for good business reasons, which include, but are not limited to the failure of the Franchisee, transferee or terms of the transfer to satisfy the terms and standards AWB generally applies to transfers and transferees at the time Franchisee proposes to make a transfer. The standards need not be in writing.

(c) Franchisee must notify AWB of any bonafide proposed transfer or sale of any rights or interests in Franchisee, the Franchise Agreement or the Franchised Business, and set forth a complete description of all terms and fees of the proposed transfer or assignment, including the proposed transferee's name, address, financial qualifications and previous five (5) years business experience.

(d) AWB or its assignee may, within thirty (30) days after receipt of such notice, purchase the interest offered on the same economic terms as those offered less any brokerage fees or commissions.

(e) If AWB fails to exercise its option to purchase the interest which is the subject of the transfer or assignment within thirty (30) days ofAWB's receipt of the notice described above, AWB shall notify Franchisee of its approval or disapproval of the proposed transfer and its terms. If AWB approves the transfer, it only may be accomplished on terms which are no more favorable to the transferee than were the terms offered to AWB.

(f) AWB may condition a transfer upon the transferee's paying AWB a transfer fee (but no initial franchise fee) and upon the transferee's executing a general release for the benefit of AWB, its employees, agents and representatives, and upon the transferee's signing AWB's then current form of Franchise Agreement. The transfer fee and training fee will be Forty Thousand Rupees (Rs. 40,000) and up to Seventy Thousand Rupees (Rs. 70,000) if AWB obtained the lead for such transfer.

(g) Franchisee may transfer to another MSA, only with AWB's prior written approval, which may be withheld in AWB's sole discretion. Such transfer will be conditioned upon Franchisee's payment of Thirty Thousand Rupees (Rs.30,000) and Franchisee's entering into AWB's then current Franchise Agreement.

(h) Upon Franchisee's death or disability (or. if Franchisee is a corporation, partnership or other entity, the death or disability of a principal owner), Franchisee's (or such principal owner's) executor, administrator, conservator, guardian or other personal representative shall transfer Franchisee's interest in this Agreement (or the principal owner"s interest) in Franchisee to a third party provided the transfer is made to the spouse, adult child, heirs or legal representative of the deceased or disabled person and such person has been approved by AWB in advance, which approval may be withheld for good business reasons. Such disposition of this Agreement or the interest in Franchisee (including, without limitation, transfer by request or inheritance) must be completed within a reasonable time, not to exceed six (6) months from the date of death or disability, and will be subject to all of the terms and conditions applicable to transfers contained in this Section. A failure to transfer Franchisee's interest in this Agreement or a principal owner's interest in Franchisee to an approved party within this period of time constitutes a breach of this Agreement. For purposes hereof the term "disability" means 'a mental or physical disability, impairment or condition that is reasonably expected to prevent or actually does prevent Franchisee or the principal owner from managing and operating the Franchised Business. Any transfer made pursuant to this Section 10.h. shall not be subject to the provisions of Section 10.d., 10.e., or 10.f.

11. Termination

AWB may terminate the Franchise Agreement, without prejudice to the enforcement of any legal or equitable remedy, immediately upon giving Franchisee written notice of such termination and the reason or cause for the termination, without providing Franchisee with an opportunity to cure the default. The following shall constitute sufficient basis terminate the Franchise Agreement:

(a) If the Franchisee fails to pay any financial obligation to AWB or to a supplier of. products or equipment approved by AWB or fails to comply with Section 9.g of this Agreement within five (5) days after AWB gives Franchisee a written notice of default;

(b) If the Franchisee fails to perform or breaches any covenant or obligation owing under the Franchise Agreement and fails to cure such non-compliance within thirty (30) days after AWB gives Franchisee written notice of default;

(c) If Franchisee uses the Licensed Marks in any way which has not been previously approved by AWB;

(d) If Franchisee attempts to divert any prospective AWB Franchisee from entering into a Franchise Agreement with AWB, or if Franchisee attempts to sell its Franchise or Franchised Business in the MSA within ninety (90) days of the date(s) AWB is scheduled to participate in a franchise or business opportunity show, conducting an in-house workshop or conducting an advertising campaign to select new franchisees in the Franchisee's MSA, without AWB's prior written approval;

(e) If Franchisee attempts to sell its Franchise or any interest in Franchisee or its Franchised Business in any MSA within ninety (90) days of the day(s) AWB is scheduled to participate in a franchise or business opportunity show, franchise conducting an in-house workshop or conducting an advertising campaign to franchisees select new ftancbisees without subfranchise's prior written approval;

(f) If Franchisee attempts to subfranchise or subdivide its Franchise rights without AWB's prior written approval;

(g) If Franchisee sells or attempts to sell any AWB Product to another wholesaler, distributor or former AWB franchisee without AWB's prior written approval;

(h) If Franchisee engages in any other activities which, in AWB's reasonable opinion, brings discredit upon the Licensed Marks or the reputation and goodwill of AWB or its Franchisees;

(i) If Franchisee files, or if Franchisee has filed against it, a voluntary or involuntary petition in bankruptcy or is adjudicated as bankrupt or insolvent; if Franchisee files any petition or answer seeking or acquising in any reorganization, arrangement, liquidation, dissolution, receivership, appointment of trustee, liquidator or examiner; if a receiver, trustee or liquidator is appointed for all or any part of Franchisee's assets; or upon the dissolution or termination of existence of Franchisee;

(j) If Franchisee sells more than fifty percent (50%) of the assets relating to its Franchised Business;

(k) If Franchisee has received from AWB, during any consecutive 24 month period, 3 or more notices of default (whether or not the notices relate to the same or to different defaults and whether or not the defaults were timely cured by Franchisee);

(l) If Franchisee abandons or fails or refuses to actively operate the Franchised Business for any period such that AWB may reasonably conclude that Franchisee does 'not intend to continue operating the Franchised Business; or.

(m) If Franchisee fails to purchase at least four (4) containers of blinds Products form AWB or an authorized Master Distributor during any calendar year following the year in which AWB executes the Franchise Agreement.

12. Obligations Following Termination Or Nonrenewal

Upon the expiration or termination of the Franchise Agreement, Franchisee shall immediately:

(a) Cease to be a Franchisee of AWB and cease to operate the former Franchised Business. Franchisee shall not thereafter, directly or indirectly, represent to the public that the former Franchised Business is or was operated or in any way connected with AWB Products, or hold itself out as a present or former Franchisee of AWB;

(b) Pay all sums owing to AWB. Upon termination for any default by Franchisee, such sums shall include actual damages, costs and expenses incurred by AWB as a result of the default;

(c) Return to AWB any and all trade secrets and confidential materials owned by AWB, and all copies thereof which may be in Franchisee's possession. Franchisee shall retain no copy or record of any of the foregoing other than its copy of the Franchise Agreement, any correspondence between the parties, and any other document which Franchisee reasonably needs for compliance with any applicable provision of law;

(d) Provide AWB a complete list of Franchisee's employees, customers, their respective addresses, all mailing lists, and any outstanding obligations Franchisee may have to any third parties, including outstanding customer orders. AWB shall have the right, but not the obligation, to fill any such outstanding customer orders generated by Franchisee, and in such event, Franchisee shall immediately reimburse AWB for any costs or expenses incurred by AWB in doing so. In addition, AWB shall have the right to cancel any orders placed by Franchisee for which delivery has not been made;

(e) Take such action as may be required by AWB to terminate, transfer or assign to AWB or its designee all telephone numbers, white and yellow page telephone references and advertisements, and all trade and similar name registrations and business licenses, and to cancel any interest which Franchisee may have in the same;

(f) Cease to use in advertising or in any manner whatsoever, any methods, procedures, or techniques in which AWB has a proprietary right, title or interest, the Licensed Marks, and other marks and indication of origin associated with the Franchise, and remove or change all trade dress, including photographs of Products, decals, posters and other indications of association with the Franchise from any vehicles, buildings, freezers, uniforms, clothing and other effects at the Franchisee's expense and in a manner satisfactory to AWB. Unless otherwise approved in writing by AWB, Franchisee must return to AWB all copies of materials bearing the Licensed Marks as specified by AWB.

(g) For one (I) year following the termination or expiration of the Franchise Agreement, the Franchisee shall not directly or indirectly own an interest in or engage in any business, in Franchisee's MSA or in surrounding areas where Franchisee has carried on the Franchised Business, which sells products that compete directly with the AWB brand Products which were sold by the Franchisee during the term of the Franchise Agreement;

(h) Franchisee understands and acknowledges that AWB shall have the right, in its sole, discretion, to reduce the scope of any covenant set forth in the Franchise Agreement or any portions thereof, without the Franchisee's consent, effective immediately upon receipt by Franchisee of written notice thereof; and Franchisee agrees that it shall comply immediately with any covenant as so modified.

(i) If all or any portion of a covenant described above is held unenforceable by a court or agency having valid jurisdiction in an unappealed final decision to which AWB is a party, Franchisee expressly agrees to be bound by any lesser covenant imposing the maximum duty permitted by law that is subsumed within the terms of such covenant, as if the resulting covenant were separately stated in and made a part of the covenants described above. Franchisee further expressly agrees that the existence of any claim it may have against AWB, whether or not arising from the Franchise Agreement, shall not constitute a defense to the enforcement by AWB of the above covenants.

13. Disclaimers

(a) Except as is ,expressly set forth elsewhere in this Agreement, AWB will not refund Franchisee's initial investment in whole or in part, unless the Products sold to Franchisee by AWB are defective, and the manufacturer does not promptly replace the defective Products.

(b) Except as set forth in the Uniform Offering Circular that has been delivered to Franchisee, AWB makes no representations whatsoever as to the actual or potential sales, income or profits a Franchisee may achieve as a result of this Agreement. Franchisee aclmowledges that the success or failure of the Franchisee's Business depends substantially upon Franchisee himself or herself.

14. Remedies

(a) Franchisee may only bring any claims he or she may have against in arbitration pursuant to the rules of the Indian Arbitration Association in Mumbai.

(b) AWB may bring any claim it may have against Franchisee in arbitration pursuant to the rules of the Indian 'Arbitration Association in Mumbai. AWB also may bring an action in any court of competent jurisdiction to enjoin any violation of this Agreement or to obtain specific performance hereof. Franchisee shall be liable to AWB for AWB's costs and attorneys' fees arising from pursuing or defending against any claims against Franchisee in arbitration or in litigation, regardless of the forum. Additionally, Franchisee agrees to reimburse AWB for any fees or expenses AWB incurs in collecting any amounts due under this Agreement.

15. Governing Law

This Agreement shall be governed by and interpreted under the laws of Florida.

16. Acknowledgemets

(a) Franchisee understands and acknowledges that AWB is not the manufacturer of the blinds which AWB sells to Franchisee and that AWB makes no representations or warranties about the blinds. AWB has multiple sources of blinds which are all similar in utility value but may have minor differences in dimensions, features and colors (e.g., the blinds currently come in either red, white or blue). The blinds do not include locks, although manufacturers and AWB may occasionally add those features at no charge. Franchisee's only contractual obligation is to AWB, and that this Agreement creates no contractual obligation between Franchisee and any manufacturer or other suppliers of Products or equipment.

(b) AWB agrees to arrange shipment of all blinds purchased at the time this Agreement is executed to Franchisee within approximately thirty (30) working days from receipt and approval of this Agreement, and receipt of payment in full, accompanied by cashier's check. certified check. money order or bank transfer. In the event of strikes, riots, insurrections, circumstances beyond AWB's control or Acts of God, this period may be extended, but under no circumstances to exceed ninety (90) working days. If AWB fails to effect shipment within such time period, Franchisee, upon request, shall have payment for said order refunded immediately.

(c) Franchisee shall be responsible for Franchisee's own federal, state and local taxes, and or compliance with all applicable laws, as well as any sales taxes due on equipment 'or Products purchased from AWB. Franchisee shall act as an independent contractor and shall be solely liable for determining the nature and applicability of all local laws which may apply to the operation of the Franchised Business in Franchisee's MSA, or where else the Franchisee conducts business.

(d) All Franchisee's purchases of AWB Products shall be made solely from AWB or an authorized Master Distributor, other than emergency purchases to fill an unexpected shortage of certain products, which purchases may be made from another Franchisee. An "AWB Product" or "Product" is any product designated as such by AWB, and which AWB makes available for purchase by Franchisee.

(e) Franchisee and AWB agree that this Agreement contains their entire understanding relative to its subject matter, and there is no reliance upon any verbal or other written representation whatsoever. AWB has not guaranteed minimum or maximum earnings; any estimate thereof is in the nature of possibilities only; earnings are primarily dependent upon the type of service and promotion rendered by the Franchisee and sales volume, which factors are beyond the control of AWB. This Agreement may be amended only in writing and signed by all parties hereto.

(f) Franchisee agrees not to use the Licensed Marks or any trademarks, service marks, names or indication which are or maybe confusingly similar to the Licensed Marks in Franchisee's name or identity. Franchisee must obtain written permission to use any of the Licensed Marks from AWB on a per use basis if such use has not previously been authorized in writing.

(g) Franchisee aclmowledges that AWB or its agent has provided Franchisee with a Franchise Offering Circular not later than the earlier of the first personal meeting held to discuss the sale of the Franchise, ten (10) business days before the execution of this Agreement, or ten (10) business days before any payment of any consideration connected to the purchase of this Franchise. Franchisee further acknowledges that Franchisee has read such Franchise Offering Circular and understands its contents.

(h) Franchisee acknowledges that AWB has provided Franchisee with a copy of this Agreement and all related documents, fully completed. for at least five (5) business days prior to Franchisee's execution hereof.

(i) Franchisee acknowledges that AWB has advised it to consult with its own attorneys, accountants, of other advisors, that Franchisee has had ample opportunity to do so, and that the attorneys for AWB have not advised or represented Franchisee with respect to this Agreement or the relationship hereby created.

(j) Franchisee acknowledges and recognizes that different terms and conditions, including different fee structure and investment requirements may pertain to different AWB Franchises offered in the past, contemporaneously herewith, or in the future, and that AWB does not represent that all Franchise Agreements are or will be identical.

(k) Franchisee acknowledges that except as is specifically set forth in this Agreement, it is not for is it intended to be a third party beneficiary of this Agreement or any other agreement or contractual relationship to which AWB is a party.

(l) This Agreement only shall become effective upon its execution by AWB's President.

(m) Franchisee agrees that the Franchised Business shall only be operated by the Franchisee or by a Manager/Employee employed by Franchisee who has previously been approved by AWB. AWB's approval of Franchisee's Manager/ Employee shall be predicated upon the Manager's execution of a confidentiality agreement in a form approved by AWB.

[Signatures on following page]

IN WITNESS WHEREOF, the parties intending to be legally bound hereby, have duly executed, sealed and delivered this Agreement.

Apollo Window Blinds Ltd.

By: ____________________

Ravi Kumar President

Date: ____________________

Franchisee

By: ____________________

Date: ____________________

By: ____________________

Date: ____________________

Schedule 1

Franchisee's Metropolitan Statistical Area ("MSA")

AWB awards Franchisee the right to operate an AWB Franchised Business pursuant to the attached Franchise Agreement in the Mentropolitan Statistical Area known as:

A map depicting the boundaries is attached here to with initials of an authorized AWB representative and Franchisee to express their agreement to its boundaries.

Schedule 2

Apollo Window Blinds Ltd.
Equipment Purchase Order

____

Name

____

Address

____

City State Zip

( ) ( )

____

________________	________________
Home Phone	Business Phone
	DATE: ________________
TO: Apollo Window Blinds Ltd. 7, Apollo Street, Wadala, Mumbai 400016	PAYMENT: ________________ All funds to be by certified check, cashier check, money order, bank wire, or credit card.
PLEASE SHIP THE FOLLOWING ITEMS:	Custom Display blinds, includes initial Point of Sale material and other initial materials.

QUANTITY	PRICE	TOTAL
______CUSTOM DISPLAY BLINDS(S)	@ Rs ________	Rs. ________
______CASES OF AWB PRODUCTS	@ Rs ________	Rs. ________
______CUSTOM BLINDS KIT(S)	@ Rs. 2,100	Rs. ________
GRAND TOTAL ON EQUIPMENT	Rs.	
TRAINING FEE	Rs. ________	
STATE SALES TAX (FLORIDA ONLY)	Rs. ________	
FRANCHISE FEE TOTAL	Rs. ________	
GRAND TOTAL	Rs. ________	

MUMBAI PURCHASERS REQUIRED TO PAY 6% BMC SALES TAX oN' EQUIPMENT
Address where Equipment is to be shipped: ________________

____

____

NOTE: All shipments will be freight collect, F.O.B. Mumbai, INDIA unless Purchaser remits balance of payment, or payment in full within fifteen (15) business days of receipt of UFOC. If Purchaser makes full payment in given time frame, Purchaser will not be required to pay freight on initial shipment of equipment or product. If not approved within five (5) business days by AWB or Purchaser, refund payment immediately to Purchaser.

APPROVED BY AWB

DATE

____

By: Ravi Kumar, President

____
Representative of AWB DATE

____
Purchaser DATE

____
Purchaser DATE

Schedule 3

APOLLO WINDOW BLINDS LTD. PERSONAL RELEASE

In consideration of, and as an inducement to, the execution of the Franchise Agreement (the "Franchise Agreement") dated __________, 20 __, by Apollo Windows Blinds Ltd. ("AWB"), a

Mumbai Corporation with its principal place of business at 7, Apollo Street, Wadala, Mumbai 400016 and ("Franchisee"), Franchisee and AWB agree as follows:

(1) Franchisee hereby grants to AWB, its agents, successors, licensees and assigns, the right to use the photograph(s) of Franchisee (and Franchisee's family as the case may be), which was provided to AWB pursuant to the Franchise Agreement (''the Photos"), along with any additional photos given to or acquired by AWB.

(2) Franchisee agrees and consents that AWB may exhibit, distribute, transmit and/or otherwise exploit the Photos as AWB may see fit, in any and all media now and hereafter known, and in advertising and/or publicity in connection therewith and the right to use Franchisee's name in any connection with any of the foregoing.

(3) Franchisee agrees that the rights granted to AWB hereunder are granted for the entire world and shall inure in perpetuity and no further compensation shall be payable to Franchisee at any time in connection therewith.

IN WITNESS WHEREOF, the parties intending to be legally bound hereby, have duly executed, sealed and delivered this Agreement.

APOLLO WINDOW BLINDS LTD.

By: ______________________
Ravi Kumar
President

Date: ______________________

FRANCHISEE

By: ______________________

Date:__________________________

By: __________________________

Date:__________________________

Schedule 4

{SECOND} ADDENDUM TO THE FRANCHISE AGREEMENT

THIS {SECOND} ADDENDUM to the Franchise Agreement (the "Agreement") by and between Apollo Window Blinds Ltd., Mumbai Corporation and ______ (hereinafter referred to as "Franchisee") is made and entered into this ________ day of __________, 20___.

Recitals

Franchisor and Franchisee entered into the Agreement on ____________, 20___. The Franchisee has obtained from a lender a loan ("Loan") in which funding is provided with the assistance of the India Small Business Administration ("SBA"). SBA requires the execution of this Addendum as a condition for obtaining the SBA assisted financing.

NOW, THEREFORE, in consideration of the mutual promises below, and for good and valuable considerations in hand paid by each of the parties to the others, the receipt and sufficiency of which the parties acknowledge, the parties agree as follows:

- The Franchise Agreement is in full force and effect, and Franchisor has sent no official notice of default to Franchisee under the Franchise Agreement that remains uncured on the date hereof.
- Provided that Franchisee complies with the provisions of Section 10 of theAgreement, Franchisor will not unreasonably withhold, delay or condition its consent to any proposed transfer or assignment by Franchisee.
- This Addendum automatically terminates on the earliest to occur of the following: (i) a Termination occurs under the Franchise Agreement; (ii) the Loan is paid; or (iii) SBA no longer has any interest in the SBA financing.

IN WITNESS WHEREOF, the parties hereto have-duly executed this {Second} Addendum on the date first written above.

APOLLO WINDOW BLINDS LTD.

By: __________________________

Its: __________________________

FRANCHISEE

By: __________________________

Its: __________________________

*On January 1, 2008, the Advertising Fund Contributions shall be increased to Five Thousand Rupees (Rs. 5,000) per year.

5.11 SUMMARY

There are no specific regulations governing the franchising industry in India. The Indian government has laid down certain rules and regulations that are to be followed in foreign collaboration, which affect the franchise industry. Limits have been laid down on the amount of royalty that can be charged by a foreign franchisor from an Indian franchisee. This amount depends on various factors such as use of the brand name, transfer of technology and processes involved. Franchisors can charge royalty for the use of only its brand name by the franchisee, without transferring any technology or taking up any responsibilities. This is a very attractive and lucrative option.

The United States with its strict UFOC requirements have ensured that the franchise industry grows in a systematic manner. India too needs to adopt and include a similar disclosure requirement if it wishes the industry to grow in a healthy manner. All franchisors must reveal at the initial stage itself, details about its business and what role it plans to play. The obligations and rights of the franchisee must be clearly defined, to prevent any misunderstanding in the future. All prospective franchisees must know the costs involved and various fees payable to the franchisor. Only then will they step up and take the risk of plunging into the market.

Most franchises are offered to individuals and are in the form of a contract. They are required to adhere to certain standards and specifications which the franchisor lays down. All expenses involved are normally born by the franchisee. Franchisors retain the sole option of changing these standards and specifications. If these are changed on a regular basis, the operating costs of the franchisee will increase as it will have to make relevant changes in its operations as per the guidelines. The law must be clear on the kind of protection franchisees have in this regard.

A franchisor can prevent the franchisee from running a similar business during the term of the agreement. This is justified to protect the interests of the franchisor. Franchisors also keep the option of giving similar franchisees to other parties, in the same area as an existing franchisee. They are absolved of any loss to the business of the original franchisee. If the franchisee is not protected from such a practice, one can expect reluctance in participation from the small Indian Businessman.

At present, certain rules and regulations pertaining to the amount of royalty that can be charged do exist. Franchisors however, do need some sort of remedy against defaulting franchisees. Any franchisor, in particular foreign franchisors will want a fast and effective system to ensure there are no bottlenecks in royalty collection.

Franchisors allow the franchisee the use of the franchisors intellectual property like trademarks, trade names, domain names, etc. Though there is reasonable protection under the Trademarks Act, 1999, franchisors would feel more comfortable if specific protection was given with regard to the franchisor-franchisee relationship. Also, termination of use of the franchisor's trademark on termination of the agreement is crucial. Besides this, where a franchisee reports infringement of the trademark, whether the franchisor can put the responsibility for protecting the trademark on the franchisee must also be made certain. Since the franchisor is the owner of the trademark, it would be logical to expect the franchisor to take such matters in his hand.

A very crucial part of any franchise agreement is the termination clause. Often franchisors restrict the franchisee from opening a similar or competitive business for a certain period after termination of the agreement. While they would explain this as protection of business interests, it operates as an agreement in restriction of trade as far as the franchisee is concerned. To what extent can this be allowed needs to be clarified and laid down.

The inherent ambiguity which accompanies the non-existence of franchise laws is perhaps the root cause of a listless Indian franchising industry today. The concerns of the parties are reasonable to say the least, and need to be addressed. India needs to take cue from the American regulations which have come up with answers to almost every difficulty created by the complex nature of a franchise relationship.

Other pertinent areas of the law which are applicable to franchise agreements are:

Intellectual Property laws;

Competition laws;

Consumer Protection laws; and

Labour laws.

5.11 SELF ASSESSMENT QUESTIONS

(1) What are the key elements of basic franchise agreement? Explain briefly.

(2) To resolve a dispute what are the options open to franchisor? Give brief details.

(3) What is arbitration? What are its advantages over civil litigation?

(4) Explain briefly:

(a) Obligations of franchisor

(b) Obligations of Franchisee

6 Chapter MARKETING IN FRANCHISING

Objectives

After going through this chapter, you will be able to understand:

- The principle of Franchise Marketing
- The forms of Franchise Marketing
- The potential marketing concerns

Structure:

While many businesses spend valuable time and money on making sure that their brochure or website is just right with the correct language and colours. It is just as important to invest in the people within the organisation, as they too are involved in the process of shaping prospective and current customers mindsets. The human contact creates or reinforces the perception of the brand, the product and service. So encourage a culture that communicates a consistent brand message with a clearly defined path to success. Often much more difficult to achieve within a franchised business as franchisees do not sit within the head office absorbing the business culture 8 hours a day. Employing these proactive tactics will protect the valuable brand.

The prospect of turning a business into a franchise operation is an attractive option for many companies. After all, it is arguably one of the world's most popular business models. However, 'Franchising Plus' partner Eric Parker believes that organization have a lot to learn in terms of being a franchisee, franchisor or prospective franchise. He offers the comment that many franchises become successful inspite of themselves, and that with better strategic marketing direction and budgeting, many could become dominant and highly-profitable forces in their industry sectors.

Most franchise budgeting formula are based on the levies that franchisors apply to their franchisees. Generally, franchisors extract a levy of between 1% and 2% of franchisee turnover to fund advertising and other such activities. Parker believes that this levy percentage is far too small. According to Parker, successful franchise operations are those that accrue at least 5% of collective turnover for marketing activity.

He goes on to say that advertising often becomes a bone of contention between franchisors and franchisees. Franchisees see the outlet down the road as being in competition with them, despite the fact that they bear the same brand name, and franchisors see the entire operation as a whole, wanting to market the brand name to the general public, and not a particular store to a select few. Parker suggests that as a rule of thumb, marketing costs should equate to between 5% and 8% of a company's annual turnover. "If franchisees pay just 2% of the turnover to franchisors for top-level marketing, the remaining 3% to 5% should be used by individual franchisees to fund marketing in their own area." He continues: "The marketing budget should be controlled by the franchisee council or franchisee co-op. These are bodies consisting of franchisees that have been elected by other franchisees to represent their best interests at meetings, regarding, among other issues, the use of advertising levies from all the franchisees. Giving the income earner more influence over how and where this budget is spent, will go a long way towards more cordial relationships..."

Parker adds that franchisees must not assume that brand- building efforts should be the responsibility of the franchisor. "Franchisees may find the temptation to do promotional marketing very strong. This tends to discount brand value. Consistently offering specials and added incentives leads customers to look only for price-specific bargains. When franchisees stop offering these, they'll go to competitors instead. Incentivised promotion has a limited place in retail marketing," he asserts.

Parker acknowledges that franchisees are not necessarily good marketers, and that given too much levy, they can do damage to the brand. "Franchisors should work a lot harder at being creative about the needs of individual franchises," he advises.

He also points out that franchisees need to be more involved with the management of the marketing budget in order to create a win-win situation for both franchisee and franchisor.

6.1 TEN KEY PRINCIPLES OF FRANCHISE MARKETING

Being part of a franchise system offers tremendous advantages such as, in most cases, instant brand recognition. But it also presents some limitations. Most, if not all, of the promotional initiatives must pass the franchisor's approval. Despite some restrictions there are plenty of opportunities for individual franchisees to help drive business.

(1) Know the Customer and Market: if a franchisee has already purchased a franchise then he should be confident that there is a demand for the product. Successful business owners know their customers and make adjustments according to cultural factors and trend.

(2) The Product or Service: this itself is an important marketing tool. In a highly competitive playing field where similar businesses are selling similar products, product naming and packaging becomes highly important.

(3) Promote the Products and Services: through advertising campaigns, public and media relations efforts, TV and radio commercials, Internet advertising and direct mail initiatives. Many franchisors will have public relations representation and provide guidance or drive campaigns at the corporate level.

(4) Position the Franchisee as an Expert: additional ways to create brand awareness include writing or contributing to articles as an expert in the field.

(5) Keep Past Customers Coming Back: through in-store promotions, loyalty programs, coupons and special offers and involvement in the community (sponsoring sporting or charity events, etc).

(6) A Web Site: is without a doubt an essential tool to getting customers. Most likely the franchisor has a Web site with the option to search for locations. Depending on the type of business, it may be appropriate for some franchisees, however, to have their own Web site for their local market.

(7) Marketing Collateral provides potential customers with information about a company. These include brochures, white papers, and sales videos. Not all franchisees require marketing collateral. These materials may not be relevant to a fast food franchise but may be necessary for others, especially those engaged in B2B franchises.

(8) Implementing a Marketing Database is a great way to log the marketing progress and keep track of customers and leads.

(9) Establish a Referral System with complimentary business owners. Another way to get referrals is through the existing client base. Franchisees can ask customers to write testimonials, act as references or offer an incentive program for them to refer the services to others.

(10) Identify Innovative Approaches for getting more business. One mistake in running a business is remaining static — if one wants to remain competitive one must find new ways for reaching the target demographic.

Qualities of Franchise Marketing Programs

Regardless of the franchise marketing mechanism chosen, the franchise selling process must be attended to with great care and attention. Even where the franchisor uses the services of a trusted franchise marketing organization, the franchisor must become intimately involved in the final selection process. The franchisor should devote the same efforts to selecting a franchisee as choosing a junior partner or key employee.

Mandatory centralized marketing programs are probably one of the greatest strengths of franchising. Pooling funds from all of the franchisees in a system gives them, collectively, much greater marketing power. This central fund can be used to do things that no single franchisee could afford, like running television advertising campaigns. The fund can also be used to hire experts to produce advertising materials of far better quality than what an individual owner could create.

These funds can also be a great source of conflict, though, because franchisees often feel that the pooled money is not being spent in the way they think it should be. This can be a huge issue in any franchise system, especially in a recession when all advertising tends to be less effective than in better times. So it is essential for anyone contemplating a franchise investment to know in advance that the company's marketing system is a good one. The following are five essential qualities of a good franchise marketing program:

(1) It Drives Customers: Plain and simple, the number one question for any franchisee to ask is whether or not the marketing fund brings enough customers to make the business successful. If the answer is yes, conflicts will be kept to a minimum. If the answer is no, watch out for World War III.

(2) **It Involves the Franchisees:** Successful franchise marketing programs typically give franchisees substantial opportunity to weigh in with their opinions. The ultimate decision-making authority is normally still reserved by the franchisor, but well-run funds get plenty of input from the people closest to the customer—the franchisees. Franchisee should look for at least a franchisee advisory group (elected or appointed) that meets with the company's marketing executives regularly to provide input on future projects and campaigns.

(3) **It Gets the Splits Right:** Marketing fund rupees are used primarily for three things. First, they cover the costs of administering the marketing effort (internal expenses, agency fees, etc.). Second, they cover the costs of producing advertising materials (print, direct mail, radio and television ads, etc.). Finally, they pay for media purchases to place these advertisements for the benefit of the contributing franchisees. A common franchisee complaint is that too much is being spent in one of these area and not enough in another. For example, the fund clearly needs to produce high-quality promotional materials, but if all of the money is spent on production, there won't be any fund left to deliver these wonderful materials to consumers. There obviously has to be a reasonable balance between these two needs. Another common conflict is over the amount spent to promote "brand-building" advertisements versus the amount spent on "customer attraction" advertisements. Many marketing department executives seem to favor the first approach, whereas most franchisees strongly favor the latter. So again, if there's not a reasonable balance between these two needs, massive conflict can result.

(4) **It is Well-Documented:** A well-thought-out and proven franchise marketing system will be carefully documented by the franchisor. Though they probably won't provide the franchisee with all of their proprietary internal marketing documentation, he can request at least the table of contents of the marketing support manuals they provide to franchisees. This will give him a good idea of the scope of the strategies they address in training franchisees to market effectively. It will also demonstrate that they have perfected their systems to the point where they have documented them in manuals and other support and training tools.

(5) It Validates Well: The surest way to find out how well the marketing program is working is to get on the phone and start asking the existing franchisees. The franchisee will find that they will be very forthcoming on this topic since few things are closer to their hearts than marketing. Be specific and ask them how well the marketing works in terms of driving customers into their business. Also ask if they think they're consistently getting good value from their contributions to any required marketing fund. If the franchisee finds a franchise system where the majority of the existing franchisees are unhappy about the way their marketing dollars are being managed, he can safely assume that he will end up unhappy. On the other hand, if most of the franchisees are pleased with the way the marketing fund is handled by the franchisor, that's a great sign. It is often found that if this is the case, the franchisees are happy about most other factors in their business as well.

Forms of Marketing in Franchising:

Marketing within a franchised organization takes on several forms and combinations:

- **Franchisor Marketing:** The franchisor is normally responsible for centralized marketing and materials production, and development of national advertising campaigns. Once this function is fulfilled, the franchisor is principally responsible for the purchase of media on a national level. It also is responsible for providing advice and approving local and regional advertising done by the franchisee.
- **Franchisee Marketing:** Franchisees are often responsible for regional and local advertising to promote their individual store. The franchisor provides informational support regarding buying behavior, media costs, and market trends. As a franchisee, franchisee has a contractual obligation to spend marketing dollars in the local market on promotions and public relations. Then, if the franchise is large enough, regional advertising is accomplished through the cooperative efforts of franchisees in a "region" that is served by a common media, often defined by the reach of the largest network television affiliate. Clearly, regional cooperatives create increased buying power for the franchise. Franchisees have to remember that although national advertising execution is a franchisor responsibility, it is funded through a contractually obligated contribution of all franchisees to a franchisor-administered fund.
- **Supplier Advertising Cooperatives:** Supplier's cooperatives in which franchisees and suppliers team up and share advertising expenses are

a common practice in franchising. One will see Pepsi in most local fast food. Not only do supplier cooperatives provide franchisors with additional financial resources, but they can also be extremely valuable in helping to leverage the brand support of a nationally recognized supplier.

- **Joint Advertising:** Joint advertising occurs when, for example, Dunkin' Donuts and Baskin Robbins, which are both owned by Allied Domecq, find ways to promote each other's products within their respective franchise systems. Franchisors have recently developed dual or triple branded outlets, with joint signage linking the two or three brands. A few years ago Allied Domecq added Togo's Eatery, a high-end sandwich offering, to its franchise brands. Of course, in addition to joint marketing, franchises are seeking operational synergy from combining brands.
- **Cross-Promotion:** Cross-promotion is a local promotion between a franchisee and another local firm that induces purchase for both entities. The product being promoted in this franchise is often completely unrelated to the other product. "If you're licensing a property like Curious George, McDonald's provides you with 30,000 distribution points to get that furry little guy in the hands of kids. Dinner at Pizza Hut might include tickets to the professional sports franchise. Another example occurs when the back of your receipt from the supermarket is a coupon for a free frankie or an ice cream. Creative marketing is a hallmark of cross-promotion.

Local Marketing

Local marketing in franchise organizations most often manifests in the form of promotional activities. As a result, franchisee will be responsible to drive activity, because it requires a high degree of knowledge of the local market dynamics. At the local level, franchisee uses a great deal of promotional activities, such as sponsoring local youth sports teams, rather than advertising to increase revenue. The franchisor provides details on target customer and buyer behavior information that is then combined with the franchisee's in-depth local knowledge to deliver highly targeted and effective promotional campaigns.

Regional Advertising

A key achievement in the life of a franchise occurs when it gets big enough to pool advertising funds for regional media purchases. In regional advertising, all franchisees within a defined geographic region are obligated to participate by contributing as much as 4 or 5 percent of their revenue to an advertising fund.

Television reach has traditionally defined the region, but there are a variety of methods. The focus on radio and television as the principle measure of marketing efficiency underpinned direct-marketing campaigns and other guerilla marketing tactics. The advantage of this program is that these tactics provide a higher level of flexibility on the part of the regional co-op because there is so much money for marketing.

Most franchises use a combination of many marketing tools. The key issue is to understand that regional differences will affect the marketing mix. Therefore, contractual obligations have to be flexible enough to meet local needs, yet they must also be measurable by the franchisor.

These events leverage the franchise's television and radio coverage. From an operational perspective, regional co-ops utilize nationally produced materials and implement them at a regional level. This usually translates into buying economies initially for radio and newspaper, and eventually for television as well. When television economies are achieved at the regional level, it begins with cable television and then moves to network television. Network television spans the nation, and a purchase at one network can satisfy several regional markets.

However, the cable television industry tends to be more fragmented.

National cable purchases are cumbersome. To deliver a national spot in cable, a franchisor would have to purchase advertising spots from several cable operators, which would diminish the economies. The same holds for newspaper and radio. In addition, radio and newspaper efficiencies at the national level are low (and sometimes negative) due to the differences in audiences in regional markets. With radio, cable television, and many newspapers, the optimal economies of scale can be achieved at the regional level.

Multiple outlet owners often dominate the decision-making process of the co-op because they contribute more to the fund. However, single-unit owners gain a disproportionate benefit, because they contribute the least and receive the same marketing benefits as the others. This dynamic tends to be less of an issue in situations where area development agreements or trade area franchises are in place, because all of the participants are approximately the same size, thus reducing the amount of conflict.

The franchisor often participates in the governance of the regional co-op through a seat on the board. Although the franchisor seldom has veto rights, its role is to offer assistance and, more importantly, to ensure that there is consistency between the regional and the national advertising strategies. Bylaws of the co-op are explicit and include voting rights for both the franchisees and the franchisor. Achieving the appropriate size to implement regional advertising cooperatives tells you that a franchise system has gained scale and should continue its growth on a national level.

National Advertising

A franchisor generally spends the money needed to produce highly professional advertising materials and distribute them on a local level to franchisees. This separates the franchise from their mom-and-pop competitors in the community early in the game in an attempt to build brand equity. As the number of outlets in a franchise system grows, the contributions by franchisees to the national advertising fund will exceed the amount needed to produce marketing materials. The balance that is left franchisor will spend on national advertising. National advertising is the holy grail of marketing economies. As the total national advertising budget expands, franchisees usually want a formal voice in the way the national money is spent. Many franchisors form an advisory council to solicit the perspective of franchisees. A franchisee will need to press the franchisor to include his marketing perspective and local market knowledge. Remember, one of the important values of a franchise relationship is the direct understanding of consumer needs and requirements, as a franchisee are the closest link to the consumer. Bringing that knowledge to the marketing decision making process is a key franchise synergy.

The advertising council consists of single unit and multiunit franchisees. The role of the council is to manage the relationship with the advertising or marketing agency (including hiring and firing), to administer funds, to determine the pricing and timing issues around promotion, and to introduce new products. This council is often considered the most significant franchisee organization within a franchise system and therefore there is great demand by franchisees to participate.

Often, the national advertising fund is held in a separate escrow account and protected with a third-party certified audit and reviewed by this council. While council review of the fund is optional, an audit is a requirement. Beware of the franchise that doesn't audit their national advertising fund.

Supplier's Cooperative Advertising

Supplier's cooperatives are most common in branded supplies, such as Coca-Cola and Pepsi. The agreement is usually initiated by setting up a fund account based on purchases between Coca-Cola and the branded retailer, such as McDonald's. For example, if McDonald's purchases a certain number of containers of beverage from Coca-Cola, then Coca-Cola will contribute a certain amount of money per container to the pool. That money can then be used to fund a certain percentage of a media purchase. Usually, there are three criteria to get supplier money: physical space in a print ad, electronic time, and brand mentions.

There are, of course, risks in using supplier cooperative advertising. For example, franchisee might have to give up some flexibility in the advertising decisions. The supplier's concern is that it has to be sure that any representation of its product is consistent with the existing brand image; otherwise, brand equity could be eroded rather than built. Suppliers may want to review and potentially veto the ad before it goes public.

There is a downside to supplier cooperative advertising. The franchised brand can become inextricably linked to the supplier's product, and if the supplier is involved in a crisis, the customer might identify both brands with the problem of the supplier.

6.2 FRANCHISORS AND THE FRANCHISEE CONSIDERATIONS FOR MARKETING

When creating for an effective expansion plan, franchisors should consider targeted markets and franchisee profiling. For a lead generating program to succeed, it is important to develop a profile of the most desirable franchise candidates. Brand positioning is crucial in marketing as it is the foundational idea of a brand, product or company that distinguishes it in some valuable way from its competitors.

Here is a simple test to determine whether the marketing strategy supports the symbiotic nature of the franchising relationship. The franchisor and the franchisee would require to answer the following:

- **Franchisees:** Is it good for our customers, my business and the brand?
- **Franchisors:** Is it good for our customers (franchisees), our business and the brand?

The answer to both the questions should be positive to start on the right note. While this is a good start, implementing successful programs requires franchisors to overcome several fundamental challenges unique to marketing a franchise brand.

The underlying communication challenge between the franchisor and franchisee is among the most pressing internal issues associated with marketing a franchise brand. Keeping the symbiotic nature of the relationship and interdependence in mind, improving communication is a strategic imperative. Stronger franchisor and franchisee communication builds a foundation of trust generating more responsive and mutually profitable businesses, and ultimately, stronger brands. However, in order to be truly successful, franchisors must also overcome three additional challenges to ultimately reach marketing and business objectives.

How do fledgling, regional and super-regional franchisors expand into areas with little or no market awareness? The proliferation of new concepts and twists on established concepts has created a veritable buyers market. The resulting dilution of the potential franchisee base should be cause for new thinking about objectives and tactics for franchise expansion, while keeping the importance of the mutually-symbiotic nature of the franchisor/franchisee relationship in mind. Consider two major factors in an effective expansion plan: targeted markets and franchisee profiling.

To develop an effective, repeatable program, try these three steps:

(1) Select a test market.

(2) Determine how many outlets would fully develop this market.

(3) Focus communications on generating leads from this territory. Using simple arithmetic, based on current lead-to close ratio and costs, one can back into how many leads to generate and the cost. The goal is to improve these ratios with successive deployments as the franchisee understands target audiences better, refine tactics and gain economies of scale.

This process will lead to a proven repeatable system with the intention of deploying in several metropolitan markets simultaneously at increasingly lower costs to meet sales targets.

The logical next question is: How does the company target potential franchisees in a given market, particularly if there is little or no brand awareness? There are significant benefits to developing a profile of the most desirable franchise candidates. Knowing who the firm is talking to and why is absolutely vital to any successful lead generating program. Look at profiling on two levels: the first is demographic and the second, more subtle and no less important level, is psychographic.

Since it is critically important to fully understand the potential audience, marketers must recognize the appropriate levers and forces that drive interest in the franchise concept. At the core, there is a baseline profile of people, with common financial and lifestyle factors that are attracted to your concept. Drilling deeper, there are emotional and psychographic denominators of those who are more likely to own the franchise and be successful.

An Overview of Marketing and the License Agreement

When the franchise relationship becomes litigious, marketing always seems to have some role in the breach, so it makes sense to see how marketing is handled in the license agreement. It should explicitly outline all fees and expenditures mandated by the franchisor. Some franchisors require payments that go beyond the advertising fee for such things as printing collateral material like point-of-sale posters. The market penetration (in number of outlets) that must be achieved to form a regional cooperative also should be detailed in the agreement. Finally, the agreement should clearly outline the governance of the national advertising mechanisms. Proper checks and balances should be in place to ensure the proper allocation of those funds.

6.3 POTENTIAL MARKETING PROBLEMS

Distribution of Benefits

One problem in marketing a franchise system is that there will not be an even distribution of the benefits of the advertising. This discrepancy should be stipulated in the license agreement and understood by the franchisees.

As a result, some advertising councils have gone as far as to stipulate that there will be an attempt to balance the benefit going forward based on the results of past media buys. Franchisees who receive disproportionate benefit from one campaign will either contribute more to the fund or receive a lower benefit on a future campaign. While this is theoretically possible, it is impractical to execute.

Franchise Marketing and Pricing Issues

Some of the pricing issues that can emerge as a result of the franchise marketing relationship include promotional campaigns, antitrust issues, and regional disputes. Promotional campaign problems occur when the franchisor wants to boost revenues without regard for the short-term effect on your profitability. The franchisor constructs a promotional campaign that often includes a price discount. The promotion is designed to drive more traffic into stores. While this might result in increased revenue, the price decrease reduces the franchisees' operating margin and might negatively affect profitability (again, at least in the short run).

However, the franchisor derives its income from a percentage of total revenue in the form of a royalty, not franchisee's profitability. So, some promotions may benefit one party at the other's expense, resulting in the franchisor making more money and the franchisee making less.

In this case, the phrase "at participating stores" is always part of the promotion; however, it is difficult for a franchisee not to participate when customers are coming in expecting the special deal from every dealer. There must be careful language written into the license agreement regarding the pricing, limitations, and franchisee purchasing options.

Marketing and the Free Riding Risk

Free riding can be pervasive throughout the franchise relationship, but it is most evident in marketing. Local marketing expenditures are fertile ground for the franchisee abuse of free riding to occur. Because a little less money spent by any individual franchisee will not affect the brand or revenue of the entire system, franchisees may be tempted to restrict their share of the spending. By holding back local dollars, the individual franchise gets a free ride on the system's brand. This problem is vexing because the expenditures in the area of local marketing are difficult to monitor. The franchisor has limited knowledge of the use of dollars spent on local marketing. For example, a franchisee could take his or her family out to dinner and charge it to the local marketing account. The franchisor would have no way of knowing. Remember, local advertising is typically a contractual requirement. The franchise system uses this requirement to increase marketing impressions and create brand equity for all outlets. Anytime the allocations of marketing funds are withheld or misused, the marketing impact is diminished for the entire franchise system. Imagine if McDonald's did not monitor contractual requirements. If each franchise misallocated only a small amount of the required local advertising expenditure (e.g., Rs. 50/month) the system wide impact would be over Rs. 150 million annually in reduced advertising.

Ralph Waldo Emerson said, "If a man can write a better book, preach a better sermon, or make a better mouse-trap than his neighbor, though he build his house in the woods, the world will make a beaten path to his door." Emerson was a talented writer, but we believe his business insight was fundamentally flawed. If you build a better mousetrap, you had better make sure the world understands why it is better and where they can get it.

Franchise marketing is the communication tool that promises the customer, "We have what you need, and you can count on us to fill that need no matter which of our locations you go to." There is usually a simple message at the core of marketing and a consistency in delivering on that message that embeds in the consumer's mind as a brand. Examples include "We'll change your oil in ten minutes," "It's time to make the donuts," "Billions and billions served," "We'll do it your way," "The Pepsi Generation," and "Just do it!" Clearly, once a product's marketing becomes part of a culture's daily vernacular, spectacular success has been achieved.

Franchise Marketing Tips For a Down Economy

by Anthony Pappas

In these cash-tight times, marketing budgets and brand-building activities are often the first cost centers to get the axe. But doing so can have serious ramifications for your business - today and in the future. Customers and prospects have very short memories. If you're not staying in front of them in multiple ways, you'll be quickly forgotten once the economy brightens and competitors move in. For franchise businesses, branding and marketing challenges are twofold: Maintain awareness of the overall brand while helping the growth of individual franchisees. Both of those tasks get a lot tougher when there's less money with which to work. But a down economy also presents opportunities to strengthen your brand and stay top-of-mind with customers. To help you get the most from your marketing dollars in these trying times, here are five brand-building tips to consider:

It's All About the Brand

Right now, many organizations are doing away with or significantly reducing brand-building activities and instead investing in activities that more directly influence sales of products or services. And while these activities aren't mutually exclusive, shutting off brand-building activities can be a tragic mistake for franchise businesses. Brand recognition and integrity are vital to a franchise's success. A solid brand is a living, breathing entity that has been carefully crafted over time. It sets customer expectations for your organization, earns their loyalty and, in some cases, may earn your organization a price premium. If your brand isn't consistently supported, it will be quickly forgotten. The good news is that your competitors are facing the same dilemmas, so evaluate your current branding strategies with an eye toward making your marketing dollars go as far as possible. One opportunity is to fill those channels your competitors are leaving, such as direct mail and broadcast media. You can often score media buys at a discount, and even modest investment can reap big rewards: Once the economy brightens and competitors rush back, customers will already be familiar with you. Online banner ads are another brand-building medium franchises may want to leverage. As with other online marketing strategies, banner ads allow you to target customers to a much greater degree than is possible with offline channels Banner ads can be paired with customized landing pages to create a positive brand experience at every click. Landing pages are typically developed to generate a specific action step for the viewer, such as filling out a form to receive a coupon or joining a loyalty or rewards program. When backed by targeted landing pages, banner ads can help turn clicks into customers, offering almost immediate ROI calculations. And today's media-buying technology allows you to identify and target very specific online audiences with relevant content to maximize results even further. Of course, the ultimate goal is to drive that interested visitor to become a real customer. By combining banner ads and corresponding landing pages with other communications and the right creative elements, you compel customers to take action both online and offline.

Nurture Current Customers

When the proverbial wheels come off the economy, it's time to refocus your branding and marketing initiatives on core customers - the lifeblood of your business. There are several strategies that can help you do this effectively. First, be sure all of your brand-building initiatives reinforce your key value propositions with this audience. Stick with the differentiating statements with which your customers have become familiar; moving your brand promise in a new direction may confuse your customers and make it more difficult to maintain or expand those relationships going forward. If you haven't yet implemented a loyalty or customer rewards program, now may be a great time to do so. To be effective, the components of your loyalty program - such as discounts on products and services or access to special events or content - must be relevant to your organization's brand philosophy and value proposition, and present real value to customers.

But a down economy also presents opportunities to strengthen your brand.

Loyalty programs are one area where it's acceptable to slightly shift your messaging and tactics to reflect current market realities - as long as you aren't diluting your brand in the process. The goal of any loyalty program is to make sure your core customers feel loved by your organization - and to give them some incentive to love you back in good times and bad.

Get Local to Find Customers

Now may be the perfect time to dive into local search to attract online users right in your backyard. Local search refers to geographically-specific search queries that look for matching business listings. So if someone conducts a search for "Pet Grooming Alexandria" and your pet grooming franchise has a location there, local search makes it much more likely your location will appear in the search results. Local search doesn't happen automatically. Identify the local search engines your customers and prospects use most (Yahoo! and Google both have local search components) and update your business listings to reflect locations, products and services, contact information and more.

Beyond Page Views

The Web is no longer a novelty channel favored by a subset of your customers. It is *the* platform for interactive customer engagement and building brand loyalty. According the Pew Internet & American Life project, 81% of Internet users go online to research products or services before they buy. That means your Web site is not just another place to reinforce your brand; an online experience that goes beyond typical metrics such as page views and unique visitors should be front and center in your brand identity strategy. Fifteen seconds and one click. That's all the time Web users will give your site if you don't clearly articulate a key message to them. Keep visitors on your site and encourage them to dig deeper by creating a compelling online brand experience. Users are closer than ever to the Web – every aspect of advertising is built to drive users to a Web site. The more compelling the experience, the more likely you are to convert visitors into customers. From a creative standpoint, there are countless ways to accomplish this.

A campaign mini-site is an increasingly popular tactic that allows you to rapidly produce an online branded experience in support of a marketing message. Think of a mini-site as an expanded landing page; it mimics the look and feel of your main Web site and other collateral as a means of reinforcing your brand while containing more specialized content. The value of a mini-site is its flexibility. It can include viral and community elements, such as online games and a blog, that beg repeated visits and interaction, or it can be a simple and straightforward tool for rapidly delivering a useful message that drives users to make a purchase.

Keep Testing

The beauty of the Web is the ability to infinitely track its performance, which is why 'click-through rates" and "cost per click" metrics have entered our daily marketing lexicon. The ability to calculate ROI and adjust budgets of competing search marketing campaigns helps you maximize every dollar you invest in this medium.

The Web is no longer a novelty channel favored by a subset of your customers.

Customer feedback should be a key component of your online testing protocol. Have a new banner ad campaign? Give customers an opportunity to comment on it directly on your Web site. The economy - and your competitors - can change directions in an instant. By soliciting feedback and combining it with the proper campaign results metrics and data, you can constantly improve on the quality and overall perception of your brand and marketing programs - today and in the future.

6.4 SUMMARY

The prospect of turning a business into a franchise operation is an attractive option for many companies. Franchisors extract a levy of between 1% and 2% of franchisee turnover to fund advertising and other such activities. Advertising has become a bone of contention between the franchisor and the franchisee. In this chapter, Parker suggests that a rule of thumb, marketing costs should equate to between 5% and 8% of a company's turnover. The marketing budget should be controlled by the franchisee council or franchisee co-operative. Further he says, the franchisees must not assume that brand building efforts should be the responsibility of the franchisor alone.

Despite some restrictions, there are plenty of opportunities for individual franchisees to help drive business, such as, know the customer and market, the product or service, promote the product and services, position the franchisee as an expert, keep past customers coming back, preparing a website and identifying innovative approaches.

However, marketing within a franchised organization takes on several forms of combinations such as, franchising marketing, franchisee marketing, and supplier advertising co-operative, joint advertising and cross promotions.

Key elements in advertising are the high degree of knowledge of the market dynamics. Advertising can be local, regional or national.

There are potential marketing problems as well, because there will not be an even distribution of benefits of advertising to all the funding franchisees. This discrepancy should be stipulated in the license agreement and must be understood by the franchisees.

Some of the pricing issues that can emerge as a result of the franchised marketing relationship include promotional campaigns, anti-trust issues and regional disputes. The franchisor constructs a promotional campaign that often included a price discount, to enhance sales but this price decrease, reduced the profitability of the franchisees.

6.5 SELF ASSESSMENT QUESTIONS

(1) List down the key principles of franchise marketing and explain any three in detail.

(2) Write a short note on the various considerations by the Franchisor and the Franchise with regards to marketing.

(3) Describe the various forms of Franchise marketing.

✠✠✠

Chapter

7 FRANCHISING IN GLOBAL SCENARIO

Objectives

After going through this chapter, you will be able to understand:

- Global scenario in franchising
- Need for franchise law in India
- International Market Entry Strategies
- Opportunities existing in International markets

Structure:

Today, India is one of the biggest emerging markets for various goods and services, ranging from bare necessities to expensive luxuries. Until 1991 due to the archaic Foreign Exchange Regulation Act, 1973 (FERA), almost all sectors of goods and services relating to the consumer markets in India were secure from the grasp of foreign investors. After the repeal of FERA and the coming into force of the Foreign Exchange Management Act, 1999 (FEMA), foreign investors found their passage into India with rules for entry becoming far more favourable. Today, a convenient medium of entry by foreign companies into the Indian market is franchising. Franchising also exists as a successful business module for local companies in India within various sectors.

The United States of America stands at the forefront of the franchise boom. Today, the legal environment in the United States is highly conducive to the healthy growth and evolution of franchising. With more than 50% of total retail businesses in the United States, 45% in Canada and 26% in Australia choosing a franchise model for expansion, the impact of franchising on retail industries across the globe is considerable. To foster the rapid and sustained growth that this channel brings, it is critical that laws to regulate the franchising business exist.

However, there are no laws enacted solely for the purpose of regulating the growing business of franchising in India, even though many nations across the world have enacted such laws. The result is that when franchisors enter India they are governed by a number of different statutes and codes rather than a single comprehensive enactment.

7.1 FRANCHISE LAWS ACROSS THE GLOBE

There are many countries which have developed comprehensive legislation to cover franchising in their respective dominions. At the federal level in the United States, the Federal Trade Commission's Rules on Disclosure Requirements and Prohibitions Concerning Franchising and Business Opportunity Ventures (1979) regulate the information a franchisor is required to supply the prospective franchisee in order to enable the franchisee to make an informed decision on the prospects of venturing into the business. The North American Security Administration Association (NASSA) has adopted a Uniform Franchise Offering Circular (UFOC) which delineates the information required to be disclosed to a prospective franchisee. Disclosure requirements under franchising are well-defined in the USA.

In 2000, the Ontario Legislature in Canada adopted the Arthur Wishart Act which deals comprehensively with disclosure requirements as well as important aspects of the franchisee-franchisor relationship such as fair dealing by each party to a franchise agreement as regards to its performance and enforcement, and the right of action for damages for breach of the duty of fair dealing.

In the United Kingdom, there exists no operative franchise-related legislation. However different aspects are governed by norms laid down by the British Franchise Association (BFA), the regulatory body of the franchise industry in the United Kingdom. These include a code of ethical conduct, disciplinary procedure, complaints procedure and appeals procedure.

The Australian government has adopted a mandatory code of conduct and has also modified the Trade Practice Act 1974 to provide for franchising. The new code imposes comprehensive disclosure requirements and provides for mandatory mediation of franchising disputes and minimum standards for franchise agreements including, inter alia, a cooling period, refrain from seeking from a franchisee a general release liability, disclosing material facts and refrain from unreasonably withholding consent to transfer of the business.

In April 2002, the Japan Fair Trade Commission (JFTC), the competition authority of Japan, published new guidelines on franchising. These guidelines contain three parts - a general description of franchising, provisions for the disclosure of necessary information (such as details of the assistance to be offered to franchisees, the nature, amount and conditions of repayment, if any, of the fee to be paid at the time of entering into a franchise agreement, etc.) at the time of the offer of a franchise and a part on vertical restraints between a franchisor and its franchisees. Under the guidelines, the failure to provide necessary information shall constitute deceptive customer inducement, which is considered an unfair trade practice.

On 31st December 2004 the Ministry of Commerce of the People's Republic of China promulgated the Measures for the Regulation of Commercial Franchises which became the sole legal framework for franchising in China. The measures became operative on 1st February 2005 and provide detailed regulations for franchising, comprising of 42 articles over nine chapters covering a wide span of areas from the franchise agreement to disclosure requirements, special rules for foreign invested enterprises and legal liabilities.

7.2 NEED FOR A FRANCHISE LAW IN INDIA

A healthy legal environment is of great importance for franchising and should include provisions pertaining to all areas that fall within the ambit of franchising. This includes, *inter alia*, commercial law relating to contracts and joint ventures and intellectual property law for protection of trademarks and know-how. Franchise arrangements are subject to an array of laws and regulations in addition to those regulating commercial contracts and intellectual property rights. There are no specific laws governing franchising in India. As a result a franchise agreement may be governed by different laws.

Primarily a franchise agreement is a contract between the franchisor and the franchisee. The first law which comes into the picture is the Contract Act 1872 which governs contracts in India. A franchise agreement will be governed by the Indian Contract Act, 1872 and the Specific Relief Act, 1963 which provides for both specific enforcement of covenants in a contract and remedies in the form of damages for breach of contract. If a party to the franchise agreement commits a breach of contract, the aggrieved party has the option to initiate a suit for specific performance in Indian courts and apply for relief in the form of a temporary or permanent injunction, which may be granted at the discretion of the court considering the balance of convenience and the interests of justice. An order granting or rejecting an injunction may be appealed by an aggrieved party.

Laws relating to taxation, property laws, insurance law and labour laws also apply to franchise transactions. Additionally, laws and regulations applying to specific sectors of goods and services will also apply depending on the franchised.

The following are the reasons why a comprehensive franchise law is required in India:

Application of Multiple Legislation

A well-defined legal structure is indispensable for the effective functioning of any business operation. The international business environment demands a well-defined suitable legislation that is complete in all respects. The lack of a comprehensive legislation on franchising in India leads to the applicability of multiple laws to a franchise transaction. This poses the following problems:

Complexities: Parties to a contract normally prefer agreements with a simple approach and encompassing all the required law procedures and rules required to be complied with. However the application of different laws to one agreement makes it complex to decide various issues arising from the agreement.

Ambiguities: Due to the necessary application of multiple legislation, ambiguities are created as to certain issues. For example, a franchisor would imagine that a certain issue is the franchisee's responsibility under one law, whereas the franchisee would think the opposite based on a different law.

Time-Consuming: Referring to multiple laws consumes a lot of time at the initial stages of a transaction as well as other points of time when the agreement is sought to be enforced. This proves to be detrimental to the smooth functioning of franchising operations in India and also makes time-bound operations involving new enterprises difficult.

Absence of Disclosure Requirements

Countries with specific franchising legislation make it imperative for parties to a franchise agreement to disclose certain factual information pertaining to the business of the parties. This ensures transparency and facilitates an informed decision. A franchisor should be required, by law, to make certain disclosure to the prospective franchisee wherein he is supposed to reveal detailed information regarding himself, his litigation and bankruptcy history, his financial position, the facilities he offers, etc. In India, in the absence of effective disclosure norms, a prospective franchisee is rendered helpless as the franchisor is under no statutory obligations to make disclosures.

In the absence of a specific statute governing the franchise agreement, the franchisor refrains from providing any information that is likely to prejudice or make a franchisee reconsider the business proposition of the franchisor. The lack of proper disclosure requirements provides a golden opportunity to a franchisor to abuse his position of importance as he is virtually under no statutory obligation to make the requisite disclosure.

Applicability of Laws of other Countries

Normally, the absence of franchise laws enables foreign franchisors to make the laws of their own country applicable to the agreements entered into with the franchisees in India. The same is the case with franchisors who enter into franchising agreements with franchisees from other countries. This proves to be an additional burden on the parties, particularly the franchisee.

Lack of Proper Format for Franchising Agreements

Due to lack of a specific format, franchisors from other countries draft agreements which are in the same format as is approved or followed in their countries. Such agreements are made to suit the specific environment of their respective countries and hence are not suitable for Indian environment.

Liability of Parties Uncertain

Due to the lack of specific legislation, the liability of either party is either determined by the agreements entered into between them or on the basis of general prevailing law. The liability clause is different in different countries, and this leads to a great discrepancy among the courts which try such disputes on liabilities.

The Central Government is currently considering a franchise law aimed at fast resolution of disputes; the proposal is expected to be placed before a sub-committee of the National Development Council. The aforesaid problems surrounding franchising in India necessitate the enactment of a specific legislation pertaining to franchising in India and providing for the gamut of activities that franchising encompasses. A special franchise law would greatly accelerate dispute resolutions and fortify the Indian retail industry.

The **Franchise Association of India** is the country's peak industry body and **franchise advisory** committed to strengthening and promoting the best practices in franchising. Franchise Association of India members are businesses and service providers united by their common concerns for the well being of the franchise marketplace.

7.3 CHECKLIST OF BASIC FRANCHISE AGREEMENT TERMS

Franchise agreements are tailored to specific situations. Thus, it is impossible to identify every term and issue that should be considered in every situation. However, the Checklist of Basic Franchise Agreement Terms will provide with a comprehensive listing of the basic terms that may be included in a franchise agreement. It also identifies many of the issues surrounding those terms that should be addressed. If a person is considering the purchase of a franchise, use of the checklist helps to understand the terms typically included in a franchise agreement and to review the agreement provided by the franchisor.

Table 7.1: Checklist for International Franchising

(1) Is the country's legal and regulatory environment for franchising: • Prohibitive • Restrictive • Conducive	(6) Is the economic and political stability of the country: • Prohibitive • Restrictive • Conducive
(2) Are import rules and customs procedures: • Prohibitive • Restrictive • Conducive	(7) The franchises currently operating in the country suggest that overall it is: • Prohibitive • Restrictive • Conducive
(3) For franchising, are tax rates: • Prohibitive • Restrictive • Conducive	(8) The effect of differences in language for the franchise: • Prohibitive • Restrictive • Conducive
(4) Are the cost availability of labour: • Prohibitive • Restrictive • Conducive	(9) The effect of cultural differences on the franchise: • Prohibitive • Restrictive • Conducive

Using the Checklist

(1) Is the country's legal and regulatory environment for franchising:

- Prohibitive?
- Restrictive?
- Conducive?

Outside the United States, most countries do not have laws that specifically address franchising. The franchise-specific laws that do exist in several countries usually pertain to disclosure agreements, but some go as far as to regulate the amount and duration of the royalties due from the franchisee. The general application laws to which the parties to franchise should pay especially close attention are those that pertain to monetary exchange, employment and intellectual property. For example in Europe, such issues as minimum wage, long statutory maternity leave, or paternity leave may affect franchising decisions. If the government regulates the import and export of currencies, it may complicate, or even prohibit, the export of the payments due. And employment laws that restrict the firing of employees could also add significant costs down the road. In terms of intellectual property, it is crucial to know whether or not the law protects the system's patents, trademarks, and copyrights. If intellectual property laws exist, franchisor must determine whether or not these laws are being purposefully and effectively enforced. Loosely enforced intellectual property laws put the logo and brand at risk and expansion in those countries carries extreme risk.

Obviously a country that forbids franchising altogether (such as Mexico before 1991), or that severely restricts currency exchange, would be considered prohibitive. If a country allows franchising but has non-existent or unenforced intellectual property laws, franchisor should consider it restrictive. One that allows franchising by law, and that enforces intellectual property laws according to international standards, is conducive to franchising.

Assessing the Country's Legal and Regulatory Environment for Franchising: Because most countries do not have very specific laws, the first order of business in determining the level of intellectual property protection in a country is to determine whether or not the country is a member or observer of the World Trade Organization (WTO). All members of the WTO must sign on the Agreement on Trade Related Aspects of Intellectual Property Rights, or the TRIPS agreement and the intellectual property law enforcement rules that it contains. Although a country's membership in the WTO is highly significant, it is important to keep in mind that this alone does not guarantee that its intellectual property laws are well enforced. For example, China and Mexico are two WTO members that have had major grievances filed against them in the area of intellectual property piracy.

(2) Are import rules and customs procedures:

- Prohibitive?
- Restrictive?
- Conducive?

The franchisor may have to import raw materials and supplies to its franchises in the given country. These inputs will range from intellectual property and training personnel to raw material, for that reason, it is important to determine the state of the country's supply infra-structure and import and customs procedures. If the franchise is a restaurant and heavy import duties are imposed upon certain food stuffs, those added costs might make the country a restrictive or prohibitive place to do business. Likewise, if customs procedures are overly complex or inconsistently applied and enforced, the effect may be deleterious to a new franchise venture. For example, McDonald's in Russia built food-processing plants to supply their restaurants and to ensure quality. Low import duties and efficient customs procedures consistent with international standards will of course be conducive to a franchising operation.

(3) Are corporate tax rates:

- Prohibitive?
- Restrictive?
- Conducive?

No one wants to do business in a country that takes too much in the way of taxes. However, the franchisee will certainly will have to pay taxes to the foreign government at its tax rate. The franchisee is already paying royalties and advertising fees to the franchisor based on revenue, not profits. Therefore, a high foreign tax rate on top of that could mean the difference between a franchise that is profitable, and one that is not. Before setting up an operation abroad, franchisor must have a complete understanding of the tax structures in place for that country. A foreign tax rate that is above 35% could be restrictive or prohibitive whereas one that is below would be conducive to franchising.

(4) Are the cost and availability of labor:

- Prohibitive?
- Restrictive?
- Conducive?

When it comes to franchising, labor affordability and availability are often key ingredients for success. In the current world environment, we often see two extremes. The first is the high cost of labor in developed countries such as Japan and Germany, in which the labor pool is limited, people are relatively well educated, and the cost of living is high. The other extreme is found in developing countries in which labor is cheap and abundant, but in which workers may be less well educated and training is difficult and/or expensive. Depending on the type of franchise, either of these extremes can be prohibitive or restrictive to franchise development. However there are many nations, such as China or the countries of Latin America that have sufficiently sophisticated labor at a lower cost than in the United States. Labor environments like these would be conducive to franchising.

(5) Is the purchasing power of the population:

- Prohibitive?
- Restrictive?
- Conducive?

The purchasing power of any given population is generally related to the issue of cost, availability and literacy of labor. We have found that education levels can be a good indicator of real purchasing power of a target segment. If 50% of the population is illiterate and only a third of the population has more than 7 years of schooling, chances are that labor costs and purchasing power will be low. Conversely, a highly educated and literate population usually indicates a high cost of labor and good purchasing power. When it comes to franchising, low purchasing power need not be an indicator of a prohibitive, or even restrictive, environment for franchising. For example, fast food franchises have done well in developing countries because they offer a relatively high-quality though inexpensive product. However if purchasing power is too low, the environment will be prohibitive, because no one will be able to afford the good or service being offered by the franchise. Thus, an environment conducive to franchising is one in which the purchasing power of the population *is appropriate to purchase* the good or service the franchisor plans to offer.

Assessing the Purchasing Power of the Population: In theory, finding the purchasing power of the population in a given country should be a matter of converting the foreign GNP per capita into U.S. dollars at the prevailing exchange rates.

But the major problem with this method is that it assumes a dollar in one country buys the same amount of good or service as it does in another. As anyone who has purchased a Pepsi in Mexico knows, prices are relative; some things are more or less expensive depending upon the country it is bought from. As a result, purchasing power is better measured using the principal of Purchasing Power Parity (PPP), which takes into account differences between countries in measures such as inflation, price and wage controls, and import tariffs. The World Bank has calculated Year 2000 Gross National Income using the PPP method for over 200 countries.

(6) Is the economic and political stability of the country:

- Prohibitive?
- Restrictive?
- Conducive?

Perhaps the greatest risks in franchising abroad are those that involve political and economic disruptions. Wars, coups *d'état*, nationalizations, runaway inflation, governments in default—these create an international businessperson's nightmare. And as we have seen over the last ten years, these events can disrupt countries that the conventional wisdom has said were safe bets. Take, for example, the truncated moves to an open economy in Venezuela or the economic morass in Japan. We gauge economic and political stability by how long a country has managed to ward off these kinds of disruptions and keep its economy and political system in relative equilibrium. A country that has experienced stability for fifty years or more is one that is conducive to international franchising. Countries in this category include those of North America and much of Western Europe, as well as Australia, and New Zealand.

Countries that have experienced disruptive turmoil in the past twenty years are restrictive, and one that is in turmoil is prohibitive to franchising. Eastern Europe is a clear example of the turmoil, risk and opportunity in the last twenty years. As always in business, with greater risk comes greater potential reward. Because almost every developing economy has experienced disruption in the past twenty years, it is up to the franchisor to do the necessary research and decide whether the return is worth the risk.

Assessing the Economic and Political Stability of the Country: The level of economic and political stability of a country is often referred to as country risk.

(7) The franchises currently operating in the country suggest that overall it is:

- Prohibitive?
- Restrictive?
- Conducive?

One of the surest ways to determine the viability of a particular country for franchising is to see which franchises are already doing business there. Chances are, if someone has achieved success, so can others. If there were no franchises at all in a given country, that location could be a prohibitive one to move into unless the franchisor is willing to commit significant resources. If there are but a few there, or if the number of franchises is declining, the country is probably restrictive of franchising. But if there are a number of franchises operating in the country, and if they have grown steadily in number, then that country is probably conducive to franchising.

(8) The effect of differences in language for the franchise:

- Prohibitive?
- Restrictive?
- Conducive?

Although language is one of the biggest hurdles in realizing international business opportunities, it is a surmountable one. The franchisor has to have all documents drawn up in duplicate, one in English, the other in the foreign language. It greatly helps if he speaks the foreign language in question, but even if he plans a large-scale overseas initiative, it may be unrealistic to expect to be fluent in ten languages. Finding bilingual franchisees whenever possible and hiring a consultant, a tax professional and an attorney from the local area who can assist him with communication and paperwork will greatly reduce the language barrier risk. Many franchisors have found that partnering with a Master Franchisee from the country in question makes the most sense. For example, Cartridge World is an Australian franchisor that sells large regional franchise rights to franchisees who can then re-sell those rights or operate the large territory. The company's business strategy combines refilling printer cartridges for inkjet and laser printers, photo copy and fax machines with fast customer service at convenient retail locations. The combination of retail and office business makes it more difficult to define territories. Larger territories make it easier for a Master Franchisee, who knows the territory better than the franchisor to build the right number of outlets. Using this method, the franchisor can manage franchisee operations for the whole country (or region, if it's a large country) and minimize the points of contact Of course he needs to find the right individual, but that is a necessary task in any relationship based business arrangement.

(9) The effects of cultural differences on the franchise are:

- Prohibitive?
- Restrictive?
- Conducive?

Unfortunately, there is no guidebook available for determining which foreign countries would be most receptive to franchising, but culture can be a make or break factor in setting up internationally. The franchisor can start by looking first at the nature of his offering or menu and then on the physical service delivery system. For instance, in India beef is not widely eaten for cultural reasons, therefore a fast-food franchise such as McDonald's must take this fact into account when developing their menu there or suffer the consequences. In other countries, décor and signage might have to be adjusted to suit local tastes, or the actual products and services offered might have to be altered. High Street locations in Great Britain often have severe signage restrictions.

The best way to get a sense of the cultural differences in a country is to go there and to see first-hand how comparable local businesses are set up. Cultural differences present a complex set of variables. For example, companies that do business with the U.S. Government must adhere to the Foreign Corrupt Practices Act wherever they trade. While we agree with this anti-corruption law, it can severely limit opportunities in cultures where bribery is a normal way of doing business, can be charged to the P&L and provide the local competition with a financial competitive advantage. Additionally, we recommend looking at what the existing franchises have done regarding cultural differences to make themselves fit in locally and to be successful.

International Market Entry Strategies: A U.S. franchisor can be lured into entering a foreign country by an enthusiastic and wealthy prospective franchisee. This generally happens when a foreign entrepreneur comes to the United States, sees or uses a U.S. franchise, and then gets excited about launching the concept in his or her home country. A large franchise fee, and the perception that if the opportunity goes poorly abroad it won't hurt the company's U.S. image, can lead the franchisor into a hastily conceived relationship. These relationships seldom result in financial success.

There are no shortcuts. Entry into a foreign country from a U.S. base is a "back to basics" task that should always begin with an examination of the opportunity using the Franchise Relationship Model.

Franchise Launching into a Foreign Country: There is a wide spectrum of strategies to enter an international market, described in Table 7.2. From left to right, the spectrum identifies the extent of franchisor involvement in the unit operations.

Table 7.2: Spectrum of Market Entrance Strategies

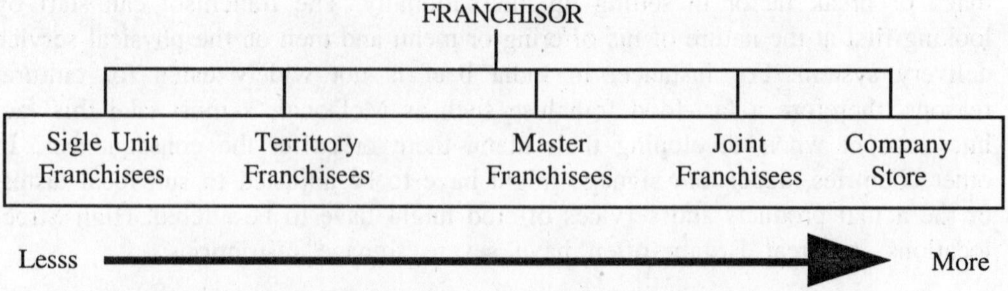

Involvement by Franchisor in International Opertions

The sale of a single franchised unit is the most problematic approach to entering a foreign market. There is typically little or no brand awareness in the foreign country. One unit is at best a "beta site," as described in earlier chapters, but with the franchisee as the risk bearer. This can seem appealing because it brings in fees with what seems to be little brand or capital risk. However, his ability to gain real market intelligence and market share, and hence his probability of success, are limited. To support the site he would have to commit major resources for training, field operations, and marketing. Putting that overhead in place for one franchised unit might not make financial sense. The franchisor may want faster growth and larger up front franchise fee and decide instead to sell territory franchise rights to a select well-capitalized franchisee.

They will be like a national of the foreign country and committed to an extensive development and operation of outlets. Marketing the sale of large franchise territories is often directed to bankers, lawyers and accountants in the targeted nation. These professionals often provide a communications conduit to wealthy business-minded nationals. Territory franchise sales usually include a large up front franchise fee and incremental payments along the way that help underwrite franchisor support. Thus he will have incentives to ramp up support for the franchisee as development increases. Multiple territory franchisees can be sold in a given country in an attempt to build critical mass. However, this "carpet bombing" approach can also magnify new country entry, operations, and marketing glitches.

The next level of involvement is to establish a relationship with a master franchisee, by selling him or her rights to share in his benefits and responsibilities in a country or section of a country. In a Master Franchisee arrangement franchisor assigns rights and responsibilities in the license agreement. The master franchisee is then responsible for opening outlets under his or her ownership or selling outlets to other franchisees that they will support in the fashion of a franchisor. That usually includes site selection, training, marketing and field operations support. The master franchisee receives a percentage of the royalty fee that a franchisor would normally receive.

An explicit partnership is the joint venture. In this case, the franchisor becomes a partner with the franchisee, bearing a percentage of both the new outlet capitalization requirements and the management functions. This is a way for the franchisor to enter a market with a partner "on the ground," but also to have significant control of the operation. However, because capital requirements are expressly shared, this scenario is also a much more capital-intensive strategy for entering a foreign country.

Lastly, the franchisor can take a "grass roots" approach similar to the strategy we recommend in the opening chapter of this book. The franchisor opens company owned stores in a methodical manner to test the service delivery system in the context of the foreign market. After initial success, the franchisor can build upon the initial markets, and upon further success, he can begin selling franchises or even offer the company owned outlets for sale to franchisees.

It is also worth mentioning the issue of physical proximity of a new base of operations from a franchisor's U.S. headquarters. Many franchisors tend to base their first international headquarters in Great Britain for several reasons: the relative close proximity to the Eastern U.S., the similarity of language and culture, and the relative closeness to other parts of Europe, Asia, and the Middle East.

Multi-Unit Opportunities Exist In International Franchising

by Larry Weinberg

Over the past 20 years or so, the world has witnessed both the incredible growth of global brands as well as an increase in the sophistication of franchise structures adopted to pursue expansion. Many would comment that with the advent of global brands, gone are the days of the mom-and-pop operation.

In a similar vein, the trend in international franchise expansion appears to be moving away from single-unit franchise development towards multiple-unit development, usually in the form of master franchising, area-development agreements and area-representative arrangements.

Many U.S. franchisors would not today even consider expansion into a new country or market unless they were able to leverage the abilities, local market knowledge and sophistication of larger candidates.

Of course, each master franchising area-development arrangement is different in its own way, but for the sake of this article the common feature is that each permits a franchisor to appoint a local party to assume some or all of the usual responsibilities of a franchisor in the local market together with a plan to open a multiple number of units.

With the increased use of multiple-unit growth strategies comes a corresponding increase in the sophistication of master franchisee candidates. What will first attract any potential candidate is the uniqueness and quality of the underlying business that is being franchised. If the business does not "wow" the candidate as a matter of first impression, then it is unlikely the candidate will look past that first casual glance.

Deeper than that, most candidates are looking for that combination of factors that provides a product or service that is either entirely new to that market or is being delivered in an entirely unique way, or in connection with an inspiring brand.

Related to that is whether the master-franchisee candidate can understand the system and believe it can be translated to the local market. Some markets are, of course, very similar to the United States in terms of language, culture and even the retail marketplace. Others are not similar but still inviting of American brands and concepts.

Every new market will be different in some way, and it is easier if both the franchisor and master-franchisee candidate recognize that possibility and address it early on in their considerations and business planning.

They will try to identify what makes the business successful in the home market and whether that similarly applies in the target market. Done right, this often requires extensive market research to determine if the business system, product or service will have a similar or different reception in target markets.

7.4 FRANCHISOR AND BRAND

Every franchise involves, at the most fundamental level, the license of a system of knowledge or know-how, together with the use of a brand, including a trademark. The master-franchisee candidate will need to consider how well known the brand and trademark are in the target market at the time the opportunity is being considered, as well as the growth potential.

The growth of the brand's recognition will surely be affected by the work to be performed by the master franchisee in the local market. But in addition, the master franchisee will be looking at the franchisor's current and future commitment to grow the brand outside the franchisor's home market.

If international expansion by the franchisor is an established long-term strategy, the master-franchisee candidate will have one reaction. If this intended international expansion is a first for the franchisor and an experiment, a different reaction should be expected. It all speaks to the franchisor's level of commitment outside the home market.

Most sophisticated master-franchisee candidates should be making an assessment of both the franchisor and the franchisor's senior management team. In particular, do they have a commitment to and a track record in international expansion through multi-unit development?

On a technical level, the master franchisee will want to know and see that the franchisor's key intellectual property, usually one or more trademarks, can be protected in the new market by way of registration. Trademarks are, of course, protected generally on a country-by-county basis.

Each master franchising area-development arrangement is different in its own way.

An important brand-related issue is the marketing of the system and advertising of products and services. Many local candidates will look to the franchisor on some level for assistance with their marketing and advertising.

At one end of the spectrum, some franchisors take responsibility for a global advertising strategy. At the other end, the master franchisee is responsible for preparation of all materials to be used in the market and for devising on its own the strategy and rollout of an advertising program. Most franchisors provide something in between.

Some franchise systems are built around the delivery of a product or service that involves the use of unique and proprietary products, services and equipment. A master-franchisee candidate should investigate whether anything of a proprietary nature is part of the system, and then if it can be made readily obtained in the new market.

In certain instances, for example, the import of certain types of ingredients is regulated or even prohibited. Both the franchisor and master franchisee should not assume that any such items can freely cross borders, even in this era of ever-growing free trade.

7.5 THE SYSTEM

A franchise is the license of a brand and a system, which involves the use of know-how and certain methodologies in operating a business. The sophisticated master-franchisee is usually expected to pay significant upfront and ongoing fees for multiple unit rights.

In return, the candidate is often looking to only acquire rights to, and to invest substantial sums in, a system that is sufficiently established and documented. This increases the likelihood of success and usually means that the master franchisee needs to do less to establish the system in the new market.

Very often, a franchise system needs to be customized to the needs of the local market, such as the changes to food recipes brought about to suit local tastes. The master franchisee will want to see how receptive the franchisor is to understanding and accepting the need for permitting changes.

Of course, none of the first four areas covered will matter unless the master franchisee sees and believes that there is a financial model to the venture that works. Every multiple-unit franchisee candidate should investigate thoroughly the expected costs in establishing and operation the business, the infrastructure that will be required in the new market (including corporate units), expected sales, costs and margins, the potential and expected return on investment, and an exit strategy.

A franchisor that is used to offering single-unit franchises in its home market may also be new to the analysis where a multiple-unit growth model is to be adopted. In a true master franchise arrangement, for instance, there will be a sharing of sub-franchisee generated fees and royalties, and this can be the subject of significant negotiation based on the obligations that the franchisor and master franchisee will assume in the relationship.

Master franchisees should look at the quality of the franchisor's training systems.

Almost every multiple-unit agreement is different, and very often this is based on the market potential for the largest market. Both sides will need a common vision of the market potential

In addition, they will, of course, need to come to terms on a form of agreement. The legal terms, and in particular those of a business nature, will have a significant impact on the master franchisee's analysis. For instance, length of term, ability to renew, the proposed development schedule and the application of local franchise laws are all issues that are important.

7.6 SUMMARY

Today, India is one of the biggest emerging markets for various goods and services, ranging from bare necessities to expensive luxuries. Until 1991 due to the archaic Foreign Exchange Regulation Act, 1973 (FERA), almost all sectors of goods and services relating to the consumer markets in India were secure from the grasp of foreign investors. After the repeal of FERA and the coming into force of the Foreign Exchange Management Act, 1999 (FEMA), foreign investors found their passage into India with rules for entry becoming far more favourable. Today, a convenient medium of entry by foreign companies into the Indian market is franchising. Franchising also exists as a successful business module for local companies in India within various sectors.

However, there are no laws enacted solely for the purpose of regulating the growing business of franchising in India, even though many nations across the world have enacted such laws. The result is that when franchisors enter India they are governed by a number of different statutes and codes rather than a single comprehensive enactment.

One of the primary factors which control the success of a franchising business in an emerging economy like India is the ability of a foreign franchisor to identify and seize the appropriate moment when the business environment is favorable and reap its rewards. Home to over a billion people, including a flourishing class of urban consumers possessing considerable amounts of disposable income together with the continued growth of the economy have strengthened India's claim to be a viable and beneficial destination for a foreign franchisor.

India offers vast openings for a franchisor to set up its business; create awareness for his products or services and exploit the enormous market offered. As a result, it comes as no surprise that India has recently been declared as the second most attractive destination for retailers among 30 emerging markets. Though current investment regulations of the Indian Government bar foreign investment in the retail sector, it hasn't deterred foreign participation. Rather than shying away from the enormous market that India offers, international companies like Marks & Spencer, the global retail chain of stores have taken to entering into different forms of franchising arrangements, ranging from just use of its trade mark for a fee to the standard model of allowing its system to be used for a franchise fee.

Before entering an international market these factors have to be considered and then an entry for franchising can be made if the conditions are favourable.

7.7 SELF ASSESSMENT QUESTIONS

(1) Explain in short the requirement of franchise law in India.

(2) Write short note on franchisor and brand.

(3) Explain in brief, the assessment of the countries legal and regulatory environment for franchising.

(4) Write in short the meaning/moving market entry strategies for franchising.

✠✠✠

8 Chapter THE WAY AHEAD

Objectives

After going through this chapter, you will be able to understand:

- Parmeters of cheeklist on franchisor
- Parmeters of checklist on franchisee.

Structure:

However happy and lucrative your working relationship with your franchise partner may be - and it ought to be excellent in every respect if you are each completely dedicated to the union - you will still want to grow and expand your own business in due course. The franchisor will seek to take on more franchisees, further building up the network. The franchisee will probably buy other franchises from the franchisor, opening new outlets. If successful growth is to occur, both parties need to review constantly their approach to franchising, spotting errors and implementing changes before moving on either to recruit the next franchisee or purchase another franchise. Only by looking back and learning from the past can you look forward and continue to be a winner.

8.1 THE FRANCHISOR'S CHECKLIST

The franchisor must regularly contemplate the following questions, taking any necessary steps to ensure that his or her answers are all positive, prior to any planned expansion.

- Are you aware of the characteristics of a reputable franchise?
- Does your franchise possess these features?
- Do you know about the different types of franchise available?
- Are you fully familiar with the changing franchise market?
- Does it remain an appealing, long-term prospect for you?
- Do you recognise the main benefits and drawbacks of franchising, along with their respective side effects?
- Do the pros outweigh the cons in your circumstances?
- Are you and your team experienced, ethical, financially sound and committed?
- Is your format proven, distinctive, complete and simple?
- Is your product and service range varied, well established and selling steadily at premium prices?
- Is the market large and growing?
- Are the financial costs and returns manageable and worthwhile?
- Can your quantitative and qualitative objectives best be achieved via this trading method?
- Does your franchise consultant play a key role in your franchising activities?
- Are you still running pilot operations for testing purposes?
- Is your trading name appropriate?
- Have you a first-class image and accumulated goodwill?
- Are your systems and procedures relevant and up to date?
- Do you offer the correct blend of prompt and efficient initial services?
- Is your front-end fee fair and non-profit making?

- Do you provide the right mix of ongoing services in a swift and proper manner?
- Is the operating manual detailed, clear and up to date?
- Is the continuing management service fee reasonable for both parties?
- Is associate (or full) membership of the British Franchise Association of benefit to you?
- Are you promoting the franchise package through the most appropriate sources?
- Are you supplying enough data to allow readers to decide whether you are well suited, and if it is worthwhile requesting further information?
- Is your franchise prospectus informing and attracting suitable would-be franchisees whilst dissuading unsuitable ones from applying?
- Does your franchise application form enable you to properly assess applicants?
- Do you know the types of personality, background, finances and goals that ought to be possessed by the ideal franchisee?
- Are you meeting candidates at their home and your head office, and asking revealing questions?
- Are you choosing the right franchisees?
- Do you liaise with an appropriately experienced solicitor before signing a franchise contract?
- Is the franchise agreement complete, clear and balanced?
- Is the franchise for a sufficient period of time?
- Are your territories evenly spread out?
- Are the rights and responsibilities fair?
- Are the terms and conditions of renewal, assignment and termination all reasonable?
- Do you fully understand the franchisor-franchisee relationship, recognising the franchisee's views?
- Do you communicate with each other at all times, exchanging ideas, suggestions and constructive criticisms?
- Do you regularly review your franchising approach, to maximise your chances of a successful future?

8.2 THE FRANCHISEE'S CHECKLIST

Similarly, the franchisee must continually think about the following queries and should be certain that his or her replies are all favourable, before any proposed growth:

- Do you know the features of an ethical franchise?
- Do you own a reputable franchise?
- Are you familiar with the various types of franchise which exist?
- Do you know the franchise industry well?
- Does it offer you an attractive, viable future?
- Are you aware of the major advantages and disadvantages of franchising, and their individual knock-on effects?
- Do the pluses exceed the minuses for you?
- Are you independent, self-disciplined, ambitious, sociable and trustworthy?
- Are you familiar with the territory, in good health and supported by your loved ones?
- Do you have sufficient money available?
- Are your personal and business goals compatible with franchising?
- Is the franchisor fully knowledgeable, totally reputable, financially secure and in possession of appropriate franchising objectives?
- Is the format completely tried and tested, distinguished, comprehensive and straightforward?
- Are the goods selling well, within a growing marketplace?
- Does the franchise package provide value for money for you?
- Does it also produce a satisfactory return on your investment?
- Is the network wholly successful?
- Is this franchise right for you?
- Do you take relevant professional advice prior to signing any binding agreement?
- Is the franchise contract fair and reasonable?
- Is the franchise long enough for you?
- Is your territory sufficiently profitable for you?

- Are you happy with each party's rights and responsibilities?
- Are the renewa1, assignment and termination clauses all even handed?
- Are you aware of the ways in which the franchisor/ franchisee partnership usually develops, sympathising with the franchisor's position?
- Do you get on well with the franchisor, having an open, communicative relationship?
- Do you often conduct a rigorous self-appraisal, to increase the prospects of your future success?

8.3 SUMMARY

To have a happy and lucrative relationship both the franchisor and the franchisee must have a checklist before planning for a planned expansion network of their business. From the point of view of franchisor, following are the important points to be thought before going for a franchise, such as

Does it remain an appealing, long term prospect for you?

Do you recognize the main benefits and drawbacks of franchising, along with their respective side effects?

Do the pros outweigh the cons in your circumstances?

Is your format proven, distinctive, complete and simple?

Is your product and service range varied, well-established and selling steadily at premium prices?

Is the market large and growing?

Can your quantitative and qualitative objectives best be achieved via this trading method?

Does your Franchise consultant playa key role in your franchising activities?

Have you a first class image arid accumulated good-will?

Are your systems and procedures relevant and up to date?

Is the operating manual detailed, clear and updated?

Is the continuing management service fee reasonable for both parties?

Are you promoting the franchise package through the most appropriate sources?

Are you supplying enough data to allow readers to decide whether you are well suited and if it worthwhile requesting further information?

Does your franchise application form enable you to properly assess applicants?

Are you meeting candidate at their home and your head office and asking revealing questions?

Do you liaise with an appropriately experienced solicitor before a franchised contract?

Similarly, the franchisee must also think the following questions, before any proposal he signs for the franchise agreement

Are you familiar with the various type of franchise that exists?

Does it offer you an attractive viable future?

Are you independent, self-disciplined, ambitious, sociable and trust worthy?

Are you familiar with the territory, in good health and supported by your loved ones?

Do you have sufficient money available?

Are you personal and business goals compatible with franchising?

Is the franchisor fully knowledgeable, totally reputable, and financially secure?

Are the goods selling well within a growing market?

Is this franchise right for you?

Do you take relevant professional advice prior to signing any binding agreement?

8.4 SELF ASSESMENT QUESTIONS

(1) Summarise the various necessary steps to be kept in mind before finalising the franchisee by a franchisor

(2) What are the important points a franchisee should look into before signing an agreement with the franchisor?

✠✠✠

Chapter 9 CASE STUDY IN RETAIL

9.1 THE 'NEW' FACES OF FRANCHISING

by Robert Purvin

Our nation, indeed the world, is mired in the worst recession in 60 years. The nightly news provides a steady diet of plummeting retail sales, corporate bailouts, downsizing, a soft real estate market and foreclosures, a healthcare crisis and record unemployment. So, with all the bad economic news, why would anybody think of buying a franchise?

Frankly, the tough economic times are precisely why many people look for opportunities that counter a suddenly unstable job market—and often look towards the benefits of franchising. The recently (and unexpectedly) unemployed may be tired of the uncertainties of the job market and be ready to fulfill a pent-up dream of business ownership. Retirees may no longer be able to afford retirement, and "unintentional" corporate refugees and people who have "downsized" careers or have seen the equity in their homes plummet may look to business ownership as a way to take charge of their lives.

Starting a business from scratch, especially in a poor economy, may present even greater economic risks. On the other hand, buying into a franchised business with an established brand offering a well-tested franchise concept can present an appealing opportunity. If the franchise opportunity has a strong track record of profitable performance and is with a franchise system with a fair franchise agreement and a collaborative franchise culture that includes an effective relationship with a strong franchisee association, the franchise option of business ownership can actually provide a strong solution to confront and withstand a troubled economy. And that's what has drawn a whole new generation of franchisees to the table during this economic downtown.

Given the promise of starting a business that has already proven itself, and perhaps has already proven to be recession-resistant, those fleeing or just locked out of the job market will find franchise investment to be well worth investigation. So, just who are the new faces of franchising? Truth be told, today's franchisees are coming from the same walks of life as previous generations. It's just that the current economic conditions have drawn even more people from several distinct areas.

Existing multi-unit owners represent one such area. Increasingly, franchisors' favorite prospects already have demonstrated business success in franchising. Just as prospective franchisees are urged to seek out a franchise system that has a proven track record, franchisors turn to existing multi-unit franchise owners looking to expand their businesses with multiple brand investments. Everybody loves a proven commodity and franchisors, as well as franchisees, are no different.

Proven Record

The franchisee who has run a successful operation at one location is far more likely to run a successful second, third, fourth location or more than the newcomer. Especially if that franchisee can recruit the staff needed to duplicate the systems and operations at additional locations. Then, it is merely a matter of having the capital or not to buy the additional franchises.

Franchising has drawn professional athletes dating back to the 1960s. And why not? Most athletes either have the capital or the ability to raise the capital to buy into a franchise-the most critical element of franchising.

Second, there are a good many athletes who realize there will come a day when they can no longer play and that planning should begin while they are still active. Franchising offers a way to transition to their post-playing days to a career with a proven brand and the resources to help them learn a business.

Finally, franchising also provides a way for athletes to capitalize on their celebrity and convert it into success in business.

The pool of candidates from corporate refugees has grown rather deep in recent months. It includes the recently downsized who have chosen to work for themselves rather than put their fate in the hands of corporate America again.

Joining them are those who did not get downsized but have grown weary of waiting for the other shoe to fall and want to control their own destiny.

Tough economic times are precisely why many people look for franchise opportunities.

As spokes in the corporate wheel, these individuals have seen how businesses run and bring a variety of skills to the table in running a franchise. While their ability to raise capital may have been impacted by the soft real estate market doing a number on their home equity, many have earned enough to be able to raise the capital to purchase a franchise.

Beyond managerial and executive skills, this group of franchisees also brings an added dimension to the table. After even, decades, of working for somebody else, these individuals are now running their own show, controlling their own fate. So rather than cruising towards retirement, these individuals are now in the game in the middle of the action. That can create an empowered, passionate franchisee willing to go that extra distance to become successful.

But a caution to those seeking to escape the corporate culture-the world of small business, even with the support of a franchise network, can be a rude awaking to those used to 'calling for office support' or requisitioning supplies from the warehouse.

Reality Check

I once had a franchisee confess that when he started his retail business he failed to evaluate that he "never had a job when he was on his feet all day," nor had he considered that he would "dislike dealing with customers on a daily basis."

Franchisees must create as well as stay within their budgets, deal directly with customers, and learn how to "fend for themselves." In most franchise systems, franchisee support comes in the form of advice – often with added expenses.

The bottom line is that running a small business - even one where the business plan is well structured and carefully laid out - is hard work and not to be undertaken without sober evaluation and consideration.

Along with the multi-unit franchise owner, the store manager brings something very valuable to the franchise table: knowledge of the business. The store manager turned franchisee also has the added value that they can actually run a franchise themselves, saving a median store manager salary in the $60,000-per-year range.

The store manager does face the challenge of raising the capital necessary to buy a franchise, but that's only part of the issue. As we all know with franchising, you not only need to raise the capital to buy your franchise, but the funding to get your operation going-even if your background is that of a store manager.

Still, the store manager-turned franchisee possesses the same intangible of the downsized corporate executive and is passionate about having a say in final decisions.

Of the five "new" faces of franchising listed here, veterans returning from duty and looking for a franchising opportunity is probably a fairly new phenomenon. Not that it hasn't happened before, but with activity overseas winding down and the economy still in tough shape, it's something we're likely to see more and more of.

The pool of candidates from corporate refugees has grown noticeably in recent months.

The veteran faces the challenges of raising capital, something difficult to fund with a military pension or wages. Still, many franchisors do offer discounts to veterans, which has helped them to become one of the "new" faces.

Whether you fall into one of these five groups or not, in tough times, the franchising option provides a particularly compelling opportunity.

However, contrary to conventional wisdom, franchising is not for independent thinkers who really are looking to calling their own shots. Franchising can be a happy medium for those who want to be in business for themselves but are willing to follow a well defined business plan.

9.2 RISK VERSUS REWARD IN THE FRANCHISE EQUATION

by Mark C. Siebert

Every year, like clockwork, books and magazines publish their franchise rankings. The franchisors who score well tout their performance and reprint the articles that call them the best franchise in their category. This, they seem to suggest, should be enough to convince any potential franchisee to fill out an application on the spot.

Of course, if there truly were a single best franchise, everyone would buy it to the exclusion of all others. In truth, however, no test, no matter how well constructed, can provide you with an answer to the single most important question: "What is the best franchise for me?"

Several things must go into each prospective franchisee's personal buying decision. How do you feel about what you will be doing? Does it seem like fun? Do you think you would be good at it? Can you see yourself doing this for the next 10 or 20 years?

Beyond the lifestyle aspects of a franchise, however, most buyers look at franchise ownership as a means to achieve financial goals. Ultimately, in making any investment decision, the two most important factors are risk and return, but a franchise investment can be very difficult to assess in those terms.

Everyone wants a no-risk franchise that offers high returns, but there is no such animal. The key lies in finding the franchise that offers the highest return for the amount of risk you are willing to assume.

Complicating matters is the fact that most buying decisions are emotional. Did you purchase your last home after hours of researching neighborhood price appreciation, construction materials and energy efficiency? Or did you start with general criteria such as schools, neighborhood and costs and look for a house you would fall in love with? How about your last car?

The purchase of a franchise is probably the biggest financial decision you will ever make-and perhaps the most emotional. Not only are you, about to invest your life's savings, you also may end up living in that business for the next 20 years. Unlike the purchase of a home or car, the purchase of a franchise is not a decision that can be easily reversed.

In many instances, a franchise investment can be riskier than other types of investments. To make this investment worth your while, it must compensate you for that incremental risk by offering an incrementally higher return. Perhaps more than any other investment, a franchise purchase demands a level of cold-eyed scrutiny that goes far beyond the emotional first blush.

Assessing Risk

With more than 4,000 franchises in the U.S. alone, the first thing that you need to do is narrow the field. A good place to start cutting is based on your likes and dislikes. If a business does not sound appealing to you, chances are good you should not be in it. Also eliminate any, you can't afford. Once you have limited your options to a manageable number, rate the remaining candidates based on risk.

Some of the risk-oriented factors you should examine include financial performance, longevity, size, turnover, management, litigation history, support and contract terms. Taken as a group, they provide excellent measures of risk.

Where do you find this information? The Franchise Handbook is a good place to start. Once you get serious about your candidates, you need to take the next step and start collecting Uniform Franchise Offering Circulars (UFOCs).

A franchisor must provide you with a UFOC at the first face-to-face meeting during which the sale of a franchise is discussed. UFOCs are also available for a minimal fee from state agencies governing franchising. The contents of a UFOC are strictly dictated and cover all of the risk factors mentioned above.

The UFOC is not the only source for this type of information, and you should not rely on it exclusively. In most states, no one other than the franchisor and its attorney reviews this document. Therefore, it is important that you talk to franchisees-both current and former and outside experts. Consult with your banker and an attorney familiar with franchising. These are important elements of conducting a thorough due diligence process.

A good technique is to assign a numerical value to each element of risk for each franchise being considered. Pay attention to which candidate has the lowest turnover level, the smallest ratio of lawsuits, the most experience, Total all the scores and use the results to draw insight regarding the risk of a specific franchise.

If there were a "best" franchise, everyone would buy it to the exclusion of all others.

Finally, determine your personal tolerance for risk. Remember that risk is relative. It is relative to who you are, to your age and to your ability to recover from a loss. It is also relative to the risks posed by other similar franchise investments. Draw a risk "line in the sand" and eliminate the franchises that have stepped over it.

Once you have eliminated those franchises that pose too great a risk, it is time to choose among the remaining candidates by assessing return. However, while some of the historical measures of risk are mandated disclosures, information on return is much harder to obtain.

Under Federal Trade Commission (FTC) Rule 436 (commonly referred to as the Franchise Rule, or simply the Rule), franchisors are not required. to provide prospective franchisees with information on unit level performance or earnings in the UFOC. As a result, some 80 percent of franchisors choose not to make these "earnings claims," a situation that, unfortunately, leaves many potential franchise buyers in the dark.

There are several alternative methods of measuring return.

Again, start by talking to franchisees. Ask very specific questions. If you ask franchisees how much profit they made last year, you might not get an accurate answer because of embarrassment over low earnings or concerns about tax liabilities.

Instead, ask more specific questions such as:

- What are your gross sales?
- What was your cost of goods sold?
- What were your labor costs?
- How much inventory do you maintain?
- What kind of inventory turnover do you achieve?
- How big is your location?

Ask questions that will allow you to construct a profit and loss statement through on your own rather than looking for a pat answer that may or may not be accurate.

Don't stop with franchisees. Speak to landlords in your area. Find out what locations are available and how much they cost. Talk to vendors on the franchisor's approved list and inquire about their charges.

Once you feel comfortable that you have created an accurate analysis of what the franchise can return, the final step is to measure that return in a consistent manner. You must avoid the temptation of gauging your projected income. Instead, measure return on investment. In essence, what you are asking here is, "How much return can I get on each dollar I invest?"

To do that, you first need to obtain one additional number: startup costs. Startup costs are a required disclosure, but franchisors use various assumptions to determine them. Your best bet is to make an educated guess on startup costs based on your own research of the franchise. You might want to seek the help of a qualified accountant for this. It pays to be conservative in this endeavor, since startup costs tend to be higher than projections.

Bypass your first year and look at projected income for years two and three. Be sure that your pro forma income statement accounts for a reasonable salary for the unit manager (even if you will be filling that job) and does not reflect debt service, depreciation or taxes. Then divide your project earnings by your startup costs to calculate your rate of return.

Ask franchisees questions that will let you develop your own profit and loss statement.

Low-risk franchises should be able to offer you consistent returns of at least 15 percent. Higher-risk franchises should offer commensurately greater rewards, or they are not worth the incremental risk. Once you have determined the risk-to-return ratio of the franchises you are considering, you will be in a much better position to make a wise investment choice.

9.3 MASTER FRANCHISEES TAKE FRANCHISING AROUND THE WORLD

by John P. Hayes, Ph.D.

While franchising continues to expand in the United States, nowhere is the growth of franchising more impressive than in the global marketplace. From Western Europe to China, from Russia to Australia to South America, franchising connects the crossroads of the world. Franchising is the sole business culture to achieve rapid global expansion and there are no signs of it slowing down.

No one would dispute that the United States leads the world in franchising. The major concepts originated in America, and several hundred of them enjoy at least a foothold in the international marketplace. Entrepreneurs in many other countries, especially those of Western Europe and Asia, have also applied the principles of franchising and developed their own concepts. Many of these companies are expanding to other countries, including the United States. When it comes to franchising, it really is a small world.

The vehicle that propels the majority of franchising's international expansion is master franchising, or licensing. Franchisors who use the master franchising paradigm contractually grant development rights for their concept to an individual or a corporation who for all practical purposes becomes a clone of the franchisor.

For example, an entrepreneur in China buys the master license rights for McDonald's and commits to develop McDonald's restaurants in China. Meanwhile, American based McDonald's, the franchisor, commits to train the Chinese entrepreneur, the master franchisee, to become its development agent and representative in China.

The Chinese entrepreneur is likely to be responsible for selling McDonald's franchises, and training and supporting franchisees in China, much the same way McDonald's trains and supports franchisees in the United States. Master franchisees usually pay a one-time licensing fee (the range is from $100,000 to $1-million or more) and share franchise fees with the franchisor. Master franchisees also pay royalties to the franchisor.

There are pitfalls to master franchising-for example, how does the franchisor manage a master franchisee in another country, and what happens if the master franchisee fails to perform or quits paying fees? But all in all it's a successful expansion strategy that has worked particularly well for American franchisors.

Once a franchisor gets the notion to build a national brand, the next logical mental leap is to build a multi-national brand, and master franchising is the safest and quickest way to get it done. The fact that franchising is growing at a faster rate internationally than in the United States is an added inducement. Plus, it helps immensely that entrepreneurs across the globe have embraced franchising and often turn to the U.S. franchise community for ideas as well as concepts that they can introduce to their own countries.

Success Story

There's no greater success story in master franchising than that of Reynaldo Concepcion, a Philippine entrepreneur who owns licenses for eight American franchise companies: Days Inn, Century 21, Pizza Inn, The Medicine Shoppe, Century Small Business Services, Hertz, Blockbuster, and Tutor Time.

Concepcion has also developed several Philippine concepts, including: Virra Mall for shopping centers, Vacation Club International for vacation ownership accreditation, Payphone Plus for public calling centers, Fitness4Less for exercise centers, and Loyola Memorial Parks for cemeteries and mortuaries.

Concepcion is a giant among master franchisees, but he's hardly alone. No one knows for sure how many master franchisees exist in the world, but the Master Franchisee Database (www.Master Franchising.com) includes more than 2,000 of them, and approximately 8% of them own more than one concept. In recent years MasterFranchising.com has surveyed master franchisees and discovered that many of them share Concepcion's idea of multi-concept ownership.

The most recent survey discovered that 30% of the Master Franchisee Database had plans to acquire another master license in 2001. Another 15% of the master franchisees said they will "eventually" purchase another master license.

While the U. S. remains the leader, when it comes to franchising, it really is a small world.

The primary reason entrepreneurs consider master franchising is the same reason that most people consider acquiring a franchise. Someone else has already paid for the mistakes! Many master franchisees say they have the wherewithal to create their own viable franchise concepts, but why bother? Money isn't usually an issue for the international investor. Quite often, in fact, the master franchisee's assets are far more impressive than the franchisor's, but why put them at risk?

Besides, master franchisees are often looking for rapid growth. They could afford to create their own concepts, but they don't want to invest years in research and development. Instead, they're in the game to score. They want to sell franchises, develop franchisees, build out a country and then do it again! Developing their own ideas would only slow them down, so they're willing to pay for the experience of a franchisor that's done it before and knows how to score.

Most master franchisees do not get started with the idea that they'll own multiple concepts. Concepcion explains that wasn't his original idea, but circumstances changed his mind.

"We were content to get our first (concept) and make that successful," he explains. "But as we began building hotels, there was an opportunity to make money on the real estate around them. This led to our interest in the Century 21 franchise. That led to the construction of commercial centers around the hotels, which led to (acquiring master licenses for) Pizza Inn, The Medicine Shoppe, and Blockbuster."

Brand Name Power

As much as anything else, master franchisees are attracted to the success of a brand name. "These (concepts) were all established names that people already knew about," continues Concepcion.

Master franchisees also recognize that multiple concepts can be operated by, as Concepcion says, "a common back office." He points out that his employees can work for multiple brands at the same time. "After the first three (concepts)," he explains, "every additional franchise requires only about 40% of the usual work. Aside from this, an economy of scale helps in lowering prices and co-branding has increased the number of potential customers."

But it takes two to become a successful master franchisee. Without a franchisor, master franchisees have no chance of succeeding. The maturation of American franchise systems embraces the success of international expansion. American franchisors, especially those who have been franchising beyond the U.S. borders for more than a few years, have come to terms with what's required internationally.

They weren't always as selective as they are today about whom they will accept as a master franchisee. Today they are providing better training, more support, and more people-power to develop their international networks. As a result, master franchisees are building more profitable and satisfying businesses and they are enjoying the relationships they have developed with franchisors.

That's not to say there aren't problems. Many master franchises have failed and at any given time many others face demise. However, recent surveys by MasterFranchising.com indicate that international franchise relationships are stronger than they've been in the past 25 or more years.

Master franchise relationships are stronger than they have been at any time in 25 years.

When MasterFranchising.com asked master franchisees to reveal their greatest challenge, 40% said it was "selling franchises." That's a common challenge among franchisors, too. 20% of master franchisees said "training" was their greatest challenge, while 10% said it was "generating franchise sales leads."

Master franchisees are taking franchising around the world, and along the way they are discovering each other and building their own international community.

9.4 FRANCHISE FULFILS LIFELONG DREAM

by Jackie McDermott

Joan Cole always wanted to work for a cosmetic company, and not just any cosmetic company - Merle Norman. When she was asked by her college professor to create a business plan of her choosing, she based the assignment on the Merle Norman franchise, even though she was working in the automotive industry at the time. She got an 'A.'

"For me, that business plan was both a safety net and a dream waiting to be realized. I knew if I ever felt uncertain about my current career, I could fall back on it. I also knew if the right opportunity presented itself, I would be ready to seize it. I kept that plan in my back pocket, waiting for the day I could put it into action," she explains.

Cole's blueprint came to life in 2002, after 20 years of working in the automotive industry, when she began running her own Merle Norman Studio in the Lakeside Mall in Sterling Heights, a northern suburb of Detroit.

"In the 1980s, some friends told me that there was a lot of money to be made in the auto field, so they helped me get a job," she says. "The money was great, and my employer offered tuition reimbursement, so I was able to go to college while I worked. I now have a B.B.A. in Management and a Master of Science in Finance."

Of course, the automotive industry is quite different from the world of cosmetics, but Cole believes her past experience helped prepare her for her current endeavors, explaining, "I was able to perfect my sales and organizational skills in a fast-paced industry, and earned managerial experience. Although I believe I possess certain innate qualities which are essential to being a good manager, such as social skills and resourcefulness, my work history undoubtedly contributed to my current success."

While Cole's experience was both lucrative and an opportunity to employ her business fortes, she still aspired to own a business in the cosmetic industry—a field which generates billions in sales each year. She explains, "I have always admired the industry, and felt that I had the desire necessary to do very well in it. I love the fashion aspect and excitement of the business. It fits my personality. I also knew that working in a female-dominated arena after years in a more male-dominated industry would be a nice change."

Cole experienced her first Merle Norman complementary makeup lesson in the early 1980s, and was instantly hooked on the products. The company is based in Los Angeles and boasts about 2,000 studios throughout the U.S. and Canada. Ms. Merle Norman, the company's founder, was an ambitious Midwesterner who began distributing her products more than 80 years ago. The company still specializes in developing and distributing its own line of skin care and cosmetics and is known for its "Try Before You Buy" policy, conceived by Ms. Norman herself. As early as the 1940s, Merle studios could be found coast to coast, offering women a nearly unprecedented chance to run their own businesses."

"Merle Norman Cosmetics, Inc. offers their customers top-quality products, an inviting studio atmosphere and superior customer service from professionally-trained beauty consultants," says Cole. "The 'Try Before You Buy' policy provides potential customers with a unique beauty experience that I believe to be unmatched by any of our competitors." In fact, *Entrepreneur* magazine recently recognized Merle Norman as America's #1 cosmetics franchise opportunity.

In the late 1990's, Cole considered opening a Studio, and even met with a Merle Norman representative. Unfortunately, they couldn't find the right location. Cole left the automotive world in February 2002, motivated not to wait until retirement to live out her dream. Fortuitously, the weekend after she left her job, she learned from a sales representative at her local Merle store that the Studio in Lakeside Mall was vacant.

"I was thinking, 'You got to be kidding me!' The timing could not have been more perfect. I had saved up some money, and really felt ready to go for it. I called Merle Norman on Monday and got the process going right away," Cole recalls. After decades of using the products herself, and fifteen years after creating her 'A'-winning business plan, she was able to open her own studio.

Although Cole's heart was set on a particular franchise, she sees many benefits to franchising in general, explaining, "Franchisees have an advantage over their non-franchisee competitors, since they have the rights to use the franchisor's brand name, trademarks, copyrights, trade secrets, logos, storefronts, and interiors. I think women see the Merle Norman brand as something they can depend on for quality products. This reputation can only work to my advantage as a business owner."

Merle Norman's home office provides sales and marketing support every step of the way, helping franchisees select their location, review their lease, and design their studio. "Subsequent to the studio's grand opening, each owner is partnered with a regional business consultant and a regional specialist who offer advice on business issues and day-to-day assistance," explains Cole, who found this type of support particularly valuable as she had never owned her own business.

Unlike other potential franchisees who struggle to choose from the myriad of attractive opportunities in the marketplace, Cole knew, and has known for 25 years, that she wanted to partner with Merle Norman. Although her mind was made up, she still understands the importance of choosing the right franchise, and offers valuable advice to those making such a decision.

"Start your journey by assessing your needs and exploring your options. Conduct a brief self-assessment of personal strengths, weaknesses, likes, dislikes and resources. These answers will help guide you through the franchise evaluation process," she advises.

"Investigate industries that interest you and try to determine which have growth potential. Narrow the choices down, and then analyze your geographic area to see if there is a market for those types of businesses," she says. "Read *The Franchise Handbook*, and go online to look up magazine and newspaper articles about the companies."

The franchise's national reputation is important, but Cole also stresses the significance of researching its local standing. "While franchises are required to submit a Uniform Franchise Offering Circular (UFOC) disclosing certain facts about their business, they are not required to disclose information on their reputation, so it is imperative that you investigate this on your own," she says. "'Google' the franchise, call your local Better Business Bureau, or even visit the nearest library to chat with the librarians-they tend to know a lot about what goes on in the community."

And of course, as Cole did years ago, write a business plan.

"You need to start every day with a plan outlining your sales targets and marketing strategy," she advises. "Follow it, review it, and change it as needed in order to meet or exceed your expectations. Work harder than your competitors to build relationships with customers, provide more knowledge and expertise than consumers are accustomed to receiving. Do all you can to coach your staff and provide ongoing training, and ask your team for feedback."

Actually, Cole has found that securing the right employees has been the most challenging aspect of franchising. "You want to find people who are as excited and passionate about the business as you are. Once they have completed the initial training, it can be challenging to keep them happy and productive enough to meet their sales goals. Coaching is an ongoing effort, and you always need to make sure your team members are creatively charged."

Cole admits that if she had to do it all over again, she would invest more time during the employee hiring and training process. She cautions, "The cost and time associated with hiring and orienting new employees can be staggering in the first couple years of business."

For Cole, owning a Merle Norman Cosmetics Studio has been her ultimate entrepreneurial dream.

9.5 BUY LOW, SELL HIGH - RETAIL REMAINS A BOOMING FRANCHISE SEGMENT

by Michael J. McDermott

Retailing has long prospered as one of the world's leading industries on the strength of a simple business model: Retailers sell products for more than it costs them to buy, inventory, market and merchandise the same products.

Sometimes the margin of profit they record on those sales is miniscule. But if they sell in large enough volume, those razor-thin margins add up to a substantial bottom line.

In retailing, maturity does not mean it is an industry lacking in franchise opportunities.

The retail sector is often described as a mature industry. Indeed, the exchange of goods and services for currency or something else of value has been the bedrock of the world's economy throughout most of recorded history. In the case of retailing, however, maturity does not mean it is an industry lacking in new opportunities-especially where franchising is concerned.

Total retail sales in the U.S. reached more than $3.9 trillion in 2006, according to estimates from the U.S. Census Bureau. That represents growth of 5.7% for the year, down a bit from previous years but still solid. Given the historically moderate inflation rate of the past several years, the difficulties of the sub-prime mortgage market collapse and weakness in the residential real estate market, growth in retail sales has been quite impressive.

A number of factors are behind that encouraging performance, including:

- Continued strength in the automotive sector, fueled by incentives offered by new car dealers and a robust used car market helped by large numbers of late-model vehicles coming off lease.
- An abundance of cash on hand, as evidenced by the record-setting increases in private equity deals completed over the past several years.
- Financial markets that, despite some rocky periods, have contributed to consumer confidence by setting new highs in important indices, including the Dow Jones Industrial Average, in 2007.

At the same time, the parameters defining the retail industry itself have been expanded with the emergence of new channels of distribution. Direct selling through Web sites, catalogs and TV shopping networks is creating new opportunities for cross-channel and multi-channel retailing. Internet sales topped

$100 billion in 2006, up from just $30 billion in 2001. Market researcher JupiterResearch projects $144 billion in online sales by 2010.

Several trends are in place that should contribute to continued growth in the retail sector over the short term. Interest rates remain at comparatively low levels, and consumers continue to have access to a substantial amount of credit. The rate of new job creation has been rising, and unemployment levels have remained relatively low. There have been few signs of any dramatic increase in inflation, and the personal savings rate is subdued, which means people are spending money.

Competition in the retail world today is probably tougher than it has ever been.

There are also some areas of concern to retailers and those considering buying a retail franchise. Consumer confidence has been on a downward track, and the correction in the residential real estate market continues.

A number of questions dog the labor market, including the looming retirement of Baby Boomers in large numbers and unresolved questions about immigration. Continuing conflicts in Iraq and Afghanistan are also contributing to a sense of unease among many consumers.

Retailing has always been an intensely competitive industry, and that is not going to change any time soon. In fact, competition in the retail world today is probably tougher than it has ever been.

Superstores and category killers have made things difficult for mom-and-pop stores and smaller chains. Big operators leverage economies of scale to offer shoppers a deeper selection of merchandise at lower prices than their smaller competitors can provide. That is a strategic advantage that is very difficult for other retailers to overcome.

Retailing may have a long and distinguished history, but it is not immune to change. According to Plunkett Research Ltd., there are 10 trends anyone interested in retailing must know to survive.

(1) "Lifestyles of Health and Sustainability (LOHAS) are creating opportunities for new products and services. Significant marketing and positioning opportunity is occurring due to shifts in consumer tastes and demands.

An affluent market is ready to buy vacation homes and wield its spending power.

"There are also shifts in budget priorities taking place," said Jack Plunkett, the research company's chief executive officer. "Consumers will pay for more for environmentally friendly products and services, for example."

Along with opportunities for new products and services, other factors influencing the LOHAS trend include evolving design, construction and regulation priorities and concerns about the conservation of energy, water, air quality and public lands. This is accompanied by growing interest in organic products.

(2) Population shifts, especially those affecting Baby Boomer and Generation Y, are creating major marketing opportunities in the retail sector. The more than 78 million Americans born between 1946 and 1964 are entering a period of their lives when they will need specialized products, services and infrastructure.

In some cases, that means an affluent target market that is ready to travel, buy vacation homes and otherwise wield the discretionary spending power that comes from high incomes and high household net worth. Generation Y, sometimes called the Echo Boomers, represents a market consisting of well-educated consumers who have growing incomes and are eager to spend. The oldest of the 75 million Americans born between 1977 and 1997 are just hitting 30, and many are ready to buy and furnish their first homes.

These consumers live a fast-paced, mobile, digital lifestyle. They embrace new technologies and leading-edge products and lean towards LOHAS, according to Plunkett's research.

(3) Ethnic markets are growing in population, income and importance in the U.S., representing an immense retail opportunity. The Hispanic population is the fastest-growing segment overall, and immigration continues at a rapid pace. The 45 million Hispanic-Americans living in the U.S. in 2007 represented 15% of the population; those figures are projected to climb to 25% and 100 million by 2043.

Changing population patterns will be evident worldwide over the coming years, with aging and shrinking populations in some areas creating unique global challenges and shortages of workers.

While the U.S. population is projected to grow 37% to 420 million by 2050, the European Union population is predicted to remain virtually unchanged at 450 million, while Japan's population is forecast to shrink by 12% to 110 million.

Today's global population of 6.5 billion will mushroom to more than 9 billion in 2050, with just nine nations accounting for 50% of that growth.

(4) Health care costs will soar, presenting challenges not only to retailers, but to employers in all industries. Current health care costs of $2.3 trillion a year ($7,500 for every man, woman and child) in the U.S. account for 16% of the

country's gross domestic product (GDP). The cost continues to grow, projected to hit $4 trillion and 19% of GDP by 2015.

Plunkett predicted that individuals and employees will bear a greater portion of health care expenses in the future, while developments such as personalized medicine and molecular diagnostics will dramatically alter the landscape. There will be an emphasis on early diagnosis and intervention, and care will finally go digital.

(5) Energy costs are creating a sea change in the retail environment. While retailers have to deal with rising energy costs, the shift is opening up huge opportunities for energy-efficient products, and energy technologies are moving to the forefront.

Those venturing into the retail field should expect an emphasis on efficiency, green buildings and smart systems. Consumer preferences and tastes in cars are likely to change, and interest in solar, wind and safer nuclear technologies will increase.

Some alternative energy sources, such as synthetics, ethanol and liquid natural gas, will be adopted quickly. Long-term solutions for additional energy resources will include deep sea wells, tar beds, oil shale and cleaner-burning coal. Businesses and consumers alike must budget for higher costs ahead.

(6) Off-shoring and globalization are creating both challenges and opportunities for retailers. This trend is enabled by advances in telecommunications and transportation, and it is creating new opportunities, especially among the growing middle and upper classes in India and China.

The emphasis in this area is on collaboration, research and development and captive off-shoring. Both India and China benefit from massive technology school graduate bases, and the governments of the two countries tend to target specific sectors, notably biotechnology and information technology.

America's role in this trend is evolving, but a clear offshoot for retailers is that U.S. consumers and businesses benefit from lower prices.

(7) The "Third Screen" is surging, and wireless transactions grow rapidly. Wireless technologies and mobile computing are expanding their capabilities, bolstering the importance of "Third Screen" devices such as cell phones and personal digital assistants (PDAs). Television and computer monitors represent the first two screens in this paradigm, but the combination of better technology, more content and greater mobility is fueling Third Screen growth. Standard 802.11G Wi-Fi already is widely available, and next-generation WiMax, which will expand the range of mobile devices up to 30 miles, is expected to boom.

Generation Y members embrace new technologies and leading-edge products.

Each year, more cell phones are sold than any other type of consumer electronics device - 800 million in 2007 alone. The number of cell phone users in the U.S. already surpasses 210 million, a number equal to two-thirds of the nation's population. The majority of new cell phones hitting the market today come with Internet capabilities built into them.

Wireless presents many marketing opportunities for retail business owners in the 21st century. They can advertise on cell phone screens, sponsor mobile video feeds, participate in active text-messaging campaigns and pursue location-based advertising programs.

(8) The Convergence Age is already upon us, as broadband prices continue to fall, opening up high-speed online access to rapidly increasing numbers of consumers. The combination of falling broadband prices and the growing use of wireless devices means that critical mass has been achieved in this area, and service offerings are proliferating, according to Plunkett Research.

More than 60 million U.S. homes and businesses subscribed to high-speed Internet connections in 2007, and the mass market tipping point has been reached. Over the next five to eight years, 80 million to 100 million homes will enjoy high-speed Internet access, and "always on" will emerge as the accepted standard.

Wireless technologies and mobile computing are expanding their capabilities.

Convergence is creating tremendous changes in the area of financial services. The cell phone is becoming a virtual credit card and debit card - a "virtual wallet" that consumers can use to pay for all kinds of purchases. Before long, cell phone-based access to all types of account information will become the industry standard.

For retailers, this trend presents key opportunities for those that can create seamless synergies among multiple channels of distribution: bricks, clicks and catalogs.

(9) Advertising is moving online, another offshoot of the convergence effect. As this trend unfolds, marketing demands more effort on the part of retailers, but the payoff is greater opportunities. "The possibilities for niche ad targeting are exceptional," Plunkett said, and such targeted advertising is particularly valuable to smaller retailers who lack the resources to compete head-to-head against the national advertising campaigns of giant retail chains.

As online advertising revenues surpass a projected $17 billion in 2007, search engines and Web sites are evolving into powerful advertising channels. Retailers have more opportunities to reach more consumers in a more accurately targeted manner than ever before.

(10) Longer-term, look for miniaturization and nanotechnology to play bigger roles. Miniaturization will make possible more-powerful processing chips, which in turn will enable enhanced electronic devices at bargain prices.

The cost of data storage has plummeted, with a 250 gigabyte hard drive costing less than $90 in 2007. Apple's popular iPod music and video player routinely sports 80 gigabytes of storage, and faster devices with even more storage are on the horizon.

Farther out, the convergence of nanotechnology with information technology will create extremely powerful semiconductors sporting up to 500 million transistors each. Better wireless networks will increase the value of enhanced mobile and personal devices, and embedded computing will detect the presence of personal portable devices. Eventually, the devices will learn their users' habits.

For would-be franchise owners searching for retail opportunities in the here-and-now, there are several things experts say they should keep in mind when weighing individual franchise offerings.

"One of the first things you have to look at is whether the franchise company has a design concept," suggested Russell Freese, a principal in R&D Consulting who has spearheaded redesign projects for franchise retail chains during his almost 30 years in visual merchandising, store design and product development. "Another thing to pay attention to is the merchandise it sells. Some prospective franchisees pay so much attention to store design and the franchisor' requirements for ownership that they forget this is all about selling something," Freese said. "Merchandise is king in retailing, and that will never change."

The majority of new cell phones hitting the market come with Internet capabilities.

Freese offered some other suggestions useful in conducting a search for a retail franchise:

- Try to be open to understanding what the company stands for. Because people are already familiar with so many of the products sold through retail franchises, their attempts at an objective business evaluation can be colored by their personal interpretation of the company based on their own usage of those products.

- Be sure that the franchise's theme, whatever it may be, is clearly conveyed to the general public and reinforced by the store design.
- Observe customers in the store to get an idea of how they feel about the company.

NOTES